Glossary of Insurance and Risk Management Terms

ABOUT IRMI

International Risk Management Institute, Inc. (IRMI) is a research and publishing organization specializing in property-casualty insurance and risk management. The firm publishes technical reference manuals, expert system software, newsletters, books, and guides. IRMI also sponsors seminars and conferences, including the annual Construction Insurance Conference. The company provides no consulting or other services that could cause a conflict of interest or interfere with its publishing priorities. Most of IRMI's researchers and editors have previous insurance or risk management experience and hold one or more professional designations. This blend of objectivity, expertise, and communication ability helps IRMI provide the insurance buyers, risk managers, agents, brokers, adjusters, auditors, attorneys, and underwriters who subscribe to its publications with practical information that helps them handle everyday business problems.

For more information on any IRMI publication call 1-800-827-4242 (in Dallas, 972-960-7693).

IRMI PUBLICATIONS

Commercial Property Insurance

Commercial Liability Insurance

Commercial Auto Insurance

Professional Liability Insurance

Manual of Rules, Classifications and Interpretations for Workers Compensation Insurance

IRMI's Workers Comp: A Complete Guide to Coverage, Laws, and Cost Containment

Risk Financing

Contractual Risk Transfer

Manufacturing Risk Management and Insurance

IRMI's Account Handling System

Construction Risk Management

The Risk Report

CGL Reporter

Litigation Management

Broad Form Property Damage Coverage

Exposure Survey Questionnaire

Guidelines for Insurance Specifications

101 Ways To Cut Business Insurance Costs

The Additional Insured Book

Classification Cross-Reference

The Wrap-Up Guide

The Alternative Market

**INTERNATIONAL
RISK MANAGEMENT
INSTITUTE, INC.**

Glossary of Insurance and Risk Management Terms

Sixth Edition

International Risk Management Institute, Inc.
Dallas, Texas

First Printing, Sixth Edition, October 1996
PRINTED IN THE UNITED STATES OF AMERICA

"This publication is designed to provide accurate and authoritative information in regard to the subject matter covered. It is sold with the understanding that the publisher is not engaged in rendering legal, accounting, or other professional service. If legal or other professional advice is required, the services of a competent professional should be sought."

From a Declaration of Principles jointly adopted by a Committee of the American Bar Association and a Committee of Publishers and Associations.

Edited by the staff of International Risk Management Institute, Inc. Designed by Bonnie Rogers.

ISBN 1-886813-23-X

International Risk Management Institute, Inc.®
12222 Merit Drive
Suite 1660
Dallas, Texas 75251-2217
972-960-7693   FAX 972-960-6037

International Risk Management Institute Inc.,®
and IRMI® are registered trademarks.

Contents

Preface..vii

Acronymns and Abbreviations..1

Glossary of Insurance and Risk Management Terms........................... 11

State Regulatory Agencies 137

Boards, Bureaus, and State WC Departments 143

Monopolistic State Funds 149

Competitive State Funds...151

Assigned Risk Plans and Pools..153

Risk Management/Insurance Organizations..155

Preface

Risk management and insurance professionals have developed a language of their own. There are many unique terms used to describe risks, insurance coverages, and risk management techniques. Many everyday words also have special meanings within an insurance or risk management context. As the art and science of risk management and insurance has become more sophisticated, this language has become more mysterious and complex. Unfortunately, this often results in miscommunication between industry professionals and those outside the industry and even between insurance industry professionals.

This Glossary was first published in 1978 to help those within and outside the insurance industry communicate effectively. In preparing and updating this Glossary, we attempt to avoid simply providing theoretical concepts, focusing instead on making this book a practical tool. For example, many definitions go beyond a simple explanation of a term by listing advantages and disadvantages of the concept or by warning of inherent problems.

Of course, the insurance industry changes continuously, and these changes result in the introduction of new terms and changes in the meaning of existing terms. We have endeavored over the years to make this Glossary grow and evolve with the industry by updating it periodically. This, the sixth edition, is no exception. Many definitions were expanded significantly while some antiquated terms were deleted. In addition, a significant number of new terms were added.

These revisions are the work of International Risk Management Institute's entire editorial staff. Terms were allocated to each of IRMI's research analysts in accordance with individual areas of expertise.

It is, of course, impossible to include all possible terms in a glossary such as this, and we welcome your suggestions for terms to include in future editions. We also welcome suggestions for improvements to the definitions contained in this edition.

Thank you for the confidence you have placed in IRMI in purchasing this Glossary. We sincerely hope you will find it to be a concise, practical, and informative translator of the unique language of insurance and risk management. May it serve you well.

Acronyms and Abbreviations

AAA............American Arbitration Association
AAI..............Accredited Adviser in Insurance
AACI...........American Association of Crops Insurers
AADA.........American Association of Dental
         Consultants
AAIS...........American Association of Insurance
         Services
AAIMCO.....American Association of Insurance
         Management Consultants
AALU..........Association for Advanced Life
         Underwriting
AAM...........Associate in Automation Management
AAMGA.....American Association of Managing
         General Agents
AAPL..........American Association of Petroleum
         Landmen
ABA ....American Bar Association, American
         Bankers Association
ABIH...........American Board of Industrial Hygienists
ABS ....American Bureau of Shipping
ABS
  RECORD...American Bureau of Shipping Record
ACAS..........Associate of the Casualty Actuarial
         Society
ACCI...........American Corporate Counsel Institute
ACEC..........American Consulting Engineers Council
ACLI............American Council of Life Insurers
ACLU..........American College of Life Underwriters
ACM ....Asbestos Containing Materials
ACORD ......Agent-Company Operations Research
         and Development
ACSC..........Association of Casualty & Surety
         Companies
ACV ....Actual Cash Value
ACWRRE....American Cargo War Risk Reinsurance
         Exchange
ADA ....Americans With Disabilities Act
ADB ....Accidental Death Benefit
AD&D.........Accidental Death and Dismemberment
ADR ....Alternative Dispute Resolution
AEIA ....American Excess Insurance Association
AFIA............American Foreign Insurance Association
AFSB ....Associate in Fidelity and Surety Bonding
AGC ....Associated General Contractors of
         America
A&H............Accident and Health (insurance)
AHERA........Asbestos Hazard Emergency Response
         Act

AHIS...........American Hull Insurance Syndicate
AI................Additional Insured
AIA..............American Institute of Architects;
         American Insurance Association
AIAF ....Associate in Insurance Accounting and
         Finance
AIC..............Associate in Claims
AICPA.........American Institute of Certified Public
         Accountants
AIDS............Acquired Immune Deficiency Syndrome
AIHA ....American Industrial Hygiene Association
AIM...........Associate in Management
AIMA..........As Interest May Appear
AIME ....Average Indexed Monthly Earnings
AIMU..........American Institute of Marine
         Underwriters
AIP..............Annual Implementation Plan
AIPLU.........American Institute for Property and
         Liability Underwriters
AIPSO.........Automobile Insurance Plans Service
         Office
AIRAC.........All-Industry Research Advisory Council
AIRB...........Aviation Insurance Rating Bureau
AISG...........American Insurance Services Group, Inc.
AL................Automobile Liability
ALC..............American Life Convention
ALCM.........Associate in Loss Control Management
ALIC ....Association of Life Insurance Council
ALIM ....Association of Life Insurance Medical
         Directors of America
ALM............Association of Lloyd's Members
ALOS..........Average Length of Stay
AMA...........American Medical Association
AMBAC ......American Municipal Bond Assurance
         Corp
AMEMIC ....Association of Mill & Elevator Mutual
         Insurance Companies
AMIC..........American Marine Insurance
         Clearinghouse
AMIM.........Associate in Marine Insurance
         Management
AMIP..........American Marine Insurance Forum
AMW ....American Monthly Wage
ANI ....American Nuclear Insurers
ANL ....Above Normal Loss
ANSI...........American National Standards Institute
AOP ....All Other Perils
AP ....Additional Premium

APA.............Associate in Premium Auditing
API..............American Petroleum Institute
APIW.........Association for Professional Insurance Women
AR...............All Risk; Accounts Receivable; Assigned Risk
ARe.............Associate in Reinsurance
ARIA...........American Risk and Insurance Association
ARM..........Associate in Risk Management
ARMI.........Associated Risk Managers International
ARP..........Associate in Research and Planning
ART............Annual Renewable Term (life insurance)
ASA............Administrative Services Arrangement; American Surety Association
...................Associate in Society of Actuaries
ASCLU.......American Society of Chartered Life Underwriters
ASIM..........American Society of Insurance Management
ASIS...........American Society of Industrial Security
ASM...........Available Seat Miles
ASME.........American Society of Mechanical Engineers
ASO............Administrative Services Only
ASPA..........American Society of Pension Actuaries
ASSE..........American Society of Safety Engineers
ASTD..........American Society of Training and Development
ATM............Automated Teller Machine
ATRA..........American Tort Reform Association
AU...............Associate in Underwriting
BAP............Business Auto Policy
BBB.............Banker's Blanket Bond
B&C............Building and Contents
BCBSA.......Blue Cross and Blue Shield Association
BCEGS.......Building Codes Effectiveness Grading Schedule
BERP..........Basic Extended Reporting Period
BFCGL........Broad Form Comprehensive General Liability (endorsement)
BFPD..........Broad Form Property Damage (endorsement)
BI.................Bodily Injury; Business Interruption
BIC..............Business Income Coverage
BM..............Boiler and Machinery Forms
B&M............Boiler and Machinery
BOP............Businessowners Policy
BOW...........Breach of Warranty
BPB............Blanket Position Bond
BPF.............Basic Premium Factor
BR...............Builders Risk
BV...............Brick Veneer (construction)
CAA............Clean Air Act

CAC............Combined Additional Coverage; Combined Auto Coverage
CAI.............Computer Assisted Instruction
CAL............Comprehensive Automobile Liability
CAPP.........Conference of Actuaries in Public Practice
CAR............Contractors All Risk (insurance)
CARE.........Concerned Alliance of Responsible Employers
CAS............Casualty Actuarial Society
CBE............Computer Based Education
CCC............Care, Custody, or Control (exclusion)
CCIA...........Consumer Credit Insurance Association
CCIC..........Conference of Casualty Insurance Companies
CD..............Certificate of Deposit
CDW..........Collision Damage Waiver
CEB............Council of Employer Benefits
CEBS..........Certified Employee Benefits Specialist
CEND.........Confiscation, Expropriation, Nationalization, and Deprivation (insurance)
CEO............Chief Executive Officer
CEPT..........Credit Equivalent By-Pass Trust
CERCLA.....Comprehensive Environmental Response Compensation and Liability Act
C&F............Cost and Freight
CFC............Controlled Foreign Corporation; Chartered Financial Consultant
CFA............Chartered Financial Analyst
CFO............Chief Financial Officer
CFP............Certified Financial Planner; Coordinated Financial Planning
CGL............Comprehensive General Liability; Commercial General Liability
CHCM........Certified Hazard Control Manager
CHFC.........Chartered Financial Consultant
CHIAA.......Crop-Hail Insurance Actuarial Association
CIC.............Certified Insurance Counselor
CICA...........Captive Insurance Company Association
CIF.............Cost, Insurance, and Freight
CIH.............Certified Industrial Hygienist
CIP.............Consolidated Insurance Program
CIRB..........Crop Insurance Research Bureau
CISR...........Certified Insurance Service Representative
CIT.............Critical Incident Technique
CLM...........Commercial Lines Manual
CLU............Chartered Life Underwriter
CMT...........Crisis Management Team
CNHI.........Committee for National Health Insurance
CNP...........Cotton Named Perils (insurance)
C/O............Completed Operations
COB...........Coordination of Benefits

COBRA .... Consolidated Omnibus Reconciliation Act
COC .... Course of Construction
COGSA .... Carriage of Goods by Sea Act
COGWA ...... Carriage of Goods by Water Act
COIL .... Conference of Insurance Legislators
COLA .... Cost of Living Adjustment
COO .... Chief Operating Officer
COPE .... Construction, Occupancy, Protection,
                Exposure
COR .... Cost of Risk
CP .... Commercial Property (forms)
CPA .... Certified Public Accountant
CPCU .... Chartered Property Casualty Underwriter
CPE .... Certified Professional Engineer
CPI .... Consumer Price Index
CPIW .... Certified Professional Insurance Women
CPL .... Comprehensive Personal Liability
               (insurance)
CPL .... Contractors Pollution Liability (insurance)
CPM .... Critical Path Method
CPP .... Certified Protection Professional;
               Commercial Property Program
CPSA .... Consumer Product Safety Act
CPSC .... Consumer Product Safety Commission
CPSM .... Certified Product Safety Manager
CPU .... Central Processing Unit
CQE .... Certified Quality Engineer
CR .... Commercial Crime Forms
CRA .... Cargo Reinsurance Association
CRE .... Certified Reliability Engineer
CRS .... Commercial Risk Services (ISO)
CSL .... Combined Single Limit
CSO .... Claim Services Only
CSO
  TABLE .... Commissioners Standard Ordinary Table
CSP .... Certified Safety Professional; Commercial
               Statistical Plan
CSR .... Customer Service Representative
CV .... Cash Value (life insurance); Coefficient of
               Variation
CVIF .... Compound Value Interest Factor
CWA .... Clean Water Act
CWR .... Countrywide Rate Pages
D&B .... Dun & Bradstreet
DAP .... Deposit Administration Plan
DB .... Decibel
DBA .... Doing Business as
DB&C .... Dwelling, Building and Contents
DCF .... Discounted Cash Flow Techniques
DDD .... Dishonesty, Disappearance and
               Destruction
DDP .... Distributed Data Processing
DEC .... Declarations Page
DED .... Deductible
DI .... Disability Income; Double Indemnity

DIC .... Difference-in-Conditions (insurance)
DIL .... Difference-in-Limits
DITC .... Disability Insurance Training Council
DMIC .... Direct Marketing Insurance Woman
DNI .... Distributable Net Income
D&O .... Directors and Officers (liability)
DOB .... Date of Birth
DOC .... Drive Other Car Coverage
DOD .... Date of Death
DOT .... Department of Transportation
DPP .... Deferred Premium Payment Plan
DR .... Daily Report
DRG .... Diagnostic Related Group
DRI .... Defense Research Institute
DTI .... Department of Trade and Industry
               (London)
EA .... Enrolled Actuary
EAP .... Employee Assistance Program; Estimated
               Annual Premium
EAR .... Erection All Risk (insurance)
EBRI .... Employer Benefit Research Institute
EC .... Extended Coverage (endorsement)
ECC .... Eastern Claims Conference
ECF .... Extended Care Facility
ECFC .... Employers Council on Flexible
               Compensation
ECO .... Extra Contractual Obligations
EDP .... Electronic Data Processing
EEL .... Emergency Exposure Limits
EEOC .... Equal Employment Opportunity
               Commission
EFT .... Electronic Funds Transfer
EIL .... Environmental Impairment Liability
EIS .... Environmental Impact Statement
EL .... Employers Liability; Expected Loss
ELP .... Excess Loss Premium (factor)
ELR .... Expected Loss Rate
EMT .... Emergency Medical Technician
ENCP .... ERISA Non-Compliance Program
E&O .... Errors and Omissions (liability)
EP .... Earned Premium
EPA .... Environmental Protection Agency
ERIC .... Erisa Industry Committee
ERISA .... Employee Retirement Income Security
               Act
ERP .... Extended Reporting Period
ERSC .... Environmental Response Services
               Contractor
E&S .... Excess and Surplus
ESA .... Employee Spending Account
ESH .... Environmental Safety & Health
ESOP .... Employee Stock Ownership Plan
ESOT .... Employee Stock Ownership Trust
ETB .... Engaged in Trade or Business
EXIMBANK Export-Import Bank of the United States

FAA.............Federal Aviation Administration
FAC.............Facultative Reinsurance
FAIR............Fair Access to Insurance Requirements
FALU...........Fellow of the Academy of Life
            Underwriting
FAP.............Family Automobile Policy
FAR.............Federal Aviation Regulations
FAS.............Free Along Side (ocean marine cargo)
FASB............Financial Accounting Standards Board
F&C.............Fire and Casualty
FCAS...........Fellow of the Casualty Actuarial Society
FCIA ....Foreign Credit Insurance Association
FCIC............Federal Crop Insurance Corporation
FCII ....Fellow of the Chartered Insurance
            Institute (British)
FCPL...........Farmers Comprehensive Personal
            Liability
FC&S..........Free of Capture and Seizure
FDA.............Food and Drug Administration
FDI ....Foreign Direct Investment
FDIC ....Federal Deposit Insurance Corporation
FECA ....Federal Employees Compensation Act
FEGLI..........Federal Employees Group Life Insurance
FELA...........Federal Employers Liability Act
FEMA ....Federal Emergency Management Agency
FET.............Federal Excise Tax
FIA ....Full Interest Admitted; Fellow of the
            Institute of Actuaries
FIC ....Fraternal Insurance Counselor
FICA ....Federal Insurance Contribution Act
FICC...........Federation of Insurance & Corporate
            Counsel
FIFO...........First in, First out
FIIC ....Fellow of the Insurance Institute of
            Canada
FIRM...........Flood Insurance Rate Map
FIRREA ......Financial Institutions Reform Recovery
            and Enforcement Act
FLMI ....Fellow of the Life Management Institute
FLSA...........Fair Labor Standards Act
FM..............Factory Mutual
FMV...........Fair Market Value
FOB............Free on Board
FOC ....Fire Office Committee Forms
FPA ....Free of Particular Average
FPAAC ....Free of Particular Average American
            Conditions
FPAEC ....Free of Particular Average English
            Conditions
FPEB..........Fire Prevention and Engineering Bureau
FR...............Fire Resistive; Farm and Ranch (forms)
FSA............Fellow of the Society of Actuaries;
            Flexible Spending Account
FSLIC ....Federal Savings and Loan Insurance
            Corporation

FTC.............Federal Trade Commission
FTCAC........Fire, Theft, and Combined Additional
            Coverage
FVD ....Full Value Declared
GA ....General Agent
GAAP.........Generally Accepted Accounting
            Principles
GAAS ....Generally Accepted Auditing Standards
GAMA ....General Agents and Managers
            Association
GAMC........General Agents and Managers
            Conference
GAO ....General Accounting Office
GAP............Garage Auto Policy
GAAP.........Generally Accepted Accounting
            Principals
GASB.........Governmental Accounting Standards
            Board
GC...............Guaranteed Cost
GCW ....Gross Combined Weight
GFCI...........Ground Fault Circuit Interrupter
GHAA ....Group Health Association of America
GIC ....Guaranteed Investment Contract
GIO ....Guaranteed Insurability Option
GKLL ....Garagekeepers Legal Liability Insurance
GL ....Garage Liability; General Liability
GNEPI........Gross Net Earned Premium Income
GNPI...........Gross Net Premium Income
GNWPI ......Gross Net Written Premium Income
GPO............Government Printing Office; Guaranteed
            Purchase Option
GULP..........Group Universal Life Program
GVW ....Gross Vehicle Weight
HB...............House Bill
HCQIA ....Health Care Quality Improvement Act
HFIE ....Huebner Foundation for Insurance
            Education
HI ....Health Insurance
HII...............Health Insurance Institute
HIAA ....Health Insurance Association of America
HLDI...........Highway Loss Data Institute
HLV.............Human Life Value
HMO ....Health Maintenance Organization
HO ....Homeowners (insurance)
HPL............Hospital Professional Liability
HPR............Highly Protected Risk
HSA............Health System Agency
HSP............Healthcare Safety Professional
HT...............Heavy Timber (construction)
HVAC ....Heating, Ventilating, and Air
            Conditioning
IAC..............Industrial Accident Commission
IADC ....International Association of Drilling
            Contractors

IAHU...........International Association of Health Underwriters

IASA ....Insurance Accounting and Systems Association

IBC ....Insurance Bureau of Canada

IBNER........Incurred but not Enough Reported

IBNR ....Incurred but Not Reported

IBNYR ....Incurred but not yet Reported

ICA ....International Claim Association; Insurance Consortium of America

ICAC ....Insurance Committee for Arson Control

ICC ....Interstate Commerce Commission; Institute Cargo Clauses

ICEDS.........Insurance Company Education Directors Society

ICIA ....International Credit Insurance Association

ICJ..............Institute for Civil Justice

ICP ....Insurance Conference Planners

ICPA...........Insurance Conference Planners Association

ICPI ....Insurance Crime Prevention Institute

IDBI............Industrial Development Bond Insurance

IDI...............Inherent Defects Insurance

IEA ....Insurance Educational Association

IFEBP..........International Foundation of Employee Benefit Plans

IGF ....Insurance Guaranteed Financing

IH................Industrial Hygiene

IHOU ....Institute of Home Office Underwriters

IIA...............Insurance Institute of America

IIAA ....Independent Insurance Agents of America

IIAC............International Insurance Advisory Council

IIC...............Insurance Institute of Canada

IICAE ....Insurance Industry Consumer Affairs Exchange

IIE ....Illinois Insurance Exchange

IIHS............Insurance Institute for Highway Safety

III ....Insurance Information Institute

IIMA...........Insurance Industry Meetings Association

IIS...............International Insurance Seminars, Inc.

IL................Interline Forms

ILCA...........Insurance Loss Control Association

ILF ....Increased Limits Factor

ILU.............Institute of London Underwriters

IM...............Inland Marine (forms)

IMCA..........Insurance Marketing Communications Association

IMUA..........Inland Marine Underwriters Association

IPA..............Independent Practice Association

IPAC...........Insurance Public Affairs Council

IPFA ....Insurance Premium Finance Association

IR ....Incident Recall

IRA ....Individual Retirement Account

IRC..............Internal Revenue Code

IRES............Insurance Regulatory Examiners Society

IRI...............Industrial Risk Insurers

IRIS.............Insurance Regulatory Information System

IRM............Improved Risk Mutuals

IRMC..........Institute for Risk Management Consultants

IRMI............International Risk Management Institute, Inc

IRPM...........Individual Risk Premium Modification

IRR.............Internal Rate of Return

IRS..............Internal Revenue Service

ISCEBS.......International Society of Certified Employee Benefits Specialists

ISO.............Insurance Services Office, Inc

ITC ....Investment Tax Credit

ITI...............Insurance Testing Institute

IVANS ....Insurance Value Added Network Services

JCAH ....Joint Commission on the Accreditation of Hospitals

JSA..............Job Safety Analysis

JUA.............Joint Underwriting Authority; Joint Underwriting Association

JV................Joint Venture

K&R............Kidnap and Ransom

LASH..........Lighter Aboard Ship

LC................Letter of Credit

LCA.............Life Communicators Association

LCF ....Loss Conversion Factor

LDF ....Loss Development Factor

LDW ....Limited Damage Waiver

LEA ....Loss Executives Association

LEL..............Lower Explosive Level

LHWCA ......Longshore and Harbor Workers Compensation Act

LIAA ....Life Insurance Association of America

LIAMA ....Life Insurance Agency Management Association

LIC ....Life Insurers Conference

LIFO............Last in, First out

LIMRA.........Life Insurance Marketing & Research Association

LIRB............Liability Insurance Research Bureau

LOC ....Letter of Credit

LOMA ....Life Office Management Association

LPG.............Liquid Petroleum Gas

LPRT...........Leading Producers Round Table

LPSO ....Lloyd's Policy Signing Office

LTA..............Lost Time Accident; Long Term Agreement

LTD ....Long-Term Disability

LUMP.........Limits Under Multiple Policy Years

LUTC ....Life Underwriting Training Council

M.................Masonry (construction)

MAAA	Member of American Academy of Actuaries
MAC	Maximum Allowable Concentration
MAELU	Mutual Debit Ordinary Life Insurance
MAP	Market Assistance Plan
MAS	Management Advisory Service
MBIA	Municipal Bond Insurance Association
M&C	Manufacturers and Contractors (insurance)
MDO	Monthly Debit Ordinary Life Insurance
MDRT	Million Dollar Round Table
MET	Multiple Employer Trust
MFL	Maximum Foreseeable Loss
MGA	Managing General Agent
MIB	Medical Information Bureau
MICA	Mortgage Insurance Companies of America
MIGA	Multilateral Investment Guarantee Agency
MIS	Management Information System
MLE	Maximum Loss Expectancy
MLEA	Multiple Line Exclusive Agent
MLR	Multiple Location Risk
MMII	Mass Marketing Insurance Institute
M-NC	Masonry–Non-Combustible (construction)
MNC	Multi-National Corporation
MOP	Manufacturers Output Policy
MORT	Management Oversight and Risk Tree
MOSB	Mercantile Open Stock Burglary (insurance)
MP	Minimum Premium; Multiple Peril
MPCI	Multi-Peril Crop Insurance
MPL	Maximum Possible Loss
MPP	Managed Premium Plan
MSBF	Money and Securities Broad Form (insurance)
MSDS	Material Safety Data Sheet
MSVR	Mandatory Securities Valuation Reserve
MTC	Motor Truck Cargo (insurance)
MVR	Motor Vehicle Record
MYSL	Multi-Year Single Limit
NAA	National Association of Accountants
NABRTI	National Association of Bar-Related Title Insurers
NACA	National Association of Catastrophe Adjusters
NACIA	National Association of Crop Insurance Agents
NACSA	National Association of Casualty and Surety Agents
NACSE	National Association of Casualty & Surety Executives
NAFI	National Association of Fire Investigators
NAFIC	National Association of Fraternal Insurance Counselors

NAHU	National Association of Health Underwriters
NAIA	National Association of Insurance Agents
NAIB	National Association of Insurance Brokers
NAIC	National Association of Insurance Commissioners
NAII	National Association of Independent Insurers
NAIIA	National Association of Independent Insurance Adjusters
NAIIO	Non-Admitted Insurers Information Office
NAIW	National Association of Insurance Women
NALC	National Association of Life Companies
NALU	National Association of Life Underwriters
NAMIC	National Association of Mutual Insurance Companies
NAPIA	National Association of Public Insurance Adjusters
NAPSLO	National Association of Professional Surplus Lines Offices
NASBA	National Association of State Boards of Accountancy
NASBP	National Association of Surety Bond Producers
NASD	National Association of Securities Dealers
NATB	National Automobile Theft Bureau
NAUA	National Auto Underwriters Association
NBCU	National Bureau of Casualty Underwriters
NBFU	National Board of Fire Underwriters
NCCI	National Council on Compensation Insurance
NCCMP	National Coordinating Committee for Multiemployer Plans
NCOIL	National Conference of Insurance Legislators
NCPI	National Committee on Property Insurance
NCSI	National Council of Self-Insurers
NCUA	National Credit Union Administration
NEBI	National Employee Benefits Institute
NEISS	National Electronic Injury Surveillance System
NEPA	National Environmental Policy Act
NFCA	National Fraternal Congress of America
NFGMIC	National Federation of Grange Mutual Insurance Companies
NFIP	National Flood Insurance Program
NFPA	National Fire Protection Association

NHAFA.......National Health Care Anti-Fraud Association
NHI.............National Health Insurance
NHTSA.......National Highway Traffic Study Administration
NIA.............National Insurance Association
NICO...........National Insurance Consumer Organization
NIDC...........National Insurance Development Corporation
NIOSH........National Institute for Occupational Safety and Health
NIPA...........National Institute of Pension Administrators
NOC...........Not Otherwise Classified
NOL.............Not Officially Lapsed
NP ....Named Perils
NPD ....No Payroll Division
NPV ....Net Present Value
NRC ....Nuclear Regulatory Commission
NSC ....National Safety Council
NSCI...........National Service Life Insurance
NSIPA.........National Society of Insurance Premium Auditors
NSP.............Net Single Premium
NSPA.........National Society of Public Accountants
NSPE.........National Society of Professional Engineers
NTSB ....National Transportation Safety Board
NVD ....No Value Declared
OASDHI......Old Age, Survivors, Disability, and Health Insurance (Act)
OCA...........Outstanding Claims Account
OCIP...........Owner Controlled Insurance Program
OCP ....Owners and Contractors Protective (insurance)
OCSLA.......Outer Continental Shelf Lands Act
OD...............Occupational Disease
OEE.............Operators Extra Expense (insurance)
OFA.............Organized Flying Adjusters
OI.................Outage Insurance
OIS.............Operating Information System
OL&T..........Owners, Landlords, and Tenants (insurance)
O&M...........Operations and Maintenance (programs)
OPIC...........Overseas Private Investment Corporation
OSHA.........Occupational Safety and Health Act
OTC.............Other Than Collision
PA...............Particular Average
PAAS..........Premium Audit Advisory Service
PAIU............Professional Association of Insurance Underwriters
PAP ....Personal Automobile Policy
PARMA ....Public Agency Risk Managers Association

PAS.............Premium Allocation System
PBGC ....Pension Benefits Guaranty Corporation
PC ....Professional Corporation
P&C.............Property and Casualty
PD ....Property Damage
PE................Professional Engineer
PEBB..........Public Employee Blanket Bond
PERT ....Performance, Evaluation, and Review Technique
PI.................Personal Injury
P&I.............Protection and Indemnity (insurance)
PIA.............Professional Insurance Agents (association); Primary Insurance Account
PIAA...........Physician Insurers Association of America
PICA...........Professional Insurance Communicators of America
PILR...........Property Loss Research Bureau
PIMA..........Professional Insurance Mass-Marketing Association
PIP ....Personal Injury Protection
PL................Professional Liability
PLE ....Primary Loss Expectancy
PLL.............Pollution Legal Liability (Insurance)
PLR ....Primary Loss Retention
PMA ....Package Modification Adjustment
PMF............Package Modification Factor
PMI.............Private Mortgage Insurance
PML............Probable Maximum Loss
POL.............Public Officials Liability
PPF ....Personal Property Floater
PPO ....Preferred Provider Organization
PR ....Pro Rata
PRD ....Pro Rata Distribution
PRIMA ....Public Risk Management Association
PRO ....Peer Review Organization
PRP............Potentially Responsible Party
PSAC..........Policy Signing and Accounting Centre (London)
PSC ....Public State Commission; Public Service Commission
PSRO ....Professional Standards Review Organization
PUC ....Public Utilities Commission
PV ....Present Value
Q Tip Trust ....Qualified Terminable Interest Property Trust
QC...............Quality Control
RAA...........Reinsurance Association of America
RAM ....Reverse-Annuity Mortgage
RC...............Replacement Cost
RCRA ....Resource Conservation and Recovery Act of 1976
RDF.............Retro Development Factor

REIT	Real Estate Investment Trust
RFIS	Remedial Feasibility Investigation Study
RFP	Request for Proposal
RICO	Racketeer Influenced and Corrupt Organizations Act of 1970
RIMS	Risk and Insurance Management Society
RM	Risk Management
RMF	Rate Modification Factor
RMIS	Risk Management Information System
ROEBI	Return on Employee Benefits Investment
ROI	Return on Investment
RP	Return Premium
RPG	Risk Purchasing Group
RPMP	Risk Premium Modification Plan
RRA	Risk Retention Act
RRG	Risk Retention Group
RRSP	Registered Retirement Saving Plan
RTW	Return to Work
SA	Society of Actuaries
SAA	Surety Association of America
SAP	Statutory Accounting Principles
SAWW	Statewide Average Weekly Wage
SB	Senate Bill
SBLI	Savings Bank Life Insurance
SCIC	Society of Certified Insurance Counselors
SCOH	Statistical Coding Occupancy Hazard
SCOPE	Supervision, Construction, Occupancy, Protection, Exposure
SCPCU	Society of Chartered Property & Casualty Underwriters
SEC	Securities and Exchange Commission
SEP	Simplified Employee Pension
SERP	Supplemental Extended Reporting Period
SEUA	Southeastern Underwriters Association
SF	Standard Fire Forms
SFR	Semi-Fire Resistive
SGLI	Servicemen's Group Life Insurance
SIA	Society of Insurance Accountants
SIC	Standard Industry Classification
SIIA	Self-Insurance Institute of America
SIPC	Securities Investor Protection Corporation
SIR	Self-Insured Retention; Society of Insurance Research
SITE	Society of Insurance Trainers and Educators
SK	Storekeepers (liability)
SL	Sprinkler Leakage
SMP	Special Multi-Peril (package policy)
S&P	Standard and Poor's
SOA	Society of Actuaries
SPBA	Society of Professional Benefit Administrators
SPECS	Specifications
SR	Short Rate
SRA	Society for Risk Analysis

SR&CC	Strikes, Riots, and Civil Commotions
SRMC	Society of Risk Management of Consultants
STD	Short-Term Disability
TCD	Treasury Certificate of Deposit
TCN	Third Country National
TDA	Tax Deferred Annuity
TDB	Temporary Disability Benefits
TEFRA	Tax Equity and Financial Responsibility Acts of 1982 & 1983
TIAA	Teachers Insurance and Annuity Association
TIL	Truth in Lending (Act)
TIRB	Transportation Insurance Rating Bureau
TIV	Total Insured Value
TLO	Total Loss Only
TLV	Threshold Limit Values
TM	Tax Multiplier
TMP	Texas Multi-Peril (package policy)
TPA	Third-Party Administrator
TRA	Tax Reform Act of 1984
TSA	Tax Sheltered Annuity
TSCA	Toxic Substances Control Act
TSDF	Treatment, Storage, and Disposal Facility
UCC	Uniform Commercial Code
UCD	Unemployment Compensation Disability
UCI	Unemployment Compensation Insurance
UCR	Usual, Customary, Reasonable (reimbursement)
UEL	Upper Explosive Level
UJF	Unsatisfied Judgment Fund
UIM	Underinsured Motorist
UIMV	Underinsured Motor Vehicle
UL	Underwriters' Laboratories; Umbrella Liability
ULC	Underwriters Laboratories of Canada
UM	Uninsured Motorist
UMPD	Uninsured Motorist Property Damage
UMV	Uninsured Motor Vehicle
UNL	Ultimate Net Loss
U&O	Use and Occupancy
UP	Unearned Premium
UPR	Unearned Premium Reserve
UPS	Uninterruptible Power System
URMIA	University Risk Management & Insurance
USGLI	U.S. Government Life Insurance
USL&HW	United States Longshore and Harbor Workers (Compensation Act)
UST	Underground Storage Tank
V&MM	Vandalism and Malicious Mischief
VGLI	Veterans Group Life Insurance
VP	Valuable Papers
VSI	Vendors Single Interest (insurance)
WA	With Average

WAEPA .... Worldwide Assurance for Employees of Public Agencies

WC .... Workers Compensation

WCRI .... Workers Compensation Research Institute

WLRT .... Women Leaders Round Table

WLUC .... Women Life Underwriters Confederation

WPA .... With Particular Average

XCU .... Explosion, Collapse, and Underground (property damage hazard)

XS .... Excess Policy

YRCT .... Yearly Renewable Convertible Term

YRT .... Yearly Renewable Term

Glossary of Insurance and Risk Management Terms

A

AAPL—See American Association of Petroleum Landmen.

abandonment—An abandonment clause in property insurance policies prohibiting the insured from abandoning damaged property to the insurer for repair or disposal. Arranging for repair or disposal is the insured's responsibility, unless the insurer elects otherwise. [*Commercial Property Insurance* V.F.33]

abatement—The act or process of diminishing the presence of a pollutant (e.g., asbestos or lead) in either degree or intensity.

absorbed dose—The amount of a chemical that enters the body of an exposed organism.

accept—To agree to insure. An insurer accepts a risk when an underwriter or agent agrees to insure it, and the essential elements of the insurance contract are known and agreed to by the parties to it. Even though a policy has not been issued, once the risk is "accepted," the insurer is obligated to pay a loss that occurs subject to the terms and conditions of the coverage agreed upon.

accident—(1) In boiler and machinery insurance, a sudden and accidental equipment breakdown that causes damage to the equipment. Boiler and machinery coverage applies to loss or damage resulting from an accident to a covered object. [*Commercial Property Insurance* XI.D.9]

(2) In liability insurance, particularly older forms, an event that must cause bodily injury or property damage in order to trigger coverage. Modern liability policies, such as the commercial general liability policy, use the broader term "occurrence" instead of "accident." See Occurrence. [*Commercial Auto Insurance* VIII.G.1]

accidental death—Death resulting directly and solely from: (1) an accidental injury visible on the surface of the body or disclosed by an autopsy, (2) a disease or infection resulting directly from an accidental injury as described, beginning within 30 days after the date of the injury, or (3) an accidental drowning.

accidental death & dismemberment (AD&D)—A type of coverage often written in conjunction with group life insurance plans. It essentially provides for (1) "double indemnity" when death is caused by an accident, and (2) defined dismemberment benefits. It will generally pay the full principal sum when death occurs or more than one member (e.g., hand, eye, or foot) is lost in an accident. One-half of the principal sum is generally paid when one member is lost.

accidental means—A condition precedent to recovery under some insurance policies requiring that the covered loss be the result of an accident rather than merely the accidental result of a nonaccidental event.

accident year data—A method of arranging loss and exposure data of an insurer, group of insurers, or within a book of business, so that all losses associated with accidents occurring within a given calendar year and all premium earned during that same calendar year are compared. Thus, regardless of individual policy periods and regardless of when a loss is reported or is paid, accident year data 1997 will include all premiums earned during 1997 and will also include all losses occurring in 1997. Rate-making organizations use both accident year data and policy year data in their analyses of rate adequacy. For example, workers compensation loss development factors promulgated by NCCI are developed from accident year data. [*Risk Financing* Appendix F] accommodation line—When an insurer accepts from an agent, broker, or the insured—whose account is otherwise satisfactory—one or more lines of coverage that would ordinarily be declined if considered strictly on the merits of the individual risk.

accountants professional liability insurance—Provides coverage for financial loss from of the delivery of professional accounting services. The policies typically exclude coverage for fraud, intentional acts, criminal acts, bodily injury, and property damage. Coverage for higher risk activities, such as investment services and Securities and Exchange Commission (SEC) work is available by endorsement. [*Professional Liability Insurance* XIII.C.1–XIII.F.303]

account current—A monthly statement to the insurance company by its agent showing premiums written, return premiums, commissions, and net amount due to or from the company.

accounts receivable coverage—Insures against loss of sums owed to the insured by its customers that are uncollectible because of damage by an insured peril to accounts receivable records. [*Commercial Property Insurance* IX.H.1]

Accredited Adviser in Insurance (AAI)—Professional designation resulting from a joint effort of the Insurance Institute of America (IIA) and the Independent Insurance Agents of America (IIAA). The program leading to this designation consists of three 13-week courses with three national exams, and is designed for all insurance production personnel in any distribution system.

acquisition cost—(1) The cost incurred by an insurer in securing business. This is usually considered to include commission to agents and brokers, and sometimes, field supervision costs.

(2) The commission paid to a reinsured company by its reinsurer to offset its agent's commission, premium taxes, and other costs of doing business—also includes reinsurance broker's commission, where applicable. [*Risk Financing* III.A.44]

action levels—(1) Regulatory levels recommended by the Environmental Protection Agency for enforcement by the Food and Drug Administration and U.S. Department of Agriculture when pesticide residues occur in food or feed commodities for reasons other than the direct application of the pesticide. As opposed to "tolerances" which are established for residues occurring as a direct result of proper usage, action levels are set for inadvertent residues resulting from previous legal use or accidental contamination.

(2) In the Superfund program, the existence of a contaminant concentration in the environment high enough to warrant action or trigger a response under the Superfund Amendments and Reauthorization Act of 1986 and the National Oil and Hazardous Substances Contingency Plan. The term is also used in other regulatory programs.

action versus the insurer provision—See Legal action against us.

act of God—An accident or event resulting from natural causes, without human intervention or agency, and one that could not have been prevented by reasonable foresight or care, e.g., floods, lightening, earthquake, or storms. This is a peril terminology found in ocean and inland marine policies.

actual cash value (ACV)—In property insurance, one of several possible methods of establishing the value of insured property to calculate the premium and determine the amount the insurer will pay in the event of loss. Although the term is seldom defined in the policy, the generally accepted insurance industry definition of actual cash value is the cost to repair or replace the damaged property with materials of like kind and quality, less depreciation of the damaged property. Courts have differed as to whether depreciation includes economic obsolescence as well as actual physical depreciation. [*Commercial Property Insurance* V.F.44 and *Commercial Auto Insurance* VIII.E.10]

actuary—An individual, often holding a professional designation, e.g., Fellow of the Casualty Actuarial Society (FCAS) who computes statistics relating to insurance, typically estimating loss reserves and developing premium rates. [*Risk Financing* I.B.1]

acute exposure—A single exposure to a toxic substance that results in severe biological harm or death. Acute exposures are usually characterized as lasting no longer than a day, as compared to continuous or repeated exposure over a longer period of time.

acute toxicity—The ability of a substance to cause poisonous effects resulting in severe biological harm or death soon after a single exposure or dose. Also, any severe poisonous effect resulting from a single short-term exposure to a toxic substance.

ACV—See Actual cash value.

additional expense coverage—See Extra expense coverage.

additional insured—A person or organization not automatically included as an insured under an insurance policy, but for whom insured status is arranged, usually by endorsement. A named insured's impetus for providing additional insured status to others may be a desire to protect the other party because of a close relationship with that party (e.g., employees or members of an insured club) or to comply with a contractual agreement requiring the named insured to do so (e.g., customers or owners of property leased by the named insured). [*Commercial Liability Insurance* VI.H and *Commercial Property Insurance* IV.G.6]

additional medical—Provides medical benefits to an insured worker over and above those provided by the statutory compensation laws of a particular state. Most state regulations provide for unlimited medical coverage for injured workers; however, in the few states where a limit remains in place, the workers compensation administrator may grant a variance to override the limit. [*IRMI's Workers Comp* VI.C.13]

additional named insured—(1) A person or organization, other than the first named insured, identified as an insured in the policy declarations or an addendum to the policy declarations.

(2) A person or organization added to a policy after the policy is written with the status of named insured. This entity would have the same rights and responsibilities as an entity named as an insured in the policy declarations (other than those rights and responsibilities reserved to the first named insured). In this sense, the term can be contrasted with additional insured, a person or organization added to a policy as an insured but not as a named insured. The term has not acquired a uniformly agreed upon meaning within the insurance industry, and use of the term in the two different senses defined above often produces confusion in requests for additional insured status between contracting parties. See Additional insured.

add-on control device—An air pollution control device, such as carbon absorber or incinerator, that reduces the level of pollutants in an exhaust gas. The control device usually does not affect the process being controlled and thus is "add-on" technology, as opposed to a scheme to control pollution effected by altering the basic process itself.

adjusted earnings—Estimated earnings of an insurer based on the growth in premiums written plus net earnings from operations.

adjusted net worth—An estimated value for a book of business and unrealized capital gains (less potential income tax on the gains), plus the capital surplus and voluntary reserves of an insurer. Other adjustments are frequently made as well.

adjuster—One who settles insurance claims. This typically involves investigation of the loss and a determination of the extent of coverage. In the context of first-party (e.g., property) insurance, the adjuster negotiates a settlement with the insured. In liability insurance, the adjuster coordinates the insured's defense and participates in settlement negotiations. Adjusters may be employees of the insurer (staff adjusters) or of independent adjusting bureaus (independent adjusters) that represent insurers and self-insureds on a contract basis. Public adjusters are consultants who specialize in assisting insureds in presenting claims to insurance companies in a manner that will maximize their recovery.

administrative order—A legal document signed by the Environmental Protection Agency (EPA) directing an individual, business, or other entity to take corrective action or refrain from an activity. It describes the violations and actions to be taken, and can be enforced in court. Such orders may be issued, for example, as a result of an administrative complaint whereby the respondent is ordered to pay a penalty for violations of a statute.

administrative order on consent—A legal agreement signed by the Environmental Protection Agency (EPA) and an individual, business or other entity through which the violator agrees to pay for correction of violations, take the required corrective or cleanup actions, or refrain from an activity. It describes the actions to be taken, may be subject to a comment period, applies to civil actions, and can be enforced in court.

administrative services only (ASO)—A group health self-insurance program for large employers wherein the employer assumes responsibility for all the risk, purchasing only administrative services from the insurer. Such administrative services include such activities as the preparation of an administration manual, communication with employees, determination and payment of benefits, preparation of government reports, preparation of summary plan descriptions, and accounting. Most employers would also purchase stop loss insurance to protect against catastrophic losses.

administrator—A person or organization appointed as fiduciary in the settlement of an estate.

admiralty law—All areas of law relating to maritime activity, including personal injury liability, property damage liability, and maritime contracts.

admitted assets—Assets whose value is included in the annual statement of an insurance company to the state commissioner of insurance.

admitted insurer—An insurer licensed to do business in a given state. [*Risk Financing* I.B.1]

admitted reinsurer—One who has substantially complied with licensing requirements of a particular state but has not taken out a license. Reinsurance effected with an admitted reinsurer is equivalent to reinsurance with a licensed reinsurer as far as taking credit for reinsurance is concerned.

ADR—See Alternative dispute resolution.

advanced wastewater treatment—Any treatment of sewage that goes beyond the secondary or biological water treatment stage and includes the removal of nutrients, such as phosphorus and nitrogen and a high percentage of suspended solids.

adverse publicity coverage—An excess and surplus lines coverage that protects the insured from loss of income resulting from adverse publicity. Coverage is usually on a named peril basis. [*Professional Liability Insurance* XVI.C.1]

adverse selection—An imbalance in an exposure group created when persons who perceive a high probability of loss for themselves seek to buy insurance to a much greater degree than those who perceive a low probability of loss.

advertising injury—A general liability coverage, combined in standard commercial general liability policies with personal injury coverage, that insures the following offenses in connection with the insured's advertising of its goods or services: libel, slander, invasion of privacy, copyright infringement, and misappropriation of advertising ideas. [*Commercial Liability Insurance* V.E]

advisory endorsement—An endorsement developed by a rating bureau and distributed to member insurers but not filed with the state insurance departments on behalf of the member insurers. Each individual insurer must make its own filing.

aerobic treatment—A process by which microbes decompose complex organic compounds in the presence of oxygen and use the liberated energy for reproduction and growth. (Such processes include extended aeration, trickling filtration, and rotating biological contactors.)

affiliated companies—Insurance companies linked together through common ownership or interlocking directorates.

afterburner—In incinerator technology, a burner located so that the combustion gases are made to pass through its flame in order to remove smoke and odors. It may be attached to or be separated from the incinerator itself.

AGC—See Associated General Contractors of America.

agency—An office where insurance is sold. It may be directed toward property and liability insurance or life and health insurance, or both. Also, it might be an independent organization or a company subsidiary group.

agency agreement—A written contract stipulating the arrangement between an insurance agency and the insurance company it represents. Important details such as ownership of renewals, commission percentages, and duties and responsibilities of each party are usually spelled out in this agreement.

agency plant—The total force of an insurer's marketing representatives.

agency system—The independent contractor approach to sales and service in insurance marketing. This is in juxtaposition to direct marketing, which uses salaried sales representatives or direct mail.

agent—A person or organization who solicits, negotiates, or instigates insurance contracts on behalf of an insurer. Agents can be independent businessmen or employees of the company.

agent's errors and omissions—Liability coverage for any act or omission of the insured (or of any other person for whose acts or omissions the insured is legally responsible), arising out of the performance of professional services for others in the insured's capacity as an insurance agent or insurance broker. [*Professional Liability Insurance* XV.A.1-XV.F.305]

agent's license—A state-issued permit under whose provisions the agent conducts business.

aggregate—(1) A limit in an insurance policy stipulating the most it will pay for all covered losses sustained during a specified period of time, usually a year. Aggregate limits are commonly included in liability policies. While not often used in property insurance, aggregates are sometimes included with respect to certain catastrophic exposures, e.g., earthquake and flood.

(2) The dollar amount of reinsurance coverage during one specified period, usually 12 months, for all reinsurance losses sustained under a treaty during such period. [*Risk Financing* I.B.1]

aggregate excess insurance—Provides coverage once the total claims for an annual period exceed a predetermined retention amount. The retention can be stated as a flat dollar amount (often calculated as a percentage of expected losses), as a percentage of standard premium, or in terms of a specific loss ratio. See Aggregate excess of loss reinsurance.

aggregate excess of loss reinsurance—A form of reinsurance that stipulates participation by the reinsurer when aggregate losses for the primary insurer exceed a certain level. [*Risk Financing* V.A.13]

aggregate limit of liability—An insurance contract provision limiting the maximum liability of an insurer for a series of losses in a given time period, e.g., a year or for the entire period of the contract. [*Commercial Liability Insurance* V.I.1-6 and *Risk Financing* I.B.1]

aggregate limits reinstatement—A clause contained in the extended reporting provisions of some claims-made policies that reinstates—for the term of the extended reporting period—the original policy limits of liability if they have been reduced or impaired by the payment of claims or by the setting of claim reserves. See Extended reporting period. [*Commercial Liability Insurance* II.C]

agreed amount clause, option or endorsement—A property insurance provision that effectively suspends the coinsurance clause until a specified expiration date. This is accomplished by a statement that the insurance amount shown in the endorsement or in the declaration is agreed to be equal to the specified percentage of value required by the coinsurance provision. [*Commercial Property Insurance* V.F.55]

agreement not to rely on government immunity—An endorsement to liability policies expressing an agreement not to rely on the statutory limitations regarding governmental immunity unless requested by the insured. It is used when public entities have limited liability or complete immunity under state statute, but this immunity or limitation of liability can be waived by the governmental entity on a case-by-case basis. Although instances where statutory limitations should be waived are rare, this endorsement leaves control with the insured.

AIA—See American Institute of Architects.

airborne particulates—The total of suspended particulate matter found in the atmosphere as solid particles or liquid droplets. Chemical composition of particulates varies widely, depending on location and time of year. Airborne particulates include windblown dust, emissions from industrial processes, smoke from the burning of wood and coal, and motor vehicle or nonroad engine exhausts.

air quality control region—A federally designated area that is required to meet and maintain federal ambient air quality standards. May include nearby locations in the same state or nearby states that share common air pollution problems.

air quality standards—The level of pollutants prescribed by regulations that may not be exceeded during a given time in a defined area.

air stripping—A treatment system that removes volatile organic compounds (VOCs) from contaminated groundwater or surface water by forcing an airstream through the water, thus causing the compounds to evaporate.

air toxins—Any air pollutant for which a national ambient air quality standard (NAAQS) does not exist (i.e., those other than ozone, carbon monoxide, PM-10, sulfur dioxide, nitrogen oxide) that may reasonably be anticipated to cause cancer, developmental effects, reproductive dysfunctions, neurological disorders, heritable gene mutations, or other serious or irreversible chronic or acute health effects in humans.

ALAE—See Allocated loss adjustment expenses.

aleatory contract—An agreement concerned with an uncertain event that provides for unequal transfer of value between the parties. Insurance policies are aleatory contracts because an insured can pay premiums for many years without sustaining a covered loss. Conversely, insureds sometimes pay relatively small premiums for a short period of time and then receive coverage for a substantial loss.

alienated premises—Premises that have been sold or given away to another or abandoned. An exclusion in the standard commercial general liability (CGL) policy states that coverage does not apply to property damage to such premises arising out of those premises. An exception to this exclusion clearly leaves coverage intact for contractors' completed operations as long as the premises were never occupied, rented, or held out for rental by the named insured. [*Commercial Liability Insurance* V.D]

alien insurer—An insurer domiciled outside the United States. See Foreign insurer. [*Risk Financing* I.B.1]

allegations—Unsupported assertions that each party intends to prove.

allocated loss adjustment expenses (ALAE)—Loss adjustment expenses that are assignable or allocable to specific claims.Fees paid to outside attorneys, experts, and investigators used to defend claims are examples of ALAE. [*Risk Financing* I.B.1]

allocated loss expense—See Allocated loss adjustment expenses above.

allocation—A term describing the process specified within the provisions of a directors & officers liability policy that apportions liability for a given claim between the individual directors/officers and the organization itself. Allocation of such liability is critical, because D&O policies written for corporations cover only the directors and officers, not the organization. Allocation disputes between insurers and insureds are frequent, given the large dollar amounts frequently at stake in high-profile D&O claims. [*Professional Liability Insurance* X.E.3]

all risk coverage—Property insurance covering loss arising from any fortuitous cause except those that are specifically excluded. This is in contrast to named perils coverage which applies only to loss arising out of causes that are listed as covered. [*Commercial Property Insurance* II.D.7]

all risks, difference-in-conditions (builders risk)—A policy maintained by a general contractor (or subcontractor) to fill coverage gaps created by a project owner's (or general contractor's) maintenance of its own builders risk program. Often the owner (or general contractor) will purchase builders risk insurance on a particular project that is not as broad as the coverage that the general contractor (or subcontractor) ordinarily purchases, or that has a much higher deductible than the general contractor (or subcontractor) ordinarily purchases.

In such cases, the general contractor (or subcontractor) can purchase a builders risk difference-in-conditions policy that covers any loss excluded or under the deductible of the owner's or general contractor's program—subject to the exclusions and deductible in the difference-in-conditions policy.

all risks, ground and flight—Provides all risk hull coverage for the described aircraft whether or not the aircraft is in flight at the time of loss. See All risk coverage.

all risks, not in motion—Provides all risk hull coverage for the described aircraft while not in motion, i.e., on the ground and not in motion under its own power. Coverage applies for a loss occurring while the aircraft is being pushed or towed. A taxiing aircraft is considered to be in motion. See All risk coverage.

alternate employer endorsement—An endorsement that provides those scheduled as alternate employers with primary workers compensation and employers liability coverage as if they were an insured in the policy. This endorsement is commonly used when a temporary help supplier (the insured) is required by its customer (the alternate employer) to protect the alternate employer from claims brought by the insured's employees. [*IRMI's Workers Comp* VI.L.1]

alternative dispute resolution (ADR)—Methods for resolving legal disputes other than full litigation through formal trial. Arbitration proceedings are the most commonly used ADR technique. [*Commercial Liability Insurance* V.L]

alternative market—A term commonly used in risk financing to refer to one of a number of risk funding techniques (e.g., self-insurance, captive) or facilities (e.g., ACE, XL) that provide coverages or services that are outside the realm of such provided by most traditional property and casualty insurers. The alternative market may be utilized by large corporations, for example, to provide high limits of coverage over a large self-insured retention; it may also be utilized by groups of smaller entities, for example, participating in a risk retention group or group captive program. Note that the distinction between traditional and alternative markets tends to blur over time as many traditional insurers expand their offering of products to encompass alternative type funding techniques, and vice versa. Also, retrospective rating plans, especially paid loss plans, are sometimes identified with the alternative market. [*Risk Financing* VIII.E.1]

alternative remedial contract strategy contractors—Government contractors who provide project management and technical services to support remedial response activities at National Priorities List (NPL) sites.

alternative risk financing facilities—Any risk financing mechanism that does not involve a commercial insurance company, e.g., captive insurers, risk retention groups, pools, and individual self-insurance. [*Risk Financing* I.A.4–5 and VIII.E.1–8]

American Association of Petroleum Landmen (AAPL)—Promulgates the Model Form Operating Agreement (AAPL Form 610).

American Institute of Architects (AIA)—Promulgator of several standard construction contracts, defining the responsibilities of contracting parties with respect to indemnification and the purchase of insurance coverage.

American Petroleum Institute (API)—Promulgator of several standard oil and gas contracts, such as the Master Rotary Drilling contract.

amount at risk—The protection element of a life insurance policy as calculated by subtracting any cash value from the face amount. It decreases over time as premiums are paid and cash value increases.

amount subject—The value that may reasonably be expected to be lost in a single fire or other casualty, depending on the protection and construction of the risk and the distribution or concentration of values. Estimating the amount subject is a major responsibility of inspectors and underwriters. See Probable maximum loss.

animal mortality insurance—A form of life insurance for livestock, zoological, and domesticated animals. Normally covers death from any cause with some exceptions as well as voluntary destruction for humane reasons. Also available on a named perils basis.

anniversary date—A date used in some types of insurance, e.g., workers compensation, when a prior policy has been canceled midterm, that governs the application of rates and experience modifiers. It prevents either the insured or the insurer from canceling a policy midterm to take advantage of a more favorable rate structure. It also may have application for changes of ownership or combinations of ownership.

For an example of how the anniversary date applies in the case of a canceled policy, assume a workers compensation policy is written for a 1-year term effective January 1, 1997. It is subsequently canceled and rewritten effective July 1, 1997. The new policy would carry an anniversary date, or anniversary rating date, of January 1,

1998. The rates effective on July 1, 1997, when the new policy is issued are those that were effective January 1, 1997, not those that are currently effective. On January 1, 1998, the anniversary rating date, the policy is endorsed to the rates and modifier effective January 1, 1998. Then, when the new policy expires July 1, 1998, and is renewed, the anniversary date becomes July 1 and stays that date until some event causes the process to begin all over.

annual aggregate deductible—(1) A deductible type program under which the insured agrees to reimburse its insurer for its own losses during the policy year up to the agreed upon annual aggregate amount. Once the insured has paid losses up to that amount, the remainder of losses for the annual period are paid by the insurer without seeking reimbursement from the insured.

(2) The amount by which a loss or applicable coverage limit is reduced in order to determine the amount of the insured's recovery. In standard property insurance practice, the deductible amount is subtracted from the amount of the adjusted loss; the insurer pays this reduced amount and the insured is responsible for the deductible amount. [*Risk Financing* I.B.1]

annual payments annuity—An annual payment over a period of time up to some maximum that requires yearly premium payments.

annual statement—A yearly report required by the state insurance commissioner detailing insurers' income, expenses, and assets and liabilities, along with other pertinent data.

annuitant—The recipient of periodic payments made over a specified period of time.

annuity—A stream of periodic payments made over a specified period of time.

annuity certain—Funds received from an annuity in the form of a guaranteed minimum number or amount of payments.

annuity due—Income received from an annuity that is paid at the beginning of a period rather than at the end.

answer—The formal written statement made by a defendant setting forth the grounds of his defense under the Codes and Rules of Civil Procedure.

anti-stacking provisions—Anti-stacking provisions are intended to avoid the application of multiple sets of deductibles or multiple sets of limits to a single loss event. They are sometimes included in insurance policies covering exposures that may occur over long periods of time, triggering coverage under multiple policies. They stipulate that, in such an event, only one policy limit or one deductible (rather than the limit or deductible under each policy) applies to the occurrence. They may also be included in liability policies to specify that all claims resulting from a single occurrence will be subject to one each occurrence limit. [*Commercial Liability Insurance* XIII.E]

antitrust liability—Violations of the Sherman and Clayton Acts that prohibit restraints of trade of monopolies. In 1982 the U.S. Supreme Court decided that cities are not immune to antitrust laws. Exclusions for alleged violations should be avoided in the public officials liability policy. [*Professional Liability Insurance* XI.C.6]

AOSC—See Association of Oilwell Servicing Contractors.

apparent agency—A legal doctrine applied in connection with estoppel stating that an agent has whatever power a reasonable person would assume that agent to have.

appeal—The plea to an appellate court for review of an order issued by a trial court.

application—A form providing the insurer with certain information necessary to underwrite a given risk. It is completed by the applicant for insurance.

application of retention—Under an excess liability policy, the practice of specifying a retention amount that applies on a different basis to different types of covered loss. For example, under most excess policies, the retention specified applies "per accident/occurrence" for losses other than occupational disease claims and "per employee" for occupational disease.

apportionment—Involves the question of "how much" each of two or more policies covering a risk, which sustained a loss, will contribute to that loss.

appraisal clause—Property insurance provision allowing either the insurer or the insured to demand a binding appraisal of damaged property in the event of a dispute as to its value and establishing the required appraisal procedure. [*Commercial Property Insurance* V.F.33]

approval—Acceptance of a given risk by an insurer because the underwriting standards of the insurer have been met.

"A" rates—Judgment rates that do not have loss experience statistics as a foundation for their development. These rates are developed by the underwriter on an individual risk basis, according to what the underwriter feels is an equitable rate commensurate with risk involved.

arbitration—Referral of a dispute to an impartial third party chosen by the parties in the dispute who agree in advance to abide by the arbitrator's award issued after a hearing at which both parties have a chance to be heard.

arbitration clause—Language providing a means of resolving differences between a reinsurer and the reinsured (or an insurer and an insured) without litigation. Usually, each party appoints an arbiter. The two arbiters select a third, or an umpire, and a majority decision of the three becomes binding on the parties in the arbitration proceedings. [*Professional Liability Insurance* VII.D.12]

architects and engineers liability coverage—A form of liability insurance that insures design professionals against errors and omissions in their work. Coverage for faulty construction work associated with projects is normally excluded under the policies. [*Professional Liability Insurance* XVII.B.1–XVII.F.303]

ARM—See Associate in Risk Management.

asbestos—A mineral fiber that can pollute air or water and cause cancer or asbestosis when inhaled. Environmental Protection Agency has banned or severely restricted its use in manufacturing and construction. Liability arising out of asbestos-related injuries is commonly excluded from coverage in umbrella policies and in some general policies as well. [*Commercial Liability Insurance* XI.D]

asbestos abatement—Procedures to control fiber release from asbestos-containing materials in a building or to remove them entirely, including removal, encapsulation, repair, enclosure, encasement, and operations and maintenance programs.

asbestos program manager—A building owner or designated representative who supervises all aspects of the facility's asbestos management and control program.

ASO—See Administrative services only.

assessment company (society or insurer)—An insurer retaining the right to assess additional charges above initial premium when those premiums are shown to be inadequate to cover the costs of operation. This is usually a mutual or reciprocal type of insurer.

asset share value—The value of a class of business to an insurer.

assigned risk plan—A method of providing insurance required by state insurance codes for those risks that are unacceptable in the normal insurance market. Every state with the exception of those which are monopolistic has an assigned risk plan which is either a stand alone entity or part of the competitive state fund. All insurers writing workers compensation coverage in the voluntary insurance market must also participate in the plan. [*IRMI's Workers Comp* III.D]

assignee—The receiver of policy rights through an assignment.

assignment—A transfer of legal rights under, or interest in, an insurance policy to another party. In most instances, the assignment of such rights can only be effected with the written consent of the insurer. [*Commercial Liability Insurance* V.M; *Commercial Property Insurance* V.C.6; and *Commercial Auto Insurance* XII.B.10]

associate—Younger attorney or one new to the practice of law. An entry-level lawyer usually works for a firm for 6 to 7 years before being eligible for consideration as a partner at a law firm.

Associated General Contractors of America (AGC)—Promulgator of several standard construction contracts that define indemnity and insurance requirements of parties to the construction project. See American Institute of Architects.

Associate in Automation Management (AAM)—Professional designation awarded by the Insurance Institute of America (IIA) upon successful completion of three national exams. The program leading to this designation consists of three 13-week courses with three national exams, and is designed for insurance practitioners who use automation in their work, supervise automated activities, or provide information services to insurance practitioners.

Associate in Claims (AIC)—Professional designation awarded by the Insurance Institute of America (IIA) upon successful completion of four national exams. The program leading to this designation consists of four 13-week courses with four national exams, and is most appropriate for experienced adjusters, claims supervisors and examiners. The program was developed with the technical and financial assistance of the National Association of Independent Insurance Adjusters.

Associate in Fidelity and Surety Bonding (AFSB)—Professional designation awarded by the Insurance Institute of America (IIA) upon successful completion of five national exams, three of which are designed specifically for this program and two of which are CPCU exams. The program leading to this designation was developed with the encouragement and technical assistance of the National Association of Surety Bond Producers and the Surety Association of America, and is designed for anyone associated with the fidelity and surety bonding industry or who has an interest in becoming proficient in the field.

Associate in Insurance Accounting and Finance (AIAF)—Professional designation awarded by the Insurance Institute of America (IIA) upon successful completion of four national exams, three of which are designed specifically for this program and one of which is a CPCU course. The program offers an opportunity to master statutory accounting principles, reporting procedures, and financial management concepts; it presumes prior exposure to general accounting principles and a working knowledge of insurance principles and coverages.

Associate in Insurance Services (AIS)—Professional designation awarded by the Insurance Institute of America (IIA) upon successful completion of four national exams, one specifically designed for this program and the three examinations in the IIA Program in General Insurance. The program leading to this designation consists of one course in total quality management for insurance personnel with an exam made available on demand, and the three general insurance courses, together with those exams.

Associate in Loss Control Management (ALCM)—Professional designation awarded by the Insurance Institute of America (IIA) upon successful completion of five national exams, two of which are designed specifically for this program and three of which are CPCU courses. The program leading to this designation is designed for individuals with job responsibilities that deal with selection, design, and implementation of loss controls.

Associate in Management (AIM)—Professional designation awarded by the Insurance Institute of America (IIA) upon successful completion of three national exams, two of which are designed specifically for this program and one which is a CPCU exam. Dealing with contemporary management principles, the program is designed for upper and middle managers as well as those who are about to move into such positions.

Associate in Marine Insurance Management (AMIM)—Professional designation awarded by the Insurance Institute of America (IIA) upon successful completion of six national exams, two of which are specifically designed for this program and four of which are CPCU programs. The program leading to this designation was developed with the technical and financial assistance of the Inland Marine Underwriters Association and the American Institute of Marine Underwriter, and is designed for individuals whose job duties or professional interests involve inland or ocean marine insurance.

Associate in Premium Auditing (APA)—Professional designation awarded by the Insurance Institute of America (IIA) upon successful completion of six national exams, two of which are designed specifically for this program and four of which are CPCU courses. The program leading to this designation was developed with the cooperation of the National Society of Insurance Premium Auditors, and is designed to enable students to perform premium audits in an organized and professional manner.

Associate in Reinsurance (ARe)—Professional designation awarded by the Insurance Institute of America (IIA) upon successful completion of four national exams, two of which are designed specifically for this program and two of which are CPCU courses. The program leading to this designation was developed with the support of the Reinsurance Section of the CPCU Society and with technical and financial assistance from the Brokers & Reinsurance Markets Association. Program completers will gain an in-depth understanding of the reinsurance business as well as a familiarity with primary insurance company exposures, coverages, and operations.

Associate in Research and Planning (ALP)—Professional designation awarded by the Insurance Institute of America (IIA) upon successful completion of six national exams, two of which are designed specifically for this program and four which are CPCU exams. Developed in cooperation with the Society of Insurance Research, the program leading to this designation is designed for insurance company personnel working in the areas of research, planning, and related decision support functions.

Associate in Risk Management (ARM)—A professional designation conferred upon individuals who successfully complete three written comprehensive examination covering all aspects of risk management. They are administered by the Insurance Institute of America.

Associate in Underwriting (AU)—Professional designation awarded by the Insurance Institute of America (IIA) upon successful completion of four national exams, two of which are specifically designed for this program and two of which are CPCU courses. The program leading to this designation is designed for agency and company underwriters, field representatives, and account managers; it assumes a working knowledge of insurance principles and coverages.

association captive—A captive insurance company formed and owned by a trade or professional association. [*Risk Financing* **IV.K.4 and IV.K.36**]

association group—Group insurance issued covering the members of an association or health insurance issued to those members on a franchise basis.

Association of Oilwell Servicing Contractors (AOSC)—Promulgator of a standard well-servicing contract.

Association of Trial Lawyers of America (ATLA)—Trade organization for plaintiff/claimant personal injury attorneys.

assume—(1) To reinsure all or part of another insurer's risk.

(2) A risk management technique involving the retention of risk (e.g., self-insurance).

assumed liability—See Contractual liability.

assumption—The amount of risk accepted by a reinsurer.

assumption endorsement—See Cut through endorsement.

assumption of risk—Based on the maxim "*volenti non fit injuria.*" If a person knows the consequences of a particular act and voluntarily accepts that risk, he/she is solely responsible for any resulting injury.

assumption of risk doctrine—A common law defense that has been used to pass the responsibility for loss or injury onto the injured party by asserting that the individual had knowledge and understanding of the hazards involved in the undertaking and is therefore not entitled to recovery for the loss. Legal decisions have eroded and narrowed the applicability of this defense. [*IRMI's Workers Comp* **III.C.2**]

assurance—Insurance. Likewise, assured is synonymous with insured as is assurer for insurer.

attained age—Age of insured on a given date. Not to be confused with nearest age.

attorney/client communication—Oral or written communication between an attorney and a client that is intended to remain confidential.

attorney work product—Documents prepared by or on direction of an attorney pursuant to the attorney/client relationship or in furtherance of pending or contemplated litigation.

attractive nuisance doctrine—A notable exception in the law relating to trespassers that imposes a special duty of care on a person maintaining an artificial condition on land which attracts children (e.g., a swimming pool). Under the attractive nuisance doctrine, children enjoy the status and protection of invitees. In some cases, the landowner has been held absolutely liable for injuries to children in connection with an attractive nuisance even though the children were trespassers.

audit—A survey of the financial records of a person or organization conducted annually (in most cases) to determine exposures, limits, premiums, etc.

automatic additional insured endorsement—A manuscript endorsement, sometimes attached to liability policies, that provides insured status automatically to any person or organization which the named insured is required by contract to add as an insured. [*Commercial Liability Insurance* VII.D]

automatic increase in insurance provision—See Inflation guard provision.

automatic insureds—Persons or organizations that are provided with insured status by the terms of an unendorsed policy. Most automatic insureds are members of groups with close ties to the named insured, such as the named insured's directors, officers, and employees. [*Commercial Liability Insurance* V.H]

automatic premium loan—An optional provision in life insurance, that, when selected, authorizes the insurer to pay from the cash value any premium due at the end of the grace period. This provision is useful in preventing inadvertent lapse of the policy.

automatic treaty—A reinsurance treaty under which the ceding company must cede exposures of a defined class that the reinsurer must accept in accordance with the terms of the treaty. [*Risk Financing* V.A.6]

automobile—A land motor vehicle, trailer, or semi-trailer designed for travel on public roads, not including "mobile equipment." This definition is important in determining whether liability coverage is afforded under an auto liability policy or a commercial general liability policy (in the case of mobile equipment). See Mobile equipment. [*Commercial Auto Insurance* VIII.G.2]

automobile liability excess indemnity—Provides excess limits for bodily injury and property damage liability for persons unable to secure more than minimum limits under their basic liability policy. This type of coverage stipulates that the primary policy must always be kept in force and is typically purchased by assigned risk plan policyholders.

average rate—A single rate applying to property at more than one location that is a weighted average of the individual rates applicable to each location.

average severity—The observed or estimated value of an average sized claim. This is determined by dividing losses by claim counts.

aviation accident insurance—Protects employees of a company or other insured personnel against the peril of aircraft accident under a master policy.

aviation hazard—A hazard associated with the peril of death or disability arising from aviation operations other than commercial aircraft exposures. Such coverage may be limited in life and health policies by exclusion or be subject to additional premium.

avoidance—A risk management technique whereby risk of loss is prevented in its entirety by not engaging in activities that present the risk. For example, a construction firm may decide not to take on environmental remediation projects to avoid the risks associated with this type of work.

awareness provisions—See Discovery provision.

B

bailee—A person or organization to whom possession of the property of others has been entrusted, usually for storage, repair, or servicing.

bailee coverage—Inland marine coverage on property entrusted to the insured for storage, repair, or servicing. It is typically purchased by businesses such as dry cleaners, jewelers, repairers, furriers, etc.

barratry—Severe misconduct by the captain or crew of a ship including but not limited to fraudulent and criminal acts that cause loss or damage to the ship or its cargo.

basic causes of loss form (ISO)—One of the four Insurance Services Office, Inc. (ISO), causes of loss forms. This form (CP 10 10) provides coverage for the following named perils: fire, lightning, explosion, smoke, windstorm, hail, riot, civil commotion, aircraft, vehicles, vandalism, sprinkler leakage, sinkhole collapse, and volcanic action. See Causes of loss forms. [*Commercial Property Insurance* **V.Q.1**].

basic extended reporting period (BERP)—The 60-day and 5-year extended reporting periods automatically provided to the insured by the 1986 ISO claims-made CGL policy when a claims-made policy is cancelled, not renewed, renewed with a laser exclusion, renewed on a basis other than claims-made, or renewed with an advanced retroactive date. [*Commercial Liability Insurance* **V.K.3**]

basic limits—The minimum limits of liability that can be purchased by an insured. [*Commercial Liability Insurance* **V.I.2**]

basic premium—In a retrospective rating plan, the policy standard premium multiplied by the basic premium factor or basic premium ratio. It provides for insurer expenses, profit, and contingencies. [*Risk Financing* **III.D.6 and III.F.5**]

basic premium factor—Used in the retrospective formula to represent expenses of the insurer, acquisition, audit, administration, and profit or contingencies, but it does not include taxes. [*Risk Financing* **III.D.6**]

basic rate—The manual shown in an insurer's rate manual at basic limits, before adjustment for such factors as increased limit of liability. This term is somewhat obsolete as respects rating manuals published by independent rating organizations since the advent of loss cost rating.

basket retention—Used in connection with self-insurance. Excess liability insurance that attaches once retained losses for several lines of coverage (e.g., workers compensation and general liability) reach a certain specified level.

beauty contest—Colloquial term used to describe a process in which clients have lawyers or firms make competing proposals for the same assignment or business.

BEN—The Environmental Protection Agency's computer model for analyzing a violator's economic gain from not complying with the law.

bench-scale tests—Laboratory testing of potential cleanup technologies.

bench trial—A trial held in front of a judge but no jury, with the judge rendering the decision.

beneficiary—A person named by the insured to receive the proceeds or benefits accruing under a life policy.

benefits—Compensation for loss and other services provided by insurance companies under terms of insurance contracts.

BERP—See Basic extended reporting period.

best available control measures (BACM)—A term used to refer to the most effective measures (according to EPA guidance) for controlling small or dispersed particulates from sources such as roadway dust, soot and ash from woodstoves and open burning of rush, timber, grasslands, or trash.

best demonstrated available technology (BDAT)— As identified by the EPA, the most effective commercially available means of treating specific types of hazardous waste. BDATs may change with advances in treatment technologies.

Best's Rating—The rating system developed and published annually by A.M. Best Company that indicates the financial condition of insurance companies. [*Risk Financing* X.A.4]

bid bond—A guarantee that a contractor will enter into the contract under consideration if it is awarded to him. The bid bond also guarantees that the contractor will supply the additional bonds required throughout the course of the project.

bifurcation—Usually refers to situations in which the issues of liability and damages are separated and tried independently.

billable hours—Generally, the number of hours a law firm requires an attorney to bill per day, month, or year to a client, firm, or administration.

bill of lading—A document that serves both as a receipt for goods being shipped and a contract defining the extent of the transporter's liability. [*Commercial Property Insurance* IX.E.1]

binder—A legal agreement issued either by an agent or an insurer to provide temporary evidence of insurance until a policy can be issued. Binders should contain definite time limits, they should be in writing, and they should clearly designate the insurer with which the risk is bound. They should also indicate the amount of insurance, the type of policy, and (in the case of property insurance) the perils insured against.

biological magnification—The process by which certain substances, such as pesticides or heavy metals, move up the food chain, work their way into rivers or lakes, and are eaten by aquatic organisms such as fish, which in turn are eaten by large birds, animals or humans. The substances become concentrated in tissues or internal organs as they move up the chain.

bioremediation—Use of living organisms to clean up oil spills or remove other pollutants from soil, water, or wastewater.

Black Lung Benefits Act—This legislation, Title IV of the Federal Coal Mine Health and Safety Act of 1969, and its various amendments provide coverage for mine workers whose exposure to coal dust has resulted in total disability or death due to chronic lung disease. The act grants coverage to address medical treatment and lost wages of the worker in the case of total disability and death benefits to the survivors and dependents in the event of death. [*IRMI's Workers Comp* VII.F.1]

blackmail settlement clause—A provision (also known as the "hammer clause" and "consent to settlement clause") found in professional liability insurance policies, that requires an insurer to seek an insured's approval prior to settling a claim for a specific amount. However, if the insured does not approve the recommended figure, the blackmail settlement clause states that the insurer will not be liable for any additional monies required to settle the claim or for the defense costs that accrue from the point after the settlement recommendation is made by the insurer. [*Professional Liability Insurance* VII.B.20]

blanket contractual liability insurance—Coverage applying to all liability assumed by the insured in contracts, whether reported to the insurer or not. Note that the term "blanket contractual liability insurance" does not address the extent of the transferred liability the policy covers, only that it is not necessary to report contracts to the insurer for listing in the policy. It is possible to have blanket broad form contractual liability insurance or blanket limited form contractual liability insurance. Contractual liability coverage was added to 1973 and earlier edition CGL policies by endorsement. Blanket broad form contractual liability coverage is incorporated into the basic provisions of the 1986 and subsequent CGL forms. [*Commercial Liability Insurance* V.D.3 and *Contractual Risk Transfer* X.B.1]

blanket fidelity bond—Coverage for employee theft of money, securities, or property, written with a per loss limit rather than a per employee or per position limit. [*Commercial Property Insurance* XII.D.6]

blanket group boiler and machinery coverage—Boiler and machinery coverage that applies to all equipment of a certain type. It contrasts with coverage applying only to individually described objects and with coverage applicable to all insurable objects (referred to as "comprehensive boiler and machinery coverage"). [*Commercial Property Insurance* XI.D.8]

blanket limit—A single limit of insurance that applies over more than one location or more than one type of coverage, or both. A blanket limit can be a hedge against the possibility of inaccurate property value estimates since the entire blanket limit can be applied to a loss at a single location. However, the coinsurance clause usually applies to the total value of all the property covered by the blanket limit. [*Commercial Property Insurance* II.D.16]

blanket medical expense—A form of health insurance that pays for all medical costs subject only to a maximum aggregate benefit.

blanket policy—A single insurance policy that covers several different properties, shipments, or locations.

blanket position bond—Coverage for employee theft of money, securities, or property, written with a limit that applies to each position named in the policy, regardless of the number of individuals holding that position. [*Commercial Property Insurance* XII.D.7]

blended rate—An "average" rate, factoring in the hourly rates of partners, associates and paralegals. Clients can sometimes negotiate with a law firm to pay a blended rate, which may be less than what a partner would bill but more than a paralegal would charge.

blowout and cratering—In the oil and gas production industry, refers to uncontrolled eruption of oil, gas, water, or drilling fluid from a well that is in the process of being drilled (blowout) or to the caving in of a well that has already been drilled. Blowouts are generally caused by the penetration of a reservoir that contains gas or oil that is under higher pressure than has been allowed for; often the oil or gas catches fire. When a well craters, often the drilling rig itself goes under with the well. Coverage for the insured's liability for damage to property of others caused by blowout or cratering is optional in the commercial general liability policy. A specialty coverage, control-of-well insurance, provides coverage for the expenses of bringing a blowout under control, the cost to clean up any resulting pollution, and damage to the property of the operator.

blowout prevention warranty—A provision found in oil and gas well drilling equipment coverage forms that makes the use of blowout preventers (high pressure valves that facilitate control of an oil well) on covered equipment a condition of coverage.

blue plan—A name for either Blue Cross or Blue Shield or an organization usually writing a service rather than a reimbursement plan.

boards, bureaus, and taxes—In retrospective rating, referring to outside charges that are levied against an insurer's written premium in an individual account. Such costs are ordinarily passed through to the insured in the retrospective plan factors. [*Risk Financing* III.D.5 and Appendix G.3]

bobtail liability—Automobile liability coverage for an owner/operator after a load has been delivered and while the truck is on the way back to the terminal. Until the point of delivery, liability is assumed by the trucking firm hiring the owner/operator. [*Commercial Auto Insurance* XIII.I.9]

bodily injury by accident limit (workers compensation)—The most the insurer will pay under Part Two, Employers Liability, for all claims arising out of any one accident, regardless of how many employee claims or how many related claims (such as a loss of consortium suit brought by the injured worker's spouse) arise out of the accident. [*IRMI's Workers Comp* VI.D.18]

bodily injury by disease, each employee (workers compensation)—A policy limit within Part Two, Employers Liability establishing the most the insurer will pay for damages due to bodily injury by disease to any one employee. [*IRMI's Workers Comp* VI.D.18]

bodily injury by disease—policy limit (workers compensation)—An aggregate limit of Part Two, Employers Liability stipulating the most the insurer will pay for employee bodily injury by disease claims during the policy period (normally a year) regardless of the number of employees who make such claims. In the event the policy is milder, the limit is reinstated for each subsequent 12 month period. [*IRMI's Workers Comp* VI.D.18]

bodily injury liability insurance—Protection against loss arising out of the liability imposed on the insured by law for damages due to bodily injury, sickness, or disease, including resulting death. [*Commercial Liability Insurance* V.L.4]

boiler and machinery insurance—Coverage for loss caused by mechanical or electrical equipment breakdown, including damage to the equipment, damage to other property of the insured, and damage to property of others. [*Commercial Property Insurance* XI.B.1]

bond—A three-party contract in which one party, the surety, guarantees the performance or honesty of a second party, the principal (obligor), to the third party (obligee) to whom the performance or debt is owed.

bonding—The process by which bonds are written.

book value—The value of an organization's assets as carried on the balance sheet in accordance with General Accepted Accounting Principals (GAAP). The book value for real and personal property is typically the original cost of the property less depreciation. The amount deducted for depreciation is calculated mathematically and may not relate to the actual condition of the property. Since book value is based on the original purchase price and an arbitrary depreciation schedule, it should never be relied on to establish insurable values. See Actual cash value and replacement cost.

boom coverage—Physical damage coverage for the boom of a crane, generally added as an endorsement to the equipment floater. The floater normally contains an exclusion for booms over a specified length while in operation unless the damage is caused by a named peril. The policy may be amended to provide coverage for the boom while not operational thereby enlarging the scope of coverage. [*Commercial Property Insurance* IX.K.7]

bordereau—A report providing premium or loss data with respect to identified specific risks. This report is periodically furnished to a reinsurer by the ceding reinsurers.

borderline risk—A person, organization, or property of doubtful underwriting quality.

Bornhuetter-Ferguson technique—An actuarial technique for developing losses to estimate their ultimate amount. An amount for expected unreported losses (derived using the reciprocal of the loss development factor) is added to actual reported losses to obtain the estimated ultimate loss for a given accident year. The technique is most useful when actual reported losses for an accident year are a poor indicator of future IBNR for the same accident year, as is often the case when there is a low frequency of loss but a very high potential severity.

borrowed servant rule—A common law legal doctrine stipulating that if an insured borrows a worker or employs a person on only a temporary basis, the insured can be held liable for the borrowed employee's actions, despite the fact that a permanentemployee-employer relationship does not exist.

boutique law firm—Firm with a very specialized realm of expertise.

brand equity—The consumer confidence, loyalty, and favorable reputation that a business' product or service has earned in the marketplace. A loss of or reduction of brand integrity can cause a substantial reduction in revenues and market share. Brand integrity can be damaged or lost as a result of many types of fortuitous events, such as product contamination or tampering incidents.

brand rehabilitation—The endeavor of rebuilding consumer confidence and loyalty in a business or product following a product tampering, contamination, or similar event. Such efforts generally involve substantial expenses to cover additional advertising, special promotions, and extra expenses to rush new product to market. These costs can be insured under product recall insurance.

brands and labels endorsement—A property insurance endorsement that grants permission for the insured to remove labels from damaged goods or mark the items as "salvage," provided the goods are not damaged in the process. Alleviates concern about potential injury to the insured's business reputation resulting from the sale of salvaged goods by the insurer. [*Commercial Property Insurance* VI.F.7]

breach—Failure to live up to the conditions or warranties contained in a contract.

breach of warranty clause—A lienholder's or lessor's interest endorsement that causes the policy to continue to protect the financial interest of a lienholder or lessor even when the insured breaches a condition, thereby voiding coverage. Any loss recoveries under this clause are payable only to the lienholder or lessor.

British business interruption coverage—See Gross profits insurance.

broadcasters liability—Legal liability to which radio and television broadcasters are subject. Defamation, invasion of privacy, and errors and omissions are among the types of claims alleged against broadcasters. Coverage for this exposure is available under media liability policies. [*Professional Liability Insurance* XVIII.C.2]

broad causes of loss form (ISO)—One of the four Insurance Services Office, Inc. (ISO), causes of loss forms. This form (CP 10 20) provides named perils coverage for the perils insured against in the basic causes of loss form (fire, lightning, explosion, smoke, windstorm, hail, riot, civil commotion, aircraft, vehicles, vandalism, sprinkler leakage, sinkhole collapse, volcanic action), plus: breakage of building glass; falling objects; weight of snow, ice, or sleet; water damage (in the form of leakage from appliances); and collapse from specified causes. See Causes of loss forms. [*Commercial Property Insurance* V.Q.1]

broad form contractual liability insurance—Contractual liability insurance that covers liability transferred in a wide variety of business contracts. This type of coverage is provided on a blanket basis by the broad form comprehensive general liability endorsement used with the 1973 CGL form and within the standard provisions of the 1986 and subsequent CGL forms. [*Commercial Liability Insurance* V.D.3 and *Contractual Risk Transfer* X.B.1]

broad form drive other car coverage—Automobile coverage available for employees, executives, or any other person who is supplied a company vehicle, but who does not own a personal vehicle, and thus does not have coverage under a personal auto policy. An endorsement may be added to the automobile policy of the company that furnishes the automobile that gives protection while the named individual or spouse is driving a car borrowed from a third party. The drive other car coverage is usually added at an additional premium charge. [*Commercial Auto Insurance* XIII.N.6]

broad form general liability endorsement—A comprehensive endorsement to be attached to pre-1986 editions of the standard general liability policy that provided coverage enhancements including: blanket contractual liability; personal injury and advertising liability; premises medical payments; host liquor liability; fire legal liability on real property; broad form property damage liability, including completed operations; incidental medical malpractice; nonowned watercraft liability; limited worldwide coverage; additional persons insured (employees); extended bodily injury coverage; and automatic coverage for newly acquired organizations. [*Commercial Liability Insurance* IV.E.1]

broad form hold harmless clause—A hold harmless clause under which the indemnitor assumes any and all liability of the indemnitee under specified circumstances, including liability arising out of the indemnitee's sole fault. Particularly with respect to construction contracts, statutes in a number of states restrict the enforceability of broad form hold harmless agreements. [*Contractual Risk Transfer* IV.D.1]

broad form named insured endorsement—An endorsement added to a liability policy to reduce the insurance administrative problems that large corporations encounter in acquiring new entities by covering all entities for which the insured is responsible. Most of these endorsements are similar to the following.

The Named Insured includes all subsidiaries, affiliated, associated, controlled or allied companies, corporations, or firms as now or hereafter constituted, for which the Named Insured has responsibility for placing insurance and for which similar coverage is not otherwise more specifically provided. [*Commercial Liability Insurance* VII.D.4]

broad form property damage (BFPD)—The liability exposure represented by the risk of loss to property in a contractor's care, custody, or control (CCC) or on which contracted operations are being performed. Because of the scope of exclusions applicable to these two risks of loss in the 1973 CGL form, an endorsement was necessary to provide coverage for the BFPD hazard. (See broad form general liability endorsement.) Coverage for the same exposure is provided automatically in 1986 edition and subsequent CGL forms by means of exceptions to the CCC and property damage exclusions. [*Commercial Liability Insurance* V.D.30]

broker—An independent solicitor of insurance for an insured. Brokers, unlike independent agents, do not usually have "binding authority" under an agency contract; therefore, they may not obligate an insurer to provide coverage prior to the insurer's consent.

brokerage department—An insurance company department that aids brokers in placing business, frequently on a worldwide basis.

builders risk—Indemnifies for loss of or damage to a building or other related property in the course of construction. Insurance is normally written for a specified amount on the building and applies only in the construction process. The valuation of the project may be approached on either a completed value or reporting form basis. Coverage customarily includes fire and extended coverage, and vandalism and malicious mischief coverage. Builders risk coverage can be extended to an all risk form as well. The builders risk policy also may include coverage for items in transit to the construction site (up to a certain percentage of value) and items stored at the site. [*Commercial Property Insurance* IX.J.1]

building and personal property coverage form (ISO)—The key Insurance Services Office, Inc. (ISO), direct damage coverage form. This form (CP 00 10) covers buildings, business personal property, and personal property of others for direct loss or damage, subject to the limits shown in the declarations for each of these categories. Also provides four additional coverages (debris removal, pollutant cleanup, preservation of property, and fire department service charges.) [*Commercial Property Insurance* V.F.1]

building ordinance coverage—Coverage available by endorsement to a standard property policy to insure against loss caused by enforcement of ordinances or laws regulating construction and repair of damaged buildings. Many communities have building ordinance(s) that require that a building which has been damaged to a specified extent (typically, 50 percent), must be demolished and rebuilt in accordance with current building codes rather than simply repaired. Unendorsed, standard property insurance forms do not cover the loss of the undamaged portion of the building, the cost of demolishing that un-

damaged portion of the building, or the increased cost of rebuilding the entire structure in accordance with current building codes. However, coverage for these loss exposures is widely available by endorsement, using the Insurance Services Office (ISO) endorsement CP 04 05, ordinance or law coverage. It used to be common to use three separate endorsements (contingent liability from building laws, demolition, and increased cost of construction) to cover this exposure. [*Commercial Property Insurance* II.D.14]

building rate—The rate charged for property insurance on a building as opposed to the rate charged for property insurance on the contents of a building. [*Commercial Property Insurance* IV.F.1]

bumbershoot—An excess liability coverage for insureds with major wet marine exposures. The policy covers both nonmarine and maritime liability exposures, i.e., protection and indemnity, general average, collision, sue and labor, as well as general liability hazards.

burglary—Theft of property from within a premises by a person who unlawfully enters or exits from the premises. [*Commercial Property Insurance* XII.D.18]

burning cost—Most frequently used in spread loss property reinsurance to express pure loss cost. More specifically, the ratio of incurred losses within a specified amount in excess of the ceding company's retention to its gross premiums over a stipulated number of years.

business auto policy—A commercial auto policy that includes auto liability and auto physical damage coverages; other coverages are available by endorsement. Except for auto-related businesses and motor carrier or trucking firms, the business auto policy addresses the needs of most commercial entities as respects auto insurance. [*Commercial Auto Insurance* Section VIII]

business income coverage—Insurance covering loss of income suffered by a business as a result of not being able to use property damaged by a covered cause of loss, during the time required to repair or replace it. There are two Insurance Services Office, Inc. (ISO) business income coverage forms: the business income and extra expense coverage form (CP 00 30) or the business income coverage form without extra expense (CP 00 32). [*Commercial Property Insurance* II.E.11]

business interruption coverage—Insurance covering loss of income suffered by a business as a result of not being able to use property damaged by a covered cause of loss during the time required to repair or replace it. Both of the Insurance Services Office's (ISO's) business income coverage forms (CP 00 30, the business income and extra expense coverage form and CP 00 32, the business income coverage form without extra expense) provide business interruption coverage, although they use the term "business income" in place of the term "business Interruption." [*Commercial Property Insurance* II.E.11]

business judgment rule—A common law liability doctrine sometimes used to absolve the directors and officers of a corporation from liability, provided it can be shown that a loss resulted from a seemingly prudent, good faith business decision that simply turned out to be incorrect, rather than a grossly negligent or fraudulent act. [*Professional Liability Insurance* III.D.16]

business legal expense insurance—Coverage for the expenses associated with defending liability claims against the insured. Does not cover expenses to defend claims that would be insured in a general liability policy or which would not be a tax deductible expense.

business use class—A classification by vehicle usage, used in classifying commercial vehicles. There are three business use classifications: service, which does not include transportation of any property except for tools, equipment, and supplies to and from jobs; retail, which includes transportation of property to and from individual households; and commercial, which applies for any other type of transportation except service and retail. [*Commercial Auto Insurance* III.G.10]

buyback deductible—A deductible contained in the basic policy that may be removed by paying additional premium when full coverage is required.

buy-out settlement clause—A provision found in media liability insurance policies allowing an insured the option to refuse settlement of a claim for an amount offered by an insurer and agreed upon by a claimant. The clause allows the insurer to tender that amount to the insured, thereby "buying out" of the claim. At that point, the insured takes complete control of the case, bearing the risk that ultimate settlement and defense costs will exceed the buy-out figure. On the other hand, if the case is resolved for less than that amount, the insured may keep the difference. [*Professional Liability Insurance* XVIII.E.11]

buy/sell agreement—A contract among members of a firm that provides for the continuation of the business through an agreement by which each principal agrees that, in the event of his death, his estate will sell his interest back to the business entity for a predetermined amount. The amount may be calculated as a fixed amount or as a variable amount, depending on business factors. The agreement is usually funded by life insurance.

C

CAA—See Clean Air Act.

calendar year experience—Experience developed on premium and incurred loss transactions occurring during the 12 calendar months beginning January 1, irrespective of the effective dates of the policies on which these transactions took place, and also irrespective of the dates of the accidents from which the loss transaction arose.

cancelable—Refers to the fact that most insurance contracts can be terminated by the insurer or the insured at any time. If an individual policy is not a cancelable policy, then it will probably be designated guaranteed renewable or noncancelable. Individual life insurance policies are noncancelable by the insurer. Most property and liability policies can be canceled.

cancellation—(1) The termination of an insurance policy or bond, before its expiration, by either the insured or the insurer. Insurance policy cancellation provisions require insurers to notify insureds in advance (usually 30 days) of canceling a policy and stipulate the manner in which any earned premium will be returned.

(2) Runoff basis means that the liability of a reinsurer under policies, which became effective under a treaty prior to the cancellation date of such treaty, shall continue until the expiration date of each policy.

(3) Cutoff basis means that the liability of a reinsurer under policies, which became effective under the treaty, prior to the cancellation date of such treaty, shall cease with respect to losses resulting from accidents taking place on and after said cancellation date. [*Professional Liability Insurance* VII.D.1]

C and F—See Cost and freight.

capacity—The largest amount of insurance or reinsurance available from a company or from the market in general. An insurer's capacity to write business is often measured and/or limited by its premium-to-surplus ratio.

capital stock—The ownership of a corporation as expressed in individually- or jointly-held shares of stock.

capital stock company—An insurance company owned by stockholders rather than by its policyholders.

capital sum—The maximum amount payable in one sum in the event of accidental death or dismemberment.

captain of the ship doctrine—A common law doctrine often used in operating room situations whereby a physician can be held liable for the actions of subordinates (e.g., nurses, technicians), based on the doctor's functioning as "the captain of the ship," because he or she controls and directs the actions of those in assistance.

captive insurance company—An insurance company subsidiary designed to cover the risks of its parent organization(s). Single owner captives are owned by one company, whereas association captives (also known as "group" or "industry" captives) are owned by and cover the risks of multiple organizations. Given capital and operating expense requirements, they are generally of interest only when applicable premiums exceed $2 million. Typically, captives retain substantial portions of each loss and then purchase reinsurance above these levels. Captives provide an alternative funding mechanism when coverage

breadth or capacity in traditional insurance markets does not meet the insureds' needs, and can also provide cost savings, cash flow benefits, and specialized loss prevention and claims services not otherwise available. Bermuda is the world's foremost domicile for captive insurers. [*Risk Financing* IV.K.1–46]

care, custody, and control (CCC)—An exclusion common to several forms of liability insurance, which eliminates coverage with respect to damage to property in the insured's care, custody, or control. In some cases, CCC has been determined to entail physical possession of the property; in others, any party with a legal obligation to exercise care with respect to property has been deemed to have that property in its CCC. [*Commercial Liability Insurance* V.D.32]

cargo insurance—Inland or ocean marine insurance covering property in transit. [*Commercial Property Insurance* IX.E.1]

carrier—An insurance or reinsurance company that insures or "carries" the insurance or reinsurance.

case management—The process relating to workers compensation claims in which the recovery and rehabilitation of an injured worker is overseen by a case manager. The goal of the case manager is to focus on the rehabilitation of the individual so that the return to work is quickened while aiding the worker in achieving preinjury physical condition. This is a concept that developed in the benefit arena and has been adapted to workers compensation. [*IRMI's Workers Comp* XIV.G.1.]

case reserves cash flow plans—Those risk financing plans that allow the insured, rather than the insurer, to derive benefits from unused funds, either in the form of unpaid loss reserves or unpaid premium dollars.

cash flow program—Any insurance rating scheme that allows the insured to hold and benefit from loss reserves until paid as claims, e.g., deferred premium plans, self-insurance, and paid loss retros. [*Risk Financing* IV.A.1–28]

cash refund annuity—An annuity payment contract that provides for refund of any principal remaining at the death of a primary annuitant.

cash surrender value—The amount of cash available to the insured in an individual life insurance policy when the insured cancels and surrenders the policy.

casualty insurance—Insurance that is primarily concerned with the losses caused by injuries to persons, and legal liability imposed on the insured for such injury or for damage to property of others.

catalytic converter—A control device that oxidizes volatile organic compounds (VOCs) by using a catalyst to promote the combustion process. Catalytic incinerators require lower temperatures than conventional thermal incinerators, thus saving fuel and other costs.

catalytic incinerator—A control device that oxidizes volatile organic compounds (VOCs) by using a catalyst to promote the combustion process. Catalytic incinerators require lower temperatures than conventional thermal incinerators, thus saving fuel and other costs.

catastrophe—A severe loss characterized by extreme force and/or sizable financial loss.

catastrophe plan—A prepared strategy detailing how a particular organization will respond to a disaster.

catastrophe policy—Name previously used for major medical insurance.

catastrophe reinsurance—A form of reinsurance that indemnifies the ceding company for the accumulation of losses in excess of a stipulated sum arising from a single catastrophic event or series of events.

catastrophic loss—Loss in excess of the working layer.

causes of loss forms (ISO)—Insurance Services Office, Inc. (ISO), commercial property forms that establish and define the causes of loss (i.e., perils) for which coverage is provided. An ISO commercial property policy consists of: one or more causes of loss forms, plus one or more coverage forms, the commercial property conditions form, and the common policy conditions form. There are four ISO causes of loss forms: the basic, broad, and earthquake causes of loss forms are named perils forms; the special causes of loss form is an all risks form. See basic causes of loss; broad causes of loss; and special causes of loss. [*Commercial Property Insurance* V.O.1]

CCC—See Care, custody, and control (CCC).

cede—When a company reinsures its liability with another. The original or primary insurer, the insurance company that purchases reinsurance, is the "ceding company" that "cedes" business to the reinsurer. [*Risk Financing* V.A.2]

ceding commission—A percentage of the reinsurance premium retained by a ceding company to cover its acquisition costs and, sometimes, provide a profit.

ceding company—The insurer that cedes all or part of the insurance or reinsurance it has written to a reinsurer. [*Risk Financing* V.A.2]

central collection point—Location where a generator of regulated medical waste consolidates wastes originally generated at various places in his facility. The wastes are gathered together for treatment on-site or for transportation elsewhere for treatment and/or disposal. This term could also apply to community hazardous waste collections, industrial, and other waste management systems.

CERCLA—See Comprehensive Environmental Response Compensation and Liability Act.

certificate—See Certificate of insurance.

certificate of insurance—A document providing evidence that certain general types of insurance coverages and limits have been purchased by the party required to furnish the certificate.

certificate of reinsurance—A brief document evidencing a reinsurance transaction, usually incorporating complete terms and conditions by reference.

cession—The portion of insurance transferred to a reinsurer by the ceding company.

cession number—A number assigned by an underwriting office to identify reinsurance premium transactions.

cestui que vie—The person on whose life contingency an insurance contract is based. It does not have to be the policyowner or policyholder but is the named insured.

CGL—See Commercial general liability policy.

chaplain or priest malpractice—Professional liability coverage protecting members of the clergy for claims arising out of their activities as priests or chaplains. This coverage is especially necessary for any counseling activities performed by these individuals, as suits against religious counselors for mental anguish have become more prevalent recently.

charter—Articles of incorporation or the rights from states or Congress to incorporate and transact business.

Chartered Life Underwriter (CLU)—Professional designation obtained by passing a series of 10 tests covering all phases of life insurance. The CLU program is administered by the American College of Life Underwriters.

Chartered Property Casualty Underwriter (CPCU)—A professional designation identifying an individual who has satisfactorily completed 10 national examinations covering all phases of property and casualty insurance and who has met ethical and experience requirements. The CPCU program is administered by the American Institute for Chartered Property Casualty Underwriters, Inc.

Chemnet—Mutual aid network of chemical shippers and contractors that assigns a contracted emergency response company to provide technical support if a representative of the firm whose chemicals are involved in an incident is not readily available.

chronic toxicity—The capacity of a substance to cause long-term poisonous human health effects. See acute toxicity.

CIF—See Cost, insurance, and freight.

circumstance—A term used in some claims-made policies as an alternative to "occurrence." A "notice of circumstance" provision is included in some claims-made policies as a way of extending coverage for events that may produce a claim, so long as notice of the "circumstance" is given to the insurer during the policy period. [*Commercial Liability Insurance* XIII.E.22]

claim—Used in reference to insurance, a claim may be a demand by an individual or corporation to recover, under a policy of insurance, for loss which may come within that policy.

claimant—The person making a claim. Use of the word "Claimant" usually denotes that the person has not yet filed a lawsuit. Upon filing a lawsuit, claimant becomes a plaintiff, but the terms are often used interchangeably.

claim expense—Expenses of adjusting claims, e.g., allocated claim expenses; court costs, fees and expenses of independent adjusters, lawyers, witnesses, and other expenses that can be charged to specific claims; and unallocated claim expenses which represent salaries and other overhead expenses that are incurred in adjustment and recording claims but which cannot be charged against specific claims.

claims adjuster—See Adjuster.

claims audit—A systematic and detailed review of claims files and related records to evaluate the adjuster's performance.

claims-made—A term describing an insurance policy that covers claims made (reported or filed) during the year the policy is in force for any incidents that occur that year or during any previous period during which the insured was covered under a "claims-made" contract. This form of coverage is in contrast to the occurrence policy, which covers an incident occurring while the policy is in force regardless of when the claim arising out of that incident is filed—1 or more years later. [*Professional Liability Insurance* VIII.C.1]

The liability coverage trigger under which a policy responds to losses for which a claim is first made against the insured during the policy period. [*Commercial Liability Insurance* II.C.1]

claims-made and reported provision—A claims-made coverage trigger requiring that a claim be both made against the insured and reported to the insurer during the policy period for coverage to apply. Such provisions, which are found most frequently in professional and D&O liability policies, often cause problems if a claim is made against an insured late in a policy period and the insured is unable to report the claim to the insurer prior to expiration of the policy. [*Professional Liability Insurance* VIII.C.1]

The liability coverage trigger under which a policy responds to losses for which a claim is first made against the insured during the policy period. [*Commercial Liability Insurance* II.C.1]

claims-made multiplier—A factor applied to rates used for a claims-made CGL policy, depending on how long an insured has been in a claims-made program. The insured receives a larger credit its first year in a claims-made program, and the credit is reduced in each subsequent year (unless the retroactive date is advanced). The credit virtually disappears in the fifth claims-made year. [*Commercial Liability Insurance* VIII.C.7]

claims reserve—An amount of money set aside to meet claims incurred but not paid as of the time of the statement.

clash cover—A form of reinsurance that covers the cedant's exposure to multiple retentions that may occur when two or more of its insureds suffer a loss from in the same occurrence. This reinsurance covers the additional retentions.

class—Group of insureds who have similar exposures and experience and are grouped together for rating purposes.

class action—A type of lawsuit which is brought by a single, affected individual, on behalf of a large group of similarly affected individuals. Class actions were created by the judicial system because frequently, the number of plaintiffs involved in a lawsuit are so numerous that it would be onerous to name and adjudicate the claims of all plaintiffs on an individual basis. [*Professional Liability Insurance* X.J.10]

class I area—Under the Clean Air Act, a Class I area is one in which visibility is protected more stringently than under the national ambient air quality standards; includes national parks, wilderness areas, monuments, and other areas of special national and cultural significance.

classification—The system of establishing classes for rating purposes.

classified insurance—Insurance for substandard risks in life and health insurance.

class rate—Rates for classes with broad dispersion of risks and low hazard. This differs from a schedule or specific rate.

clause—A section of a policy contract, or of an endorsement attached to it, dealing with a particular subject in the contract, e.g., the "insuring clause" or the "coinsurance clause."

Clean Air Act (CAA)—A federal act regulating the emission of harmful pollutants into the air. It requires corporations to list pollutants that may adversely affect human health and establishes air quality standards. The CAA contains provisions for civil and criminal penalties and enforcement through citizen suits.

cleanup fund—Life insurance policy purchased specifically to fund the final expenses associated with the insured's death (e.g., funeral expenses).

Clean Water Act (CWA)—A federal act that requires monitoring of discharges into U.S. waters. The CWA contains provisions for abatement actions, penalties, fines, and imprisonment of responsible parties.

closed-loop recycling—Reclaiming or reusing wastewater for nonpotable purposes in an enclosed process.

CLU—See Chartered Life Underwriter.

codefendant—More than one defendant being sued in the same litigation or more than one person charged in the same complaint.

coding—The process of translating alphabetic and numeric information into a concise numeric form for statistical or internal recording.

coinsurance provision—A property insurance provision that penalizes the insured for not purchasing a limit of insurance at least equal to a specified percentage (commonly 80 percent) of the value of the insured property. The coinsurance provision stipulates that the insured will recover no more than the following: the amount of insurance purchased (the limit of insurance) divided by the amount of insurance required (the value of the property on the date of loss multiplied by the coinsurance percentage), less the deductible. [*Commercial Property Insurance* II.D.15]

coinsurer—One who shares the loss sustained under an insurance policy. Usually refers to an insured property owner who fails to purchase enough insurance to comply with the coinsurance provision and who, therefore, suffers part of the loss himself.

collapse additional coverage—Coverage under the ISO broad and special causes of loss forms (CP 10 20 and CP 10 30) for collapse of a building due to specified causes (such as weight of snow, ice, or rain). There is no coverage for collapse due to design error, or to collapse due to faulty workmanship or materials if the collapse occurs after construction is complete. [*Commercial Property Insurance* V.R.42]

collateral agreement—A transfer of all or some of the rights of the owner of personal property (including a life insurance policy) to another party (the assignee) as security for the repayment of an indebtedness. Once the debt is repaid, the assigned property rights usually revert back to the assignor (the original property owner).

collateral estoppel—Issues that were actually litigated between two parties may operate as an "estoppel" as to those issues in other litigation. For example, a truck is shown to be defective in design due to placement of its fuel tank. Collateral estoppel might prevent this same issue of defect being litigated over and over again in subsequent trials. This is a key consideration when the same issue is being litigated in different cases all around the country.

collateralization of cash flow programs—Under cash flow programs (e.g. retrospectively-rated plans), substantial portions of the ultimate premium for coverage are not due until the insurer has actually paid claims. Therefore, the insurer is assuming a credit risk (in addition to an insurance risk). This creates the need for collateralization of such programs. Additionally, cash flow programs must be collateralized as a result of statutory requirements (i.e., virtually all states require organizations self-insuring their workers compensation exposures to purchase bonds securing these obligations).

collateral source rule—A procedural rule followed by the courts in many states that prohibits informing the jury that the plaintiff has received money for his or her injuries from other sources, such as from his or her employer's workers compensation policy or an insurance policy covering another defendant.

collateral value insurance—Insurance that guarantees the value of property pledged as collateral for a loan. The amount of recovery under such a policy is the difference between the liquidated value of the collateral to the creditor and the outstanding loan balance at the time of liquidation. Such insurance is written primarily in connection with short- to medium-term equipment loans.

collection commission—Commission paid to an agent based on a percentage of premiums actually collected in the debit market.

collection fee—The amount charged by a life insurance agent allowed as compensation for premium collection in lieu of commission.

collision insurance—A form of automobile insurance that provides for reimbursement for loss to a covered automobile due to its colliding with another vehicle or object or the overturn of the automobile. This covers only damage to the automobile itself as "auto" is defined in the policy. [*Commercial Auto Insurance* VIII.E.3]

combination crime coverage—Plan 1 of the commercial crime insurance program promulgated by Insurance Services Office, Inc. (ISO). Any combination of the following forms can be used to structure a crime insurance program under plan 1: employee dishonesty; forgery or alteration; theft, disappearance, and destruction; robbery and safe burglary—other than money and securities; premises burglary; computer fraud; extortion; premises theft and robbery outside the premises; lessees of safe deposit boxes; securities deposited with others; and robbery and safe burglary—money and securities. [*Commercial Property Insurance* XII.D.26]

combination plan reinsurance—A form of combined reinsurance which provides that the reinsurer will indemnify the ceding company the amount of covered loss in excess of the specified retention, subject to a specified limit and a fixed quota share percent of all remaining losses after deducting the excess recoveries on each risk.

combination policy—See Package policies.

comment period—Time provided for the public to review and comment on a proposed EPA action or rulemaking after publication in the Federal Register.

commercial appropriation—The unauthorized use of the name or likeness of a person (either a private individual or a celebrity) for commercial purposes. Commercial appropriation could, for example, involve publishing a picture of a celebrity taken with the owner of a restaurant indicating that the celebrity endorses the establishment. Coverage for such claims is afforded under media liability insurance policies. [*Professional Liability Insurance* XVIII.C.3]

commercial crime program—A portfolio of coverage forms, rating rules, and procedures for insuring the crime exposures of business entities, promulgated by Insurance Services Office, Inc. (ISO) and the Surety Association of America. [*Commercial Property Insurance* XII.D.1]

commercial general liability (CGL) policy—A standard insurance policy issued to business organizations to protect them against liability claims for bodily injury and property damage arising out of premises, operations, products and completed operations; and advertising and personal injury liability. The commercial general liability policy was introduced in 1986 and replaced the comprehensive general liability policy.

commercial property conditions form (ISO)—Attached to every Insurance Services Office, Inc. (ISO), commercial property policy, this form (CP 00 90) establishes the policy provisions with respect to the following issues: concealment, misrepresentation, and fraud; control of property; insurance under two or more coverages; legal action against the insurer; liberalization; no benefit to bailee; other insurance; policy period and coverage territory; transfer of recovery rights against others (subrogation). [*Commercial Property Insurance* V.C.6]

commercial property coverage forms (ISO)—Insurance Services Office, Inc. (ISO), commercial property forms that define, limit, and explain what property or property interest is covered. An ISO commercial property policy consists of: one or more coverage forms, one or more causes of loss forms, the commercial property conditions form, and the common policy conditions for The most widely used ISO commercial property coverage forms are the building and personal property coverage form (CP 00 10) and the business income and extra expense coverage form (CP 00 30). See Causes of loss forms and commercial property program. [*Commercial Property Insurance* VI.C.1]

commercial property program—A portfolio of coverage forms, policywriting procedures, and rating rules for insuring the property loss exposures of business entities, promulgated by Insurance Services Office, Inc. (ISO), This program uses a modular approach; in addition to declarations and any endorsements, an ISO commercial property policy consists of one or more coverage forms; one or more causes of loss forms; the

commercial property conditions form; and the common policy conditions form. [*Commercial Property Insurance* VI.B.1]

commercial waste management facility—A treatment, storage, disposal, or transfer facility which accepts waste from a variety of sources, as compared to a private facility which normally manages a limited waste stream generated by its own operations.

commission—A certain percentage of premium produced that is retained as compensation by insurance agents and brokers. Also known as acquisition cost. [*Risk Financing* III.A.44]

commissioner—The title of the head of most State Insurance Departments.

commissioners standard ordinary 1958 mortality table—The mortality table approved by the National Association of Insurance Commissioners as a standard for evaluation and computation of nonforfeiture values for whole life insurance policies.

commissions of selling agents coverage—Coverage for reduction in sales commissions for selling agents when the manufacturer they represent cannot deliver the product because of damage to or destruction of the manufacturer's plant. Coverage is limited to the reduction in gross selling commissions less noncontinuing expenses.

common accident—An accident in which two or more persons are injured.

common carrier—A commercial individual or organization carrying persons or property from one place to another for payment, e.g., a trucker. As contrasted with contract carriers, a common carrier is one that transports or handles the goods of the general public. [*Commercial Auto Insurance* XI.C.3]

common disaster—A situation in which the insured and the beneficiary of a life insurance policy appear to die simultaneously without evidence of who died first.

common law—Unwritten law developed primarily in England that has been extended to the United States, except for the state of Louisiana, which follows the Napoleonic Code.

common law defenses—Defenses to suits for liability claims based in common law. Such defenses include, but are not limited to: assumption of risk, lack of proximate cause, last clear chance, and no negligence on the part of the defendant.

common law liability—Responsibility imposed on a party by law based on custom, as opposed to liability imposed by statute.

common policy conditions—The part of the insurance policy typically relating to cancellation, changes in coverage, audits, inspections, premiums, and assignment of the policy. The commercial lines policy forms portfolio promulgated by Insurance Services Office, Inc., takes a modular approach to structuring policies. A commercial lines policy is made up of a declarations page, the common policy conditions, one or more coverage forms, and endorsements that modify the coverage forms. The common policy conditions form (IL 00 17) is used with the commercial property, general liability, and crime forms to specify the conditions applicable to the policy. [*Commercial Auto Insurance* XII.B.1]

community property—A law (which applies in only a minority of states) stipulating that at the time of divorce, husband and wife are each entitled to one-half of the total earnings and property acquired during marriage.

community rating—Rating based on the experience of a community in which the insureds reside, with reference to age, sex, occupation, or health.

commutation—Provides an insured under a financial reinsurance contract with a premium credit for better than expected loss experience. [*Risk Financing* V.D.3]

commutation provision—A provision in a finite risk insurance contracts mandating the return of a portion of the premium paid if loss experience is more favorable than projected. The inclusion of a commutation provision in a finite risk insurance contract converts the arrangement into a quasi self-insurance fund. [*Risk Financing* V.D.1]

commutation rights—The right of a beneficiary to receive a lump sum payment rather than continuing under an installment option selected for settlement of a life insurance policy.

comparative negligence—The rule used in negligence cases in some states that provides for computing both the plaintiff's and the defendant's negligence, with the plaintiff's damages being reduced by a percentage representing the degree of his or her contributing fault. If the plaintiff's negligence is found to be greater than the defendant's, the plaintiff will receive nothing.

compensating balance plan—An insurance cash flow plan whereby the insurance company, in an account specifically set up for the plan, collects premiums and deposits them in the insured's bank. Although the account is in the insurer's name, the insured's bank recognizes the funds as the insured's compensating balance, freeing the insured's funds. [*Risk Financing* IV.C.1]

compensatory damages—A sum of money to which a plaintiff is entitled that, so far as is possible, makes amends for the actual loss sustained. See Punitive damages.

competitive state funds—State-owned and operated facilities that compete with commercial insurers in writing workers compensation insurance specific solely to that state. The states with these funds are Arizona, California, Colorado, Idaho, Kentucky, Louisiana, Maine, Maryland, Minnesota, Missouri, Montana, New Mexico, New York, Oklahoma, Oregon, Pennsylvania, Rhode Island, Texas, and Utah. [*IRMI's Workers Comp* V.O.1]

complaint—The original or initial pleading by which an action is commenced under the Codes and Rules of Civil Procedure. The pleading sets forth a claim for relief which includes: (1) a short and plain statement of the grounds upon which court had jurisdiction, (2) a short and plain statement of the claim stating the pleader is entitled to relief, and (3) a demand for judgment for the relief sought.

completed operations—Under a general liability policy, work of the insured that has been completed as called for in a contract; or work completed at a single job site under a contract involving multiple job sites; or work that has been put to its intended use.

composite rating—A method of rating insurance premiums on a singular rate developed to apply to all coverages according to a selected exposure basis. It facilitates a policy's audit process. [*Risk Financing* III.A.24]

comprehensive auto coverage—Coverage under an automobile physical damage policy insuring against loss or damage resulting from any cause, except those specifically precluded. It covers losses such as fire, theft, windstorm, flood, and vandalism, but not loss by collision or upset. [*Commercial Auto Insurance* VIII.E.1]

comprehensive boiler and machinery coverage— Boiler and machinery coverage that applies to all insurable objects. There are two types: standard comprehensive coverage applies to all objects except production machinery; extended comprehensive coverage applies to all objects including production machinery. Contrasts with blanket group boiler and machinery coverage, which applies to all objects within specified categories of objects, and with coverage applying only to individually described objects.

Comprehensive Environmental Response Compensation and Liability Act (CERCLA)—A federal act establishing a system for reporting facilities where hazardous wastes are or have been disposed of, treated, or stored. It also encompasses trust funds financed by certain taxes to be used for cleanup costs. CERCLA also establishes very broad liability standards for hazardous waste incidents that require liable parties to reimburse trust funds which finance cleanup operations.

comprehensive general liability (CGL) policy—See Commercial general liability (CGL) policy.

comprehensive 3-D policy—Term taken from a now defunct Insurance Services Office, Inc. (ISO), crime program. The coverage of a comprehensive 3-D policy is most closely approximated by the current ISO crime coverage Plan 1 (combination crime—separate limits). Plan 1 allows the insured to select any or all of the 11 basic ISO crime coverage forms; each coverage is subject to a separate limit of insurance.

compulsory insurance—Any form of insurance that is required by law. In Massachusetts and New York, for example, automobile liability insurance is compulsory for all automobile owners. [*Commercial Auto Insurance* IV.C.1]

compulsory insurance requirements (international insurance)—When foreign countries require businesses to purchase certain types of insurance coverage in order to operate in the country, e.g., fire insurance on certain types of buildings, automobile liability, workers compensation, or inland marine on goods transported by trucks. Fre-

quently, these coverages must be purchased from an admitted insurer in the host country or from the foreign government itself.

computer crime insurance—Policy covering computer theft of money, securities, and other property. Some forms also cover computer theft of information and computer vandalism. See Computer fraud coverage form.

computer fraud coverage form—An Insurance Services Office, Inc. (ISO), crime coverage form (CR 00 07) that insures against theft of money, securities, or property by using a computer to transfer covered property from the insured's premises or bank to another person or place. No coverage is provided for theft of information or for computer vandalism. [*Commercial Property Insurance* XII.D.19]

concealment—A willful act of holding back information that may be pertinent to the issuance of an insurance policy even though not asked about that particular subject. A concealment can result in the voiding of a policy. [*Commercial Auto Insurance* VIII.F.9]

concurrent causation—A theory adopted by some courts which holds that if a given loss has more than one cause, and at least one of the causes is covered by the policy, the loss is covered even if the policy specifically excludes another cause of the loss. For example, a court might determine that a property policy that specifically excludes from coverage damage caused by flood does cover a flood loss when the municipality's negligence in improperly installing a sewage system is a concurrent cause of the loss. [*Commercial Property Insurance* V.R.2]

concurrent insurance—Two or more policies covering the same exposure and having the same policy period and type of coverage trigger. It is important for primary and excess liability policies to be concurrent. [*Professional Liability Insurance* VII.F.15]

conditional binding receipt—A receipt in life insurance which guarantees that if the risk is accepted, the named insured is insured from the date of issuance of the receipt.

conditionally renewable—A contract of health insurance stating that the policy is renewable under certain conditions as defined in the contract.

conditional vesting—A vesting agreement in a contributory pension plan in which the vested benefit is predicated on nonwithdrawal of the insured's contributions.

condominium association coverage form (ISO)—The Insurance Services Office, Inc. (ISO), commercial property coverage form (CP 00 17) that covers buildings and personal property owned by condominium associations. Very similar to the building and personal property coverage form, except that the language is tailored to address the needs of condominium associations. [*Commercial Property Insurance* VI.C.9]

confiscation, expropriation, nationalization, and deprivation insurance—Political risk coverage (commonly referred to as CEN or CEND insurance) purchased by businesses that have an ownership interest in property abroad, to cover loss resulting from government nationalization of the property or other action by the government that effectively deprives the insured of the property or restricts its operations. Coverage may be structured to insure such current assets as bank accounts, intercompany or bank loans, accounts receivable, inventory, retained earnings, supplies, and work in progress. Deprivation coverage, which insures against the risk of a government action preventing use of the asset (such as denying a permit to run a plant), can be added to the basic CEN policy.

conflict of laws—Inconsistency or difference between the laws of different states. That part of the law of each state which determines what effect is given to the fact that the case may have a relationship to more than one state.

consequential bodily injury suits—A type of lawsuit insured by the employers liability coverage of a workers compensation policy. In this type of legal action, a member of the injured worker's family purports to have an injury which directly results from the injury to the employee. Often, mental injuries are alleged. Legislative action in many states has narrowed the applicability of this type of lawsuit. [*IRMI's Workers Comp* VI.D.5]

consequential loss—A loss that arises as a result of direct damage to property, e.g., loss of rent. Some types of consequential loss are insurable under standard direct damage or time element coverage forms; others are not.

conservator—A person or organization appointed by a court of law to manage an insurer that is financially impaired or in danger of insolvency.

consolidated insurance program (CIP)—A centralized insurance program for large (e.g., $100 million) construction projects under which one party, such as the owner (an OCIP) or the general contractor (a CCIP), procures insurance on behalf of all the other parties (e.g., owner, general contractor, and subcontractors). This contrasts with the typical approach under which each party is responsible for purchasing its own insurance. When properly administered, CIPs can substantially reduce the insurance costs associated with construction projects. Typically, the coverages provided under a CIP include builders risk, commercial general liability, workers compensation, and umbrella liability.

construction ban—If, under the Clean Air Act, the EPA disapproves an area's planning requirements for correcting nonattainment, the EPA can ban the construction or modification of any major stationary source of the pollutant for which the area is in nonattainment.

constructive total loss—Property damage loss that is treated as a total loss because the cost of repairing the damaged property exceeds the value of the property.

contents rate—Property insurance rate on personal property, most of which is likely to be contained within a building. [*Commercial Property Insurance* IV.F.1]

contestable clause—The portion of a life insurance policy setting forth the conditions under which an insurer may contest or void the policy.

contingency reserve—Reserve in excess of legal requirements to provide for unexpected contingencies (sometimes called "contingency surplus").

contingent annuitant—Secondary beneficiary to an annuity policy.

contingent beneficiary—Secondary beneficiary who receives policy benefits if the primary beneficiary predeceases the named insured under a life insurance policy.

contingent business interruption insurance—Coverage for income loss suffered by the insured when its operations are suspended as a result of damage from a covered cause of loss to the property of a key supplier or customer, or to a leader location (a nearby business that attracts customers to the insured's business). [*Commercial Property Insurance VI.L.2*]

contingent commission, agents—A commission paid to an agent that depends on the profit the company has realized from the agency's underwriting operations.

contingent commission or profit commission—In reinsurance, an allowance payable to the ceding company in addition to the normal ceding commission allowance. It is a predetermined percentage of the reinsurer's net profits after a charge for the reinsurer's overhead, derived from the subject treaty.

contingent liability from operation of building codes—See Building ordinance coverage.

continuance—To put off a hearing or trial until a later date. (If engaged in by an insurer or a corporate defendant, it is unconscionable delay or bad faith. When done by the court, it is called a continuance.)

continuation of coverage in bankruptcy provision—A clause in an insurance policy requiring an insurer to provide coverage even though an insured has declared bankruptcy. [*Commercial Auto Insurance VIII.F.8 and Professional Liability Insurance VII.D.15*]

continuous treatment rule—A common law liability doctrine stating that if a physician has treated a patient over a period of time, only the policy limit applying at the time the claim is made is the one that applies. This rule prevents a "stacking of limits" situation where the total policy limits (that were available during the entire course of treatment) could otherwise be applied to a claim of this type. The continuous treatment rule can also be applied to other professionals, most frequently to lawyers and accountants, whose services for a given case or engagement sometimes take place over several years. [*Professional Liability Insurance III.C.13*]

contract—An agreement between two or more parties exhibiting the following necessary characteristics: mutual assent, competent parties, a valid

consideration, and legal subject matter. Insurance policies are a form of contract.

contract attorney—A lawyer typically hired by a law firm to handle a specific case or several cases. The attorney agrees to do the work pursuant to an agreement he or she has with the hiring firm or attorney. It is often less costly for the law firm since it does not have the usual overhead of a salaried employee.

contract bond—Guarantees the performance of obligations assumed under contract. This type of bond is utilized most often in the construction industry but does have application in other industries.

contract carrier—A commercial individual or organization carrying persons or property of certain customers only, rather than the goods of or the public in general. Unlike a common carrier, a contract carrier has a right to choose or refuse to convey passengers or freight for payment. [*Commercial Auto Insurance XI.C.3*]

contract of adhesion—A contract offered intact to one party by another under circumstances requiring the second party to accept or reject the contract in total without having the opportunity to bargain over the wording. Insurance policies are contracts of adhesion and, as such, are construed strictly against the party writing them (i.e., the insurer).

contractor controlled insurance program (CCIP)—See Consolidated insurance program.

contractor's limitation endorsement—An endorsement usually attached to umbrella policies of contractors and construction-related entities imposing limits or exclusions on the umbrella's coverage with respect to one or more of the following exposures: explosion, collapse, and underground (XCU) hazard; care, custody, and control; contractual liability; damage to work (broad form property damage); professional liability; joint ventures; and wrap-ups. Some endorsements operate to make the umbrella coverage following form over the coverage provided for these exposures in the underlying policy. However, other versions of the endorsement impose more restrictive conditions or even absolute exclusions. It is desirable to confirm that following form coverage is provided over explosion, collapse, underground, broad form property damage, and contractual liability coverage, as provided within the primary layer. [*Commercial Liability Insurance* XI.E.1]

contract ratification indemnity—A type of political risk insurance that pays a proportion of the contractor's start-up costs that may not be recoverable from the purchaser/employer in the event that an overseas contract is not finalized for reasons outside the contractor's control. It is common practice for contractors/sellers to place orders and mobilize a plant at site as soon as a foreign contract is signed. However, if at this stage certain conditions remain to be fulfilled before a contract becomes binding upon both parties, the contractor/seller could be liable for all expenses so incurred should the conditions precedent not be met, and the contract is, therefore, never ratified. Contract ratification indemnity coverage is designed to insure this exposure.

contract repudiation indemnity—Provides coverage for economic losses arising out of the unilateral cancellation of a contract as a result of direct or indirect actions of a foreign government or its agents under circumstances in which the insured is not in breech of contract. The coverage is usually purchased by importers, exporters, and contractors.

contractual liability—Liability imposed upon an entity by the terms of a contract. As used in insurance, the term refers not to all contractually imposed liability, but to the assumption of the other contracting party's liability under specified conditions.

contractual liability insurance—Insurance that covers liability of the insured assumed in a contract. Under the standard commercial general liability (CGL) policy, such coverage is limited to liability assumed in any of a number of specifically defined insured contracts, or to liability that the insured would have even in the absence of the contract. [*Commercial Liability Insurance* V.D.3 and *Contractual Risk Transfer* X.C.1]

contractual risk transfer—The use of contractual obligations such as indemnity and exculpatory agreements, waivers of recovery rights, and insurance requirements to pass along to others what would otherwise be one's own risks of loss.

contributory negligence—Negligence of a plaintiff constituting a partial cause or aggravation of his or her injury. This doctrine bars relief to the plaintiff in a lawsuit if the plaintiff's own negligence contributed to the damage. Contributory negligence has been superseded in many states by other methods of apportioning liability. See Comparative negligence.

controlled insurance program—See consolidated insurance program

controlled master insurance program—An insurance program for a multinational business wherein the coverage terms and conditions apply on a blanket basis to all of the insured's international operations. Local underlying policies are issued overseas to support the centralized program. Unlike global insurance programs, master insurance programs do not typically include the United States in their coverage territory; a separate domestic program is usually arranged for U.S. multinationals under this approach.

control technique guidelines (CTG)—A series of EPA documents designed to assist states in defining reasonable available control technology (RACT) for major sources of volatile organic compounds (VOC).

convertible—A policy that may be changed to another form without evidence of insurability. Usually used to convert term life insurance to permanent insurance.

cooperation clause—A policy provision compelling the insured to assist an insurer in defending claims under a policy. The rationale behind this provision is that the insured, rather than the insurer, is in a much better position to ascertain certain information about claims that are critical to the defense process. [*Commercial Auto Insurance* VIII.F.3]

cooperative insurance—Insurance for fraternal societies, employee associations, industrial associations, trade unions, or other mutual associations.

corporate counsel—In-house attorney or an outside law firm that handles corporate matters for a business client.

corridor deductible—A health insurance deductible that applies between the basic layer and the major medical layer.

cost and freight (C and F)—One of several standard terms of sale for exports and imports. C and F indicates that the buyer must obtain transit insurance on the newly purchased goods, since the price paid by the buyer includes the cost of goods and all freight charges, but not insurance.

cost, insurance, and freight (CIF)—One of several standard terms of sale for exports and imports. CIF indicates that the seller must obtain transit insurance on the goods, since the price paid by the buyer includes the cost of goods, insurance while they are in transit, and all freight charges. See cost and freight (C and F); free alongside (FAS); and free on board (FOB).

cost of hire endorsement—See Rental cost reimbursement endorsement.

cost of suit coverage—Coverage for defense of suits that fall within a self-insured retention or deductible, where the basic policy does not provide the defense.

cost of well control—See Operators extra expense.

cosurety—One of a number of sureties participating in a bond. The two types of cosurety are unlimited in which each surety is jointly and severally liable for the full bond amount, and limited in which each surety is responsible for the payment of a stated limit of liability.

counsel selection provision—A provision sometimes found in professional liability insurance policies that gives the insured the right to select or have a voice in selecting defense counsel in the event that a claim is made against the insured during the policy term. Such provisions are important because a professional's reputation is heavily at stake in every claim. [*Professional Liability Insurance* VII.B.23]

countersignature—The signature of a licensed agent or representative on a policy that validates the contract.

courthouse steps settlement—A settlement or resolution reached just before a dispute is set to go to trial; may or may not literally be a settlement agreed to on the courthouse steps. Try to avoid these.

court reporter—A person transcribing verbatim the dialogue at a trial or a deposition.

cover—(1) A contract of insurance.

(2) To effect insurance.

(3) To include within the coverage of a contract of insurance.

coverage—Used synonymously with "insurance" or "protection."

coverage trigger—The event that must occur before a particular liability policy becomes applicable to a given loss. Under an occurrence policy, the occurrence of injury or damage is the trigger; liability will be covered under that policy if the injury or damage occurred during the policy period. Under a claims-made policy, the making of a claim triggers coverage. Coverage triggers serve to determine which liability policy in a series of policies covers a particular loss. [*Professional Liability Insurance* VIII.B.1–VIII.H.13]

The event that must occur before a particular liability policy becomes applicable to a given loss. Under an occurrence policy, the occurrence of injury or damage is the trigger; liability will be covered under that policy if the injury or damage occurred during the policy period. Under a claims-made policy, the making of a claim triggers coverage. Coverage triggers serve to determine which liability policy in a series of policies covers a particular loss. [*Commercial Liability Insurance* II.C.1]

cover note—A document used to provide evidence of insurance if policy documents are not immediately available. (This term is most commonly used outside the United States.) A cover note will show, among other things, the name of the insurer and insured, brief details of the property or risk insured, the coverage and the total amount of insurance. It is similar to a "binder" in U.S. insurance parlance.

CPCU—See Chartered Property Casualty Underwriter.

cradle-to-grave or manifest system—A procedure in which hazardous materials are identified and followed as they are produced, treated, transported, and disposed of by a series of permanent, linkable, descriptive documents (e.g., manifests). Commonly referred to as the cradle-to-grave system.

credentialing liability—Liability arising from a hospital's wrongful denial of staff privileges to an otherwise competent, qualified physician or health care professional. Coverage for this exposure is typically afforded under a hospital directors & officers liability policy. [*Professional Liability Insurance* **X.M.1**]

credibility—(1) An actuarial term describing the degree of accuracy in forecasting future events based on statistical reporting of past events.

(2) The weight assigned or assignable to observed data in contrast to that assigned to an external or broader based set of data. Credibility is used to provide a measure of the relative predictive value of the data being reviewed. Weights can be determined through detailed formulas or by judgment. The weight assigned should generally increase with the number of risks in the observed data, and should decrease with higher levels of variability in the observed data.

credit carry-forward—In reinsurance, the transfer of credit or profit from one accounting period under a long-term reinsurance treaty to the succeeding accounting period.

criteria pollutants—The 1970 amendments to the Clean Air Act required the EPA to set National Ambient Air Quality Standards for certain pollutants known to be hazardous to human health. The EPA has identified and set standards to protect human health and welfare for six pollutants: ozone, carbon monoxide, total suspended particulates, sulfur dioxide, lead, and nitrogen oxide. The term, "criteria pollutants" derives from the requirement that the EPA must describe the characteristics and potential health and welfare effects of these pollutants. It is on the basis of these criteria that standards are set or revised.

criticism—A correction suggested by a rating bureau, which, if not complied with, can result in a fine.

crop-hail insurance—Specialty property coverage for hail damage to growing crops.

cross-complaint—An action brought by defendant against the plaintiff.

cross-complaintant—The "plaintiff" named in the cross-complaint.

cross-defendant—The party named as a defendant in the cross-complaint.

cross-liability coverage—Coverage in connection with a suit brought against an insured by another party that has insured status under the same policy. Cross-liability coverage is provided as an intrinsic feature of the standard commercial general liability policy, by means of the "separation of insureds" condition. Some umbrella and professional liability policies contain insured-versus-insured exclusions that eliminate cross-liability coverage. [*Commercial Liability Insurance* **V.J.16** and *Contractual Risk Transfer* **XI.C.4**]

cross-liability endorsement—An endorsement that alters or clarifies the application of a liability policy to cross-liability claims. The term is most commonly intended to mean an endorsement that provides cross liability coverage. However, the term should be used with caution as the original cross-liability endorsements were exclusions that deleted this coverage.

cross purchase—A form of business life insurance in which each member of a group purchases insurance on the other members of the group in order to assure continuance of the business in the event one of the principals becomes disabled or dies.

Cumis **council**—The 1984 California Court of Appeals decision in *San Diego Federal Credit Union v Cumis Insurance Society, Inc.* held that where an insurer is defending under a reservation of rights, a conflict of interest exists between the economic and litigation interest of the insurer and the insured. Under these circumstances, the traditional right of the insurer to select counsel and control the defense effort is lost. As a result, the insured selects counsel and controls the defense, but the insurer must pay the defense costs. Such counsel, selected and controlled by the insured at the expense of the insurer, is known as *Cumis* counsel.

cumulative collusive excess cover—A reinsurance contract under which the ceding company further reduces its net exposure that has been reinsured under a share agreement.

cumulative injury—A type of workers injury which arises from the repetition of mentally or physically traumatic job tasks over an extended length of time. Examples of injuries which fall into this category are carpel tunnel syndrome and hearing loss. [*IRMI's Workers Comp* XIV.R.3]

current disbursement—The pay-as-you-go technique to funding a pension plan. It is used today in Social Security and is known as the most costly method of pension funding.

current service benefit—The portion of an insured's pension benefit that has accrued due to credited service in a given time period.

custom bond—Bond required by the U.S. Customs Service which guarantees the payment of duties or taxes due by law on all goods directly or indirectly imported or exported to or from the United States as well as the reporting of statistical data relating to the shipments involved. The

bond may be issued on either a single or continuous form.

cutoff—A termination provision in a reinsurance contract under which the reinsurer is not liable for losses taking place after the date of termination. See Cancellation.

cut through endorsement—A reinsurance contract endorsement providing that, in the event of the cedant's insolvency, the reinsurer will pay any loss covered by the reinsurance contract directly to the insured. Also called an "assumption endorsement."

CWA—See Clean Water Act.

D

daily reports—Skeleton copies of the policies prepared for the agent and the insurer.

data processing coverage—All risk property insurance for electronic data processing equipment (computers), computer programs, and data. Typically includes coverage for perils to which such property is especially susceptible: mechanical breakdown, electrical injury, and changes in temperature and humidity. Also referred to as "electronic data processing" or "EDP" coverage. [*Commercial Property Insurance* IX.F.1]

data processors errors and omissions coverage—Insures liability arising from errors and omissions in performing data processing for outside entities on a fee basis. Coverage is usually on a claims-made policy form. The policy provides no coverage for bodily injury or property damage liability which can create a coverage gap for certain data processing applications, e.g., in medical analysis whereby an error in a diagnostic computer program causes bodily injury. Further, when one organization provides services for sister companies or its own subsidiaries, coverage would not normally apply to errors and omissions claims by these companies or subsidiaries.

date of issue—Date on which the contract was issued by the insurer.

death benefit—The amount payable by a life insurance policy in the event of the death of the named insured.

Death on the High Seas Act (DOHSA)—Provides a federal remedy for the death of seamen or other individuals arising from negligence, strict liability, or the unseaworthiness of a vessel and occurring on the high seas that is beyond 3 nautical miles from shore on a worldwide basis. Legal proceedings must be initiated within 3 years of the accident by a representative of all survivors of the deceased individual. Damages awarded are based on actual monetary loss and do not extend to encompass such usual compensable expenses as medical and funeral costs. Additionally, the award may be reduced but not eliminated by the contributory negligence of the deceased. [*IRMI's Workers Comp* VII.C.6 and *Contractual Risk Transfer* XIV.E.4]

death rate—The number of deaths occurring per 1,000 people.

debit agent—An agent who works on the debit or industrial life insurance system. Debit agents visit the houses of their insureds to collect premiums.

debit life insurance—Industrial life insurance, i.e., life insurance purchased primarily by people with low income levels under which the premium is collected weekly, biweekly, or monthly.

debit system—The system of collecting life insurance premiums on a weekly or monthly basis involving an actual visit by the agent.

debris removal—Coverage for the cost of removal of debris of covered property damaged by an insured peril. This coverage is included in most commercial property insurance policies. [*Commercial Property Insurance* II.D.6]

decennial liability—An insurance coverage required of contractors by owners in some foreign countries such as France that covers the costs to rectify a total or partial collapse of the construction. It draws its name from the fact that it covers this risk for 10 years following completion of the project.

declaration—(1) A statement by the applicant for insurance, usually relative to underwriting information. Sometimes, as in most casualty and property policies, this is copied into the policy.

(2) The front page of a policy that provides the named insured, address, policy period, location of premises, policy limits, and other policy information. Also known as the information page.

declination—The act of rejecting an application for insurance.

deductible—A portion of covered loss that is not paid by the insurer. Most property insurance policies and some liability insurance policies contain a per-occurrence deductible provision that stipulates that the deductible amount specified in the policy declarations will be subtracted from each covered loss in determining the amount of the insured's loss recovery. In property insurance, the deductible is usually subtracted from the amount of the loss, whereas in liability insurance, the deductible is usually subtracted from the policy limit. See franchise deductible; self-insured retention (SIR); and waiting period deductible. [*Commercial Property Insurance* II.D.20]

deductible, annual aggregate—See Annual aggregate deductible.

defamation—Any written or oral communication about a person or thing that is both untrue and unfavorable. Media liability and general liability policies typically provide coverage for claims alleging defamation (although general liability policies exclude such coverage for insureds engaged in media businesses). [*Professional Liability Insurance* XVIII.C.2]

default—A failure, specifically the omission or failure to perform a legal or contractual duty.

defendant—In a civil trial, the party against whom the suit has been brought.

Defense Base Act—Legislation that extends the Longshore and Harbor Workers Compensation Act to apply to certain categories of employees working overseas. The three general divisions of covered employees are: (1) those working on military bases acquired from a foreign government after 1940, (2) employees of contractors and subcontractors engaged in public work projects for the U.S. government outside the continental United States and (3) individuals employed outside the continental United States by a U.S. employer whose purpose it is to provide welfare or other such services to the Armed Forces as approved by the Secretary of Defense. [*IRMI's Workers Comp* VII.E.1]

defense clause—An insurance provision in which the insurance company agrees to defend, with respect to insurance afforded by the policy, all suits against the insured, even if the suits are false or fraudulent. [*Commercial Auto Insurance* VIII.D.1 and *Commercial Liability Insurance* V.C.3]

deferred group annuity—A retirement plan under which a paid-up annuity is purchased each year for each employee. The sum of these benefits is paid as monthly income at the time of retirement.

deferred payment merchandise—Coverage for merchants, distributors, and manufacturers of products who sell their wares using time payment plans. This coverage can be on a vendor's only form, which covers the insured for the unpaid balance due the vendor until the property is fully paid for, or on a vendors and vendees dual interest form, which covers the vendor for the entire cost of the item until the final payment is made. The vendors and vendees dual interest form covers both the purchaser and the seller in the event there is a loss to the merchandise before it is fully paid off. The purchaser does not have to continue making payments on an item which is no longer in use, and the vendor can maintain the goodwill aspects of terminating the customer's payments.

deferred premiums—Periodic premium payments, usually monthly, at no interest. Used most frequently with casualty coverages. [*Risk Financing* IV.A.3]

deficit carry-forward or carry-back—The transfer of debit or loss from one accounting period to another under a reinsurance treaty.

defined benefit plan—A pension plan providing a specific benefit for each employee. The employer is required to make adequate contributions to the plan to fund the promised benefits. No individual accounts are maintained as is done in defined contribution plans.

defined contribution plan—A pension plan calling for definite annual contributions by the employer, but with no specific benefit promised to the employee. The employee's benefits are ultimately determined by the amount contributed plus the investment income. See Defined benefit plan.

delay clause—An ocean marine insurance exclusion that eliminates coverage for loss of market and other consequential loss resulting from delayed voyages, regardless of the cause of the delay even if from an insured peril.

delivery—The actual placing of an insurance policy in the hands of the insured.

demolition coverage—See Building ordinance coverage.

demurrer—A pleading usually filed by the defendant attacking the legal sufficiency of a complaint.

deposition—Pretrial testimony of a witness under oath, without the presence of a judge or jury, for the purpose of discovering evidence relevant to a lawsuit's issue.

deposit policy—A contract entered into where the insured puts on deposit with the insurance company a sum of money, which fund, in turn, is managed by the company for the insured.

deposit premium—The premium deposit required by the insurer on forms of insurance subject to periodic premium adjustment. Also called "provisional premium." [*Risk Financing* I.B.3]

depreciation—The decrease in the value of property over a period of time, usually as result of age, wear and tear from use, or economic obsolescence. Actual physical depreciation (wear and tear from use) is subtracted from the replacement cost of insured property in determining its actual cash value; courts in some jurisdictions have allowed insurers to deduct depreciation due to economic obsolescence as well. [*Commercial Property Insurance* II.D.15]

deprivation—Economic loss to an investor or contractor resulting from an inability to utilize or access equipment located in a foreign country due to political circumstances. Coverage for exposure of this type is available through political risk insurance subject to a waiting period.

derivative suits—A type of lawsuit brought by one or more stockholders, on behalf of the corporation, alleging financial loss to the organization. The alleged harm must be to the corporation as a whole, such as the diminishing of the corporation's assets, for shareholders to pursue an action derivatively. Any recovery in such suits inures to the benefit of the corporation itself as opposed to the shareholders who institute the action. [*Professional Liability Insurance* X.J.9]

designated pollutant—An air pollutant which is neither a criteria nor hazardous pollutant, as described in the Clean Air Act, but for which new source performance standards exist. The Clean Air Act does require states to control these pollutants, which include acid mist, total reduced sulfur (TRS), and fluorides.

design-build professional liability insurance—Affords professional liability coverage for firms that function as both the designer and general contractor on a construction project. [*Professional Liability Insurance* XVII.E.32]

designer bugs—Popular term for microbes developed through biotechnology that can degrade specific toxic chemicals at their source in toxic waste dumps or in groundwater.

destroyed medical waste—Regulated medical waste that has been ruined, torn apart, or mutilated through thermal treatment, melting, shredding, grinding, tearing, or breaking, so that it is no longer generally recognized as medical waste, but has not yet been treated (excludes compacted regulated medical waste).

destruction and removal efficiency (DRE)—A percentage that represents the number of molecules of a compound removed or destroyed in an incinerator relative to the number of molecules that entered the system (e.g., a DRE of 99.99 percent means that 9,999 molecules are destroyed for every 10,000 that enter. 99.99 percent is known as "four nines." For some pollutants, the RCRA removal requirement may be as stringent as "six nines.")

deviation—A rate or policy form differing from that published by a rating bureau.

difference-in-conditions (DIC) insurance—An all risk property insurance policy that is purchased in addition to a named perils property insurance policy to obtain coverage for perils not insured against in the named perils property insurance policy (usually, flood and earthquake.) See All risks, difference-in-conditions (builders risk). [*Commercial Property Insurance* VII.D.1]

difference-in-limits clause (DIL)—A provision contained in the master international insurance program that provides excess limits over the limits of local underlying policies.

direct damage—Physical damage to property, as distinguished from time element loss, such as business interruption or extra expense, that results from the inability to use the damaged property. [*Commercial Property Insurance* II.D.1]

direct discharger—A municipal or industrial facility which introduces pollution into the environment through a defined conveyance or system, such as outlet pipes or smokestacks.

direct filtration—A method of treating water which consists of the addition of coagulant chemicals, flash mixing, coagulation, minimal flocculation, and filtration.

directors and officers liability insurance—Insures corporate directors and officers against claims, most often by stockholders and employees, alleging financial loss arising from mismanagement. The policies contain two coverages: the first reimburses the insured organization when it is legally obligated (typically by corporate charter or state statute) to indemnify corporate directors and officers for their acts; the second provides direct coverage to directors and officers when the organization is not legally obligated to indemnify them. D&O forms are written on a claims-made basis, generally contain no explicit duty to defend the insureds, and typically exclude intentional/dishonest acts and bodily injury and property damage. [*Professional Liability Insurance* X.B.1–X.M.7]

direct selling system (direct marketing)—A distribution system within the insurance industry through which insurance policies and coverages are marketed by employees of the insurance company rather than independent agents.

direct writer—An employee of a direct writing insurer who is involved in the direct selling system.

direct writing carrier—An insurer that deals with its insured without the use of agents or brokers.

direct written premium—The premiums collected without any allowance for premiums ceded to reinsurers.

disability—A condition that incapacitates a person in some way so that he cannot carry on his normal pursuits. The definition of "disability" in disability income policies varies substantially and should be carefully examined. Disability may be total, partial, permanent, or temporary, or a combination of these.

disability benefit—The amount payable under a disability income policy or provision in the event of disability of the named insured.

disability income insurance—Health insurance that provides periodic payments to replace income lost when the insured is unable to work as a result of sickness or injury. The definition of "disability" found in disability income policies varies substantially and should be carefully examined.

disappearing deductible—A formula deductible that decreases as the amount of loss increases and disappears entirely to provide full coverage when the loss reaches a specified amount. Disappearing deductibles were once commonly used in property insurance policies.

discovery—Investigation of the facts of a claim or the alleged proximate cause of an injury. Discovery may include such activities as interrogatories, depositions, expert examination of a product, and review of a plaintiff's medical history.

discovery cover—Coverage for losses that are discovered during the term of a reinsurance treaty, regardless of when they occurred.

discovery period—The period of time after expiration allowed an insured to identify and report losses occurring during the period of a policy or a bond. [*Commercial Property Insurance* **XII.D.3**]

discovery provision—Found mainly in professional liability insurance policies written with claims-made coverage triggers. Discovery provisions permit insureds to report incidents or circumstances that may result in claims in the future. Discovery provisions, which are also know as "awareness" or "notice of potential claim" provisions, allow an insured to lock in coverage for such events so that coverage will apply under the current claims-made policy, regardless of how far in the future a claim is eventually made in conjunction with the incident that has been reported. [*Professional Liability Insurance* **VIII.C.9**]

discovery rule—A rule of common law indicating that the statute of limitations on bringing a claim does not begin to run until the date on which a claimant actually discovers (or should have discovered) an injury or loss—rather than on the date when the wrongful act giving rise to the injury or loss took place. The rule has the effect of lengthening the normal statute of limitations applicable to many types of claims.

discrimination—(1) The act or process of evaluating insurable risks and determining premiums on the basis of likelihood of loss. Insurance laws prohibit "unfair discrimination," i.e., the formulation of rates on the basis of criteria that do not fairly measure the actual risk involved.

(2) Unfair treatment of or denial of rights to persons on the basis of certain arbitrarily chosen attributes or characteristics, such as race, sex, religion, or nationality. Suits alleging discrimination are excluded from coverage under many forms of liability insurance, but may be covered as a form of personal injury under some umbrellas. [*Commercial Liability Insurance* **XI.D.11**]

disease loading—An additional premium charge included in certain workers compensation classification code rates which reflects specific disease hazards relative to the operations involved and therefore the increased exposure to loss.

dismemberment—In accident and health insurance policies, the definition encompasses loss of both hands, both feet, or the sight of both eyes, one hand and one foot, or the sight of one eye and one hand or foot. A fixed benefit is paid to insureds who suffer certain types of dismemberment under these policies.

dismissal—An order or judgment finally disposing of an action, suit, motion, etc. without a trial involved.

dividend accumulation—Dividends paid by life insurers that may be added to the cash value. These accumulated dividends will also earn income for the insured.

dividend addition—An option regarding payment of dividends to insureds that is offered by some life insurers, particularly mutual companies. There are a number of alternative ways dividends may be paid, such as in cash, as an increase to the policy's cash value, or as a paid-up addition. Under this alternative, the dividend is used to purchase a paid-up single premium increase in the policy's face value, thereby increasing the death benefits.

dividend options—Varying ways in which insureds may elect to receive dividends under a life insurance policy. Dividends may be received in the form of cash payments, as increases to the policy's cash value, or as paid-up additional insurance.

dividends—A partial return of premium to the insured based on the insurer's financial performance or on the insured's own loss experience. Insurers cannot legally guarantee the payment of dividends. [*Risk Financing* **III.B.10**]

divisible contract clause—Provides that violation of the conditions of the policy at one location will not void the coverage at other locations.

domestic insurer—An insurer admitted by and formed under the laws under the state in which insurance is written.

domicile—A term used to describe the location or venue in which a captive insurer is licensed to do business. There are a number of factors that must be considered in selecting the best domicile for a given captive, including: capitalization and surplus requirements, investment restrictions, income and local taxes, formation costs, acceptance by fronting insurers and reinsurers, availability of banking and other services, and proximity considerations. [*Risk Financing* IV.K.28]

dose response—The degree to which a biological organism's response to a toxic substance quantitatively shifts as its overall exposure to the substance changes. For example, a small dose of carbon monoxide may cause drowsiness; a large dose can be fatal.

dose-response assessment—Estimating the potency of a chemical.

dose-response relationship—The quantitative relationship between the amount of exposure to a substance and the extent of toxic injury or disease produced.

double indemnity—Payment by a life insurance policy of two times the face value when death results from an accident, e.g., an auto accident, as opposed to a health problem, e.g., cardiac arrest.

double protection—A form of life insurance combining whole life with an equal amount of term, with the term expiring at a future date, usually age 65.

dram shop liability—Liability imposed upon those in the business of serving alcoholic beverages for loss arising out of the intoxication of patrons. [*Commercial Liability Insurance* V.D.5]

"D" ratio—Factor used in the experience rating plan to separate the expected losses into primary and excess losses. A "D" Ratio is the normal ratio of primary expected losses to the total expected losses, and varies by state and by classification code. [*Risk Financing* III.A.17]

drive away collision—Collision coverage in a garage policy is applicable only within a 50-mile radius of the dealership. Drive away collision coverage deletes this distance exclusion and affords coverage for the pick up or delivery of vehicles to or from a point greater than 50 miles from the dealership. [*Commercial Auto Insurance* XIII.K.2]

drive other car endorsement—A form that can be added to an automobile insurance contract giving protection while the insured is driving a car other than the one named in the policy [*Commercial Auto Insurance* XIII.N.6]

drop down provision—A clause in umbrella policies providing that the umbrella will "drop-down" over reduced or exhausted underlying policy aggregate limits. Some umbrellas maintain their own coverage terms when they drop down; others assume those of the primary policy. [*Commercial Liability Insurance* XI.B.21]

druggist liability insurance—A form of professional liability insurance protecting the druggist against suit arising out of the filling of prescriptions, misdelivery of drugs, and other operations.

dry pipe sprinkler system—An automatic sprinkler system that can be used in an unheated building without risk of freezing and subsequent bursting of pipes, because the system fills with water only when the sprinkler heads are triggered by the heat of a fire.

dual agency—A situation in which an individual may serve as an agent for two parties in the same transaction. For instance, court cases have held that insurance brokers can function as agents of (and therefore owe legal duties to) both insureds and insurers in the same transaction.

dual capacity—The principle, defined in a number of court cases, that a business may stand in relation to its employee not only as employer, but also as supplier of a product, provider of a service, owner of premises, etc. When a work-related injury arises out of one of these secondary relationships, the exclusivity of workers compensation as a source of recovery to the injured worker may be challenged, and the employee may be allowed to bring suit against the employer. Such actions are covered by the employers liability insurance of the standard workers compensation policy.

dwelling property coverage forms—Alternative forms to homeowners policies that may be used to insure physical damage to dwellings and personal property. Unlike homeowners forms, these policies do not insure liability or medical payments exposures. There are three dwelling property forms in the Insurance Services Office, Inc., forms portfolio, the basic form (DP 00 01), the broad form (DP 00 02), and the special form (DP 00 03). The basic form covers only damage from fire, lightning, and internal explosion, but additional perils can be covered by endorsement. The broad form covers direct damage to dwellings and personal property on a broad named perils basis. The special form covers direct damage to dwellings and appurtenant structures on an all risks basis while covering personal property on a broad named peril basis.

E

earned premium—When a premium is paid in advance for a certain period, the company receives or "earns" a portion of the premium as time elapses during that period.

earned reinsurance premium—The amount of premium allocated to the portion of the policy period that has elapsed at any given point in time. Reinsurance premiums are usually paid at the inception of the underlying policy to which they apply. Reinsurers recognize the premium as being earned as time elapses during the underlying policy period.

earnings insurance—A type of business interruption insurance that uses a monthly limit on loss recovery in lieu of a coinsurance clause. The declarations show both a total limit of insurance and the portion of that total limit (expressed as a fraction: 1/3, 1/4, etc.) applicable to loss in each month following the direct damage loss. The monthly limit of indemnity coverage option in the Insurance Services Office, Inc. (ISO), business income coverage forms approximates the coverage provided under an earnings insurance form. [*Commercial Property Insurance* V.K.37]

earth movement or earthquake exclusion—An exclusion found in most property insurance policies (even all risk policies) eliminating coverage for loss resulting from earth movement, except ensuing fire. The exclusion may apply only to earthquake or to all forms of earth movement; the same is true of the endorsements used to add back coverage. [*Commercial Property Insurance* V.Q.13 and *Contractual Risk Transfer* XIV.P.4]

earthquake coverage—Typically excluded (along with other earth movement) from most property insurance policies, except ensuing fire. In most cases, earthquake coverage must be purchased by endorsement to a difference-in-conditions policy or to an all risks policy. Normally, the coverage provided is subject to a per occurrence sub-limit, an annual aggregate limit, and a separate deductible. [*Commercial Property Insurance* VII.C.11 and *Contractual Risk Transfer* XIV.P.4]

EC endorsement—See Extended coverage endorsement.

ecological risk assessment—The application of a formal framework, analytical process, or model to estimate the effects of human actions on a natural resource and to interpret the significance of those effects in light of the uncertainties identified in each component of the assessment process. Such analysis includes initial hazard identification, exposure and dose-response assessments, and risk characterization.

economic damages—An award to an injured person in an amount sufficient to compensate for his or her actual monetary loss. Examples of monetary damages include awards for lost wages and medical expenses.

EDP coverage—See Data processing coverage.

educators legal liability insurance—A form of liability insurance designed to cover a broad range of nonbodily injury/nonproperty damage liability claims that are made against the administrators, employees, and staff members of both schools and colleges. ELL, which is also known as "school board legal liability insurance," is a hybrid of traditional D&O and E&O coverages. Typical claims covered by ELL include: wrongful termination, wrongful dismissal, failure to grant tenure, and negligent counseling. [*Professional Liability Insurance* XI.T.1]

effective date—The date on which an insurance binder or policy goes into effect and from which time protection is provided.

efficacy insurance—Provides coverage in the event that a project does not meet the technical level of performance required by the contract. The policy provides the funds required to pay the debt service costs and may be modified to reimburse the insured for capital expended so that the project may be brought up to the expected performance level. This type of coverage is often sought for high tech projects such as co-generation facilities.

EIL insurance—See Environmental impairment liability insurance.

elective benefits—When disability income policies allow the insured the option to take a specified sum for certain minor injuries instead of receiving the disability benefit. A schedule in the policy specifies the elective benefits available.

electrical damage or injury exclusion—An exclusion contained in most property insurance policies eliminating coverage for damage to electrical appliances caused by artificially generated currents, except for ensuing fire or explosion. Coverage for this exposure is available under a boiler and machinery policy. [*Commercial Property Insurance* V.Q.21]

electronic data processing (EDP) coverage—See Data processing coverage.

electronic funds transfer system coverage—A financial institution crime coverage which relates to the erroneous transferring of funds to or from the checking or savings account of a customer based upon instructions fraudulently transmitted by a nonemployee. There are two categories of this type of fraud coverage, voice initiated and telefacimile, and they may be added by rider to the bank or credit union bond or issued separately under the financial institution computer crime form. [*Commercial Property Insurance* XII.S.2]

elevator insurance—Insurance on elevators and their operation written to cover the perils of collision and liability.

eligibility period—That period of time during which members of a given group may enroll in a group benefits program (e.g., 401-K plan, health insurance, disability insurance, or life insurance).

elimination period—A waiting period or a probationary period that must run before benefits are payable under a disability income plan or policy.

ELP factor—See Excess loss premium factor.

EMAP data—Environmental monitoring data collected under the auspices of the Environmental Monitoring and Assessment Program (EMAP). All EMAP data share the common attribute of being of known quality, having been collected in the context of explicit data quality objectives (DQOs) and a consistent quality assurance program.

emergency medical technician (EMT) and paramedics professional liability—Coverage to protect a municipality or an independent EMT service organization and its employees against liability arising from paramedical services. There is usually no coverage for dishonest acts, paramedics' performance in administering general anesthesia, punitive damages, or medical malpractice claims against a paramedic who is also a physician, surgeon, or dentist. [*Professional Liability Insurance* XVI.M.1–20]

emergency response values—Concentrations of chemicals, published by various groups, defining acceptable levels for short-term exposures in emergencies.

employee assistance program (EAP)—A compendium of services provided by the employer for the employee to address the treatment as well as prevention of mental and addictive behavioral problems. Other issues which can create stress in the life of the employee such as interpersonal and familial relationships are also included in the scope of the EAP. The major purpose of the EAP is to assist the employee in maintaining a good mental outlook and therefore be a highly productive and well adjusted worker. [*IRMI's Workers Comp* XIII.E.1]

employee benefit programs—Benefits, such as health and life insurance, provided to employees at the workplace, usually paid for totally or in part by the employer.

employee benefits liability—Liability of an employer for an error or omission in the administration of an employee benefit program, such as failure to advise employees of benefit programs. Coverage of this exposure is usually provided by endorsement to the general liability policy but may also be provided by a fiduciary liability policy.

employee dishonesty coverage—Coverage for employee theft of money, securities, or property, written with either a per loss limit, a per employee limit, or a per position limit. [*Commercial Property Insurance* XII.D.6]

employee leasing—Is a permanent staffing method under which an employee leasing company (sometimes called a labor contractor) provides all or most of its client's employees. The benefits associated with this type of arrangement include reduced administrative costs, access to risk management services like safety and loss control, and higher quality, more cost effective employee benefits. [*IRMI's Workers Comp* XII.B.1]

Employee Retirement Income Security Act (ERISA) liability—Liability under the Employee Retirement Income Security Act of 1974 for the exposure arising out of the responsibility as an officer or fiduciary of a company for the handling of pension funding and other employee benefit plans. Should the fiducial responsibility be breached, the individual is personally liable for the loss. This resulting exposure is usually excluded from the general liability policy, even when employee benefits liability coverage is purchased. However, coverage may be purchased in the form of a separate fiduciary liability policy.

employees as additional insureds—A form of general liability endorsement used with pre-1986 CGL forms to provide insured status to employees of the named insured business. Employees are automatically insureds under current editions of the CGL coverage form; no endorsement is necessary to effect this coverage. [*Commercial Liability Insurance* V.H.3]

employers excess indemnity insurance—Insurance coverage purchased by employers that do not subscribe to the Texas workers compensation law. They are usually purchased in conjunction with occupational accident policies, and reimburse the employer for liability settlements and judgments applying to pain/suffering, permanent disfigurement, and lost future earnings. [*Risk Financing* IV.J.7]

employers liability coverage—This coverage is provided by Part 2 of the basic workers compensation policy and pays on behalf of the insured (employer) all sums that the insured shall become legally obligated to pay as damages because of bodily injury by accident or disease sustained by any employee of the insured arising out of and in the course of his employment by the insured.

employment-at-will doctrine—A legal doctrine holding that absent a contract for a specified duration, both employers and employees are free to terminate the employment relationship at any time, with or without cause, and with or without notice. In recent years, however, both courts and legislatures have developed a number of exceptions to this doctrine, a factor largely responsible for a marked increase in claims alleging wrongful termination. [*Professional Liability Insurance* XX.I.4]

employment practices liability insurance (EPLI)—A form of liability insurance covering wrongful acts arising from the employment process. The most frequent types of claims alleged under such policies include: wrongful termination, discrimination, and sexual harassment. The forms are written on a claims-made basis and generally exclude coverage for large-scale, company-wide layoffs. In addition to being written as a stand-alone coverage, EPLI is frequently available as an endorsement to directors & officers liability policies. [*Professional Liability Insurance* XX.I.1]

EMT and paramedics professional liability—See Emergency medical technician (EMT) and paramedics professional liability.

encapsulation—The treatment of asbestos-containing material with a liquid, either covering the surface with a protective coating or embedding fibers in an adhesive matrix, to prevent release of the asbestos into the air.

endangerment assessment—A study to determine the nature and extent of contamination at a site on the National Priorities List and the risks posed to public health or the environment. The Environmental Protection Agency (EPA) or the state conducts the study when a legal action is to be taken to direct potentially responsible parties to clean up a site or pay for it.

endemic disease coverage—Specifies that workers compensation and employers liability coverage will apply to injury or death of an employee arising out of a disease that is peculiar to a foreign country, even though the disease is not covered under the workers compensation or occupational disease laws of the designated state. [*IRMI's Workers Comp* VI.L.11]

endowment insurance—A form of life insurance that pays the face value to the insured either at the end of the contract period or upon the insured's death. This is in contrast to life insurance, which pays the face value only in the event of the insured's death. It is also in contrast with the concept of a pure endowment, which pays the face value only if the insured lives to the end of the policy period. Endowment insurance is basically a savings plan with an element of insurance designed to protect the savings plan in the event of premature death. As such, this type of insurance is very expensive and has limited usefulness, e.g., retirement saving, saving for the purpose of making a charitable contribution, and the establishment of an education fund for the insured's children.

enforceable requirements—Conditions or limitations in permits issued under the Clean Water Act, Section 402 or 404, that, if violated, could result in the issuance of a compliance order or initiation of a civil or criminal action under federal or applicable state laws. If a permit has not been issued, the term includes any requirement, which in the Regional Administrator's judgment, would be included in the permit when issued. Where no permit applies, the term includes any requirement which the RA determines is necessary for the best practical waste treatment technology to meet applicable criteria.

enforcement decision document (EDD)—A document that provides an explanation to the public of the Environmental Protection Agency's selection of the cleanup alternative at enforcement sites on the National Priorities List.

engineering insurance—In the United Kingdom, a policy which provides boiler and machinery inspection services as well as coverage for the pressure vessel and any internal accidents. Outside the United States, particularly in the United Kingdom, a property policy provides coverage for property damage resulting from a boiler explosion; but, not for damage to the object itself. Coverage for the boiler and inspection services must be separately arranged under an engineering insurance policy.

entire contract clause—A standard insurance contract provision that limits the agreement between the insured and the insurer to the provisions contained in the contract. The clause functions primarily for the protection of the insured. [*Commercial Auto Insurance* VIII.C.1]

entity coverage—Affords direct coverage of the insured organization under a D&O liability policy. Typically, corporate D&O forms only reimburse the insured organization when it is legally obligated to indemnify corporate officers and directors for their acts on behalf of the organization. However, if a lawsuit *specifically* names the insured organization as a defendant, the standard D&O policy does not provide coverage. Entity coverage which, until recent years, was only provided under D&O policies written for nonprofit organizations and healthcare institutions, is designed to cover the organization directly—in addition to its directors and officers. A number of corporate D&O forms will not provide an entity coverage endorsement for an additional premium. [*Professional Liability Insurance* X.E.7]

environmental assessment—An analysis prepared pursuant to the National Environmental Policy Act to determine whether a federal action would significantly affect the environment and thus require a more detailed environmental impact statement.

environmental audit—An independent assessment of the current status of a party's compliance with applicable environmental requirements or of a party's environmental compliance policies, practices, and controls.

environmental impact statement—A document required of federal agencies by the National Environmental Policy Act for major projects or legislative proposals significantly affecting the environment. A tool for decision making, it describes the positive and negative effects of the undertaking and cites alternative actions.

environmental impairment liability (EIL) insurance—A specialized insurance policy that covers liability and sometimes cleanup costs associated with pollution. [*Commercial Liability Insurance* VI.V.1 and *Contractual Risk Transfer* XVII.P.1]

equipment floater—Property insurance covering equipment that is often moved from place to place. A form of inland marine insurance. See [*Commercial Property Insurance* IX.K.1]

ERISA liability—See Employee Retirement Income Security Act liability.

ERP—See Extended reporting period.

error or omission in reporting endorsement—A liberalization of the reporting requirements of property policies when written on a property value reporting basis. Such policies require the insured to report insurable values on a monthly, quarterly, or semiannual basis and as a result have very stringent reporting procedures that, unless adhered to, could cause claim settlement problems. A typical error or omission in reporting endorsements reads as follows.

It is agreed that this insurance shall not be prejudiced by any inadvertent omission in reporting of values hereunder, or unintentional error in amount, if prompt notice is given to this company as soon as said omission or error becomes known and deficiency of premium, if any, be made good.

errors and omissions clause—A provision, usually in an obligatory reinsurance treaty, stating that an error or omission in reporting a risk which falls within the automatic reinsurance coverage under such treaty shall not invalidate the liability of the reinsurer on such omitted risk.

errors and omissions insurance—An insurance form that protects the insured against liability for committing an error or omission in performance of professional duties. Generally, such policies are designed to cover financial losses rather than liability for bodily injury and property damage. [*Professional Liability Insurance* XIX.B-F]

estate plan—A plan for the systematic liquidation of one's estate. Conservation of estate assets is the uppermost consideration.

estimated premium—A preliminary figure that may be adjusted to reflect the extent of coverage provided under a given contract.

estoppel—A legal doctrine restraining a party from contradicting its own previous actions if those actions have been reasonably relied upon by another party. For example, an insurer that has repeatedly accepted late premium payments from an insured may be estopped from later canceling the policy on the basis of nonpayment because the insured has been reasonably led to believe that late payments are acceptable.

evidence—Anything that can be used to prove or disprove an alleged fact.

evidence of insurability—Underwriting information needed for an insurance policy.

excess and surplus lines insurance—Any type of coverage that cannot be placed with an insurer admitted to do business in a certain jurisdiction. Risks placed in excess/surplus lines markets are often substandard as respects adverse loss experience, unusual, or unable to be placed in conventional markets due to a shortage of capacity.

excess cover—Coverage whose limits apply once the amount of primary insurance under another policy has been paid.

excess insurance—(1) A policy or bond covering the insured against certain hazards, and applying only to loss or damage in excess of a stated amount, or specified primary or self-insurance.

(2) That portion of the amount insured that exceeds the amount retained by an entity for its own account. See Net line.

excess interest—Interest credited to the policy account of an insured in excess of the minimum amount stated in the policy.

excess liability "follow form" policy—Excess insurance that is subject to all of the terms and conditions of the policy beneath it. In the event of a conflict, it is the underlying policy provisions that take precedence. Many excess liability policies state that they are follow form except with respect to certain terms and conditions. When this is the case, the excess liability policy is not truly on a follow form basis.

excess liability policy—A policy issued to provide limits in excess of an underlying liability policy. The underlying liability policy can be, and often is, an umbrella liability policy. An excess liability policy is no broader than the underlying liability policy; its sole purpose is to provide additional limits of insurance.

excess limit—The highest amount of insurance that will be offered in a given situation in excess of basic limits.

excess line broker—A broker licensed to place insurance not available in the domestic state, through insurers licensed in states other than where the broker operates. Also known as a "surplus lines broker." [*Professional Liability Insurance* IV.J.2]

excess loss premium (ELP) factor—A factor used to calculate the charge to an insured under a retrospective rating plan to limit individual losses to a specified level. In other words, with ELP, the insured elects to limit the effect of any single loss in return for additional premium. [*Risk Financing* III.D.9]

excess of loss ratio reinsurance—See Stop loss.

excess of loss reinsurance—A form of reinsurance that indemnifies the ceding company for the portion of a loss that exceeds its own retention. It is generally used in casualty lines. [*Risk Financing* V.A.13]

excess per risk reinsurance—Excess of loss reinsurance that indemnifies the ceding company against the amount excess of the specified retention with respect to each risk involved in each occurrence. This coverage is written subject to a specified limit and is generally used in property lines. [*Risk Financing* V.A.12]

excess workers compensation insurance—A type of coverage available for risks that choose to self insure the majority of workers compensation loss exposures. Two categories of coverages are available: specific, which controls loss severity by placing a cap on losses the insured must pay arising out of a single occurrence, and aggregate, which addresses loss frequency by providing coverage once a cumulative per occurrence loss limit is breached. [*IRMI's Workers Comp* XI.T.8; *Commercial Liability Insurance* XII.F.1; and *Risk Financing* IV.E.10]

exchange transfer embargo indemnity—Insurance on the transfer risks created when an overseas sale by the insured is paid in the currency of the buyer's country, and the payment is deposited to the insured's account in the buyer's country. It is also possible to secure insurance where a contract is taken in currency other than that of the buyer's country if the same fund transfer risk is apparent.

exclusion—A provision of an insurance policy or bond referring to hazards, circumstances, or property not covered by the policy.

exclusive agency system—An insurance distribution system through which agents represent only one company or a group of companies under similar management.

exclusive remedy—A component of workers compensation statutes that bars employees injured on the job from making a tort liability claim against their employers. The benefits provided under workers compensation are the sole remedy available to injured employees. There are exceptions to this rule varying from state to state which do provide the employee with a legal venue. The failure to obtain and maintain insurance as well as willful negligence on the part of the employer are two types of such deviations. [*IRMI's Workers Comp* VIII.C.5]

executor—The fiduciary specified by a will to settle a deceased's given estate.

exemplary damages—Damages in excess of that amount needed to compensate for the plaintiff's injury, awarded in order to punish the defendant for malicious or wanton conduct; also called "punitive damages."

ex gratia payment—A voluntary payment made by the insurance company in response to a loss for which it is not technically liable under the terms of its policy.

ex-medical coverage—Workers compensation insurance without medical coverage. The insured pays all medical and hospital services required by law. [*IRMI's Workers Comp* VI.L.7]

ex parte hearings—Where due to extenuating circumstances, a party seeks immediate relief from the court.

expatriate—A person living and working in a country other than his own homeland.

expected loss—Estimated loss frequency multiplied by estimated loss severity, summed for all exposures. This measure of loss refers to a best estimate of the total losses of a particular type, e.g., workers compensation or general liability, of an organization that is expected during a given period (normally one year). [*Risk Financing* II.B.9]

expected morbidity—The expected instance of sickness or injury for a given group over a given period of time.

expected mortality—The expected instance of death for a given group over a given period of time assumed in setting life insurance rates.

expected or intended—A general liability policy exclusion for injury or damage that is expected or intended from the standpoint of the insured. An exception to the exclusion may provide coverage for liability from the use of reasonable force in the defense of persons or property (by someone such as a security guard). [*Commercial Liability Insurance* V.D.1]

expediting expense coverage—Coverage under a property or boiler and machinery policy for expenses of temporary repairs and costs incurred to speed up the permanent repair or replacement of covered property or equipment. On most extra expense forms, the recovery of expediting expenses is limited to the extent that the expenses serve to reduce the loss. However, coverage can be arranged to provide full reimbursement. [*Commercial Property Insurance* II.E.15]

expense—The cost of operating the insurance business exclusive of losses or claims.

expense allowance—Compensation paid to life insurance agents over and above commission to reimburse them for certain expense items incurred in doing business.

expense constant—A fixed, flat expense charge applied to every workers compensation policy in states using advisory rates. The charge applies in addition to the premium developed for that policy and recognizes that some of the administrative costs associated with writing a workers compensation policy do not vary with the amount of premium and should, therefore, not be included in the factors that are used to develop rates. [*IRMI's Workers Comp* XI.C.5]

expense loading—The amount added to the pure premium to cover expenses. [*Risk Financing* III.A.43]

expense ratio—The percentage of premium used to pay all the costs of acquiring, writing, and servicing insurance and reinsurance. [*Risk Financing* I.B.4]

expense reserve—A liability item for expenses incurred but not reported.

experience—(1) The loss record of an insured or of a class of coverage.

(2) Classified statistics of events connected with insurance, of outgo or of income, actual or estimated.

experience modification—The actual process by which the factor developed through experience rating is applied to the premium of the insured. [*IRMI's Workers Comp* XI.C.5; *Commercial Liability Insurance* VIII.E.5; and *Commercial Auto Insurance* III.F.2]

experience modifier—A factor developed by measuring the difference between the insured's actual past experience and the expected or actual experience of the class. This factor may be either a debit or credit and, therefore, will increase or decrease the standard premium in response to past loss experience. When applied to the manual premium, the experience modification produces a premium that is more representative of the actual loss experience of an insured. [*IRMI's Workers Comp* XI.C.5; *Commercial Liability Insurance* VIII.E.5; and *Commercial Auto Insurance* III.F.2]

experience rating—As respects workers compensation, the method in which the actual loss experience of the insured is compared to the loss experience that is normally expected by other risks in the insured's rating class. The resulting experience modification factor is then applied to the premium of the insured. In other casualty lines, the actual loss experience of the insured is generally compared to the actual loss experience of risks in the same industry to again develop a modifying factor for application to the insured's premium. [*IRMI's Workers Comp* XI.D.1; *Commercial Liability Insurance* VIII.E.5; and *Commercial Auto Insurance* III.F.2]

expert—An individual who has special training, skill, experiences, or knowledge so as to be qualified to render an authoritative opinion in a particular area of scientific, technical, or professional expertise.

expiration—The termination date of an insurance contract.

expiration file—A record kept by agents of policies that have expired or are about to expire.

expiration notice—A written notice to the insured that coverage is about to expire.

export and/or import embargo indemnity—Coverage of loss that occurs when import restrictions imposed by the government of the buyer's country or an export embargo in the seller's country frustrates an overseas contract. Similarly, should a contract include goods manufactured in a third country, substantial additional costs might be incurred if export restrictions were imposed in the subcontractor's country; or, in circumstances where subcontracted goods were being imported into the main contractor's country, an import embargo on such goods may be imposed. It is possible to cover losses incurred when contracts are frustrated in this way by means of an export/import embargo indemnity.

exposure—The state of being subject to loss because of some hazard or contingency. Also used as a measure of the rating units or the premium base of a risk. [*Risk Financing* I.B.4]

exposure base—The basis to which rates are applied to determine premium. Exposures may be measured by payroll (as in workers compensation or general liability), receipts, sales, square footage, area, or man-hours (for general liability), or per unit (as in automobile), or per $1,000 of value (as in property insurance). [*Risk Financing* I.B.4]

exposure-in-residence theory—A legal theory, applicable in certain latent injury cases, holding that injury occurs continuously while the injurious substance is within the injured person's body. [*Commercial Liability Insurance* V.C.11]

exposure survey—Process used by risk managers to identify an organization's risks of loss. May include interviews with management and operating personnel, physical inspections, financial statement reviews, and contract reviews.

expropriation—Nationalization or confiscation by a host country government of a multinational's investment (e.g., plant, inventory, equipment). If compensation is offered at all, it is usually far below fair market value.

extended coverage (EC) endorsement—An endorsement to a standard fire policy adding coverage for the following perils: windstorm, hail, explosion (except of steam boilers), riot, civil commotion, aircraft, vehicles, and smoke. The extended coverage perils are now included in most property policies without the need for a separate endorsement.

extended discovery period—A provision of coverage in claims-made policies, for claims brought against the insured following cancellation of the policy if the event(s) that caused the damage or injury occurred prior to the policy's cancellation. [*Commercial Liability Insurance* V.K.1]

extended discovery provisions—A clause that allows an insured to report (and ultimately receive coverage for) claims that are made against it after the expiration of a claims-made policy period. Also known as "extended reporting provisions" or "tail" coverage.

extended period of indemnity endorsement or option—Adds coverage under a business interruption policy for loss of income suffered during a specified period of time (e.g., 30, 60, 90 days) after the damaged property has been repaired. In the absence of this endorsement or option, business interruption coverage typically ends on the date the damaged property is repaired or replaced. See [*Commercial Property Insurance* V.K.42]

extended reporting period (ERP)—A designated period of time after a claims-made policy has expired during which a claim may be made and coverage triggered as if the claim had been made during the policy period. [*Commercial Liability Insurance* V.K.1]

extended term insurance—A nonforfeiture provision in a whole life policy that uses cash value to purchase term insurance equal to the existing amount of life insurance.

extortion coverage form G—An Insurance Services Office, Inc. (ISO) form (CR 00 08) that insures against loss of money, securities, and other property surrendered away from the premises as a result of a threat to do bodily harm to the insured, an employee, a relative, or invitee who is or allegedly is being held captive. Broader coverage, often at a reduced premium, can often be obtained by purchasing a separate kidnap and ransom policy from an insurer specializing in this field. [*Commercial Property Insurance* XII.D.20] extra expense coverage—Coverage for expenses in excess of normal operating expenses that are incurred to continue operations after a direct damage loss. Extra expense coverage is appropriate for service businesses whose property is not essentially income-producing (banks, insurance agencies, and doctors' offices), and for businesses that would find it imperative to continue operating regardless of cost (newspapers, dairies), perhaps by using a competitor's facilities. [*Commercial Property Insurance* II.E.4 and *Contractual Risk Transfer* XIV.P.7]

extra percentage tables—A form of substandard rating using mortality or morbidity tables for certain impaired health conditions.

extra premium—A premium charge added to the premium for a class rate because of extra hazardous exposures.

extraterritorial coverage—The extension of state workers compensation law to provide benefits for workers hired in the state; but injured while working in another state. There is usually a maximum placed on the amount of time an employee can spend outside the state of hire and still file a claim in that state. This term is also used in international insurance to denote coverage for work related injuries occurring outside the boundaries of the country of hire. [*IRMI's Workers Comp* III.C.5]

extremely hazardous substances—Any of 406 chemicals identified by the Environmental Protection Agency as toxic, and listed under Superfund Amendments and Reauthorization Act of 1986 Title III.

F

FAA special waiver—See Federal Aviation Administration special waiver.

face amount—Generally used to mean the amount of insurance provided.

facility emergency coordinator—Representative of a facility covered by environmental law (e.g., a chemical plant) who participates in the emergency reporting process with the Local Emergency Planning Committee (LEPC).

factory firms—Term used to describe law firms that are big, very billing-oriented, with a great emphasis on teams of attorneys handling cases in almost an assembly-line fashion.

factory insurance association—An organization of capital stock insurance companies which underwrite certain industrial risks.

factory mutuals (FMs)—Three affiliated insurers (Allendale Mutual, Protection Mutual, and Arkwright Mutual) who specialize in insuring property that qualifies as highly protected risk (HPR) property. The FMs are direct writers who reinsure each other and share common loss control, claims handling, and research services. [*Commercial Property Insurance* IV.M.3]

facultative—A form of reinsurance whereby each exposure which the ceding company wishes to reinsure is offered to the reinsurer and is contained in a single transaction. The submission, acceptance, and resulting agreement is required on each individual risk that the ceding company seeks to reinsure. That is, the ceding company negotiates an individual reinsurance agreement for every policy it will reinsure. However, the reinsurer is not obliged to accept every or any submission. [*Risk Financing* V.A.7]

facultative obligatory treaty—The hybrid between the facultative versus treaty approach. It is a treaty under which the primary insurer has the option to cede or not cede individual risks. However, the reinsurer must accept any risks that are ceded. [*Risk Financing* V.A.5–8]

faithful performance coverage—Responds to crime policy losses arising out of the failure of an individual to faithfully execute duties required by company bylaws or those prescribed by law as in the case of a public official or employee. Although this coverage may be required occasionally in the private sector, the majority of the time it is written for public entities. [*Commercial Property Insurance* XII.F.23]

false pretense, trick, and device—Refers to an exclusion in the physical damage coverage portion of a garage coverage form eliminating coverage for losses the insured suffers due to the fraudulent acts of others. Examples of false pretense include a customer absconding with an automobile on the pretense of test-driving it; the insured selling an automobile and receiving a bad check for it; and the insured selling an automobile and being instructed to deliver it to the wrong party because of fraudulent instructions. The exclusion can be negated by adding false pretense coverage on the garage liability policy. This endorsement covers the insured when a covered automobile is taken in a fraudulent manner. It also covers losses caused by the insured's acquiring an automobile from someone who did not have legal title to the vehicle. Coverage is most needed by automobile dealers but may also be desired for banks that sell repossessed autos to the public. [*Commercial Auto Insurance* IX.F.8 and XIII.K.3]

FAS—See Free alongside.

FC&S warranty—See Free of capture and seizure warranty.

feasibility study—A study undertaken to determine whether a contemplated risk financing program is feasible for an organization or group of organizations. An actuarial analysis is often done in conjunction with a feasibility study. The term is often used in reference to studies that attempt to ascertain whether or not the formation of a captive insurance company is a viable risk financing alternative under a given set of circumstances. [*Risk Financing* IV.K.14]

Federal Coal Mine Health & Safety Act (FCMH-SA)—Legislation passed in 1969 which provides no fault coverage for employees injured while working the coal mines located in the United States. A key component of the law is Title IV which deals with Black Lung Disease. See Black Lung Benefits Act. [*IRMI's Workers Comp* VII.F.1 and *Contractual Risk Transfer* XIV.E.5]

Federal Employers Liability Act (FELA)—A federal statute that provides for a liberalization of the rules for determining tort liability applicable to the liability of railroads to their employees for personal injury. Under normal tort rules, the injured party must prove negligence on the part of the defendant, and the absence of contributory negligence or assumption of risk on his own part. Under FELA, the employee need only show that any negligence on the part of the employer contributed to the injury. However, contributory negligence on the part of the employee reduces the recovery in proportion to the negligence attributable to the employee. The practical effect of this law, as interpreted over the years by the courts, has virtually been to impose a strict liability law on railroads with respect to injury to their employees in a manner very similar to workers compensation, but without the limitation on benefits provided under the workers compensation laws. [*IRMI's Workers Comp* III.C.14]

Federal Insurance Contribution Act (FICA)—Establishes a payroll tax to assist in the funding of social security benefits.

Federal Savings and Loan Insurance Corporation (FSLIC)—A U.S. government entity that insures savings deposits in savings and loan associations up to a maximum limit. See Federal Employers Liability Act (FELA).

FICA—See Federal Insurance Contribution Act.

fidelity bond—See Employee dishonesty coverage.

fiduciary—A person entrusted with the responsibility for the property or assets of another.

fiduciary bond—Guarantees that the individuals or legal entities appointed by the court to oversee the property of others will execute those appointed duties in good faith and be accountable for any deficits which may occur.

fiduciary liability—The responsibility on trustees, employers, fiduciaries, professional administrators, and the plan itself with respect to errors and omissions in the administration of employee benefit programs as imposed by the Employee Retirement Income Security Act of 1974.

fiduciary liability endorsement—A bank's fiduciary liability endorsement that can be added to the general liability policy. The fiduciary liability endorsement provides general liability protection for the financial institution, its executive officers or employees, trust beneficiaries, and others as delineated in the endorsement for bodily injury or property damage liability arising out of the ownership, maintenance, or use of property in any trust for which the named insured is acting in a fiduciary or representative capacity. Trust accounts may possess property from which liability exposures arise, and the financial institution has a liability exposure arising from this property due to its control of the property. The endorsement extends the financial institution's general liability policy to provide coverage for these liability exposures. Certain policy provisions and exclusions are altered slightly in order to remain applicable to the insured trust.

financed insurance—The payment of life insurance premiums with borrowed funds, usually from the cash value of the contract.

financial guarantee insurance—Insurance that covers financial loss resulting from default or insolvency, interest rate level changes, currency exchange rate changes, restrictions imposed by foreign governments, or changes in the value of specific goods or products.

financial institution bond—Used to insure banks and other financial institutions against employee dishonesty, burglary, robbery, forgery, and similar crime exposures. Previously called a "bankers blanket bond." Coverage may be provided on the standard form 24 promulgated by the Surety Association of America or on a special form drafted by the insurer. [*Commercial Property Insurance* XII.L.1]

financial responsibility law—A statutory provision requiring owners of automobiles to provide evidence of their ability to pay damages arising out of operations of the automobile. [*Commercial Auto Insurance* IV.C.1]

financial statement—A firm's operating statements, including balance sheet and profit and loss statement, along with associated information. Financial statements are frequently requested by underwriters when they provide both new business and renewal quotations. This is because an insured's financial condition is an important factor in assessing its insurability, commitment to loss control programs, and ability to pay premiums.

finite risk insurance—An insurance contract that shifts the risk of loss from an insured to an insurer during a stated number of years. Such contracts are subject to a specific limit of liability and also include a "commutation feature" (i.e., a refund to the insured) if loss experience is better than expected. Part of the investment income derived from the insured's premium payment is also rebated to the insured. In lieu of an underwriting profit that an insurer seeks from a traditional insurance policy, a finite risk insurance contract provides the insurer with an administrative fee for writing and maintaining the contract plus a relatively stable investment income which is earned on the insured's premium payments. [*Risk Financing* V.D.1]

fine arts coverage—Inland marine property insurance for works of art, typically written on a valued basis. [*Commercial Property Insurance* IX.I.1]

fire department service charge coverage—Coverage in a property insurance policy for charges imposed by a fire department for their services in fighting a fire, usually subject to a separate limit of insurance, such as $1,000. [*Commercial Property Insurance* V.F.16]

fire legal liability coverage—Coverage for the insured's liability for fire damage to premises rented to the insured. Included in the 1986 commercial general liability policy, but subject to a separate limit of insurance. This coverage can also be provided in a property policy. See Legal liability coverage form. [*Commercial Property Insurance* VI.C.24; *Commercial Liability Insurance* V.D.44; and *Contractual Risk Transfer* X.C.3]

fire-resistive construction—Exterior walls, floors, and roof of masonry or fire resistive material with a fire resistance rating of at least 2 hours. This is one of six basic construction types used in categorizing buildings for Insurance Services Office, Inc. (ISO), *Commercial Lines Manual* rating purposes. The other five construction categories are: frame, joisted masonry, noncombustible, masonry noncombustible, and modified fire resistive.

fire wall—A wall designed to prevent the spread of fire from within one part of a building to another. True fire walls are rated according to the number of hours that the wall is expected to withstand a fire, e.g., a 2-hour fire wall.

first class mail coverage—A policy providing all risk coverage for shipments of the insured and shipments between the insured's offices of negotiable and nonnegotiable securities and detached coupons by first class mail. Also covered are shipments of nonnegotiable securities and detached coupons from the insured to others.

first dollar coverage—Insurance coverage that provides for the payment of all losses up to the specified limit without any use of deductibles.

first dollar defense coverage—A coverage feature of some liability policies in which retentions do not apply to defense costs, even if no indemnity payments are made in conjunction with a claim. Thus, if an insurer were to expend $10,000 on defense of a claim and nothing for indemnity, the insured would not be required to pay any out-of-pocket costs for defense. [*Commercial Liability Insurance* XIII.E.5]

first dollar defense, umbrella—An umbrella or professional liability policy provision under which the insurer agrees to indemnify the insured for costs of claims defense in the self-insured retention area.

first named insured—The person or entity listed first on the policy declarations page as an insured. This primary or first named insured is granted certain rights and responsibilities that do not apply to the policy's other named insureds. Examples of additional rights of first named insureds are the receipt of cancellation notice and return premiums. Unique responsibilities include the notice of loss requirements and premium payment obligations. [*Commercial Auto Insurance* XII.B.1]

first party insurance—Insurance applying to the insured's own property or person.

first surplus reinsurance treaty—The sharing of risk by a reinsurer with the ceding company on a pro rata basis, excess of a specific retention. The proportion is sometimes fixed and sometimes varied according to different classes of risks and the net retentions which the insurance company keeps for its own account.

flat—Without interest, service, additional charges, or adjustments. For example, when a premium is quotes on a "flat" basis, no additional premiums (or refunds) will be due under the policy, regardless of loss experience or changes in exposure during the term of coverage.

flat cancellation—The cancellation of a policy as of its effective date, before the company has assumed liability. This requires the return of paid premium in full.

flat commission—A fixed commission rate.

flat dividend—A policyholder dividend paid to the insured as a flat percentage of the premium, usually 5 and 15 percent. Dividends are not guaranteed and can be paid only after the insurance company's board of directors declares a dividend.

flat rate—A fixed rate not subject to adjustment, regardless of loss experience or changes in exposure during the term of coverage.

fleet—For classifying commercial vehicles under the business auto policy, five or more automobiles. Less than five is considered nonfleet. The distinction is made for statistical coding purposes. It does not have an effect on the rating factors. [*Commercial Auto Insurance* III.G.6]

fleet automatic, auto—In automobile insurance, provides physical damage coverage automatically to all newly acquired automobiles owned by the insured. Premium charges for these automobiles are made either through a reporting form or an audit at the end of the policy period. The term is one which was used before the advent of the business auto coverage form when a physical damage endorsement was added to the commercial auto liability policy to afford such coverage. Two versions of the endorsement were available: fleet automatic and nonfleet automatic. The business auto policy equivalent to physical damage fleet automatic is covered auto symbol 2, 3, or 4. [*Commercial Auto Insurance* VIII.C.12]

fleet of companies—A number of insurance companies under the same management.

fleet policy—An insurance contract applying to a number of vehicles, usually with the requirement that they be under common ownership.

floater policy—An inland marine property insurance policy that covers personal property wherever it may be within the policy territory. [*Commercial Property Insurance* IX.B.1]

flood coverage—Coverage for damage to property caused by flood. May be available by endorsement to an all risks policy or to a difference-in-conditions policy. Normally, the coverage provided is subject to a per occurrence sublimit, an annual aggregate limit, and a separate deductible. Coverage may also be available from the National Flood Insurance Program (NFIP). See Flood exclusion. [*Commercial Property Insur-*

ance VII.C.10 and *Contractual Risk Transfer* XIV.P.4]

flood exclusion—A provision found in nearly all property insurance policies (even in all risk policies) eliminating coverage for damage by flood. May also eliminate coverage for other types of water damage, such as seepage and sewer backup. Flood coverage can sometimes be provided by endorsement. If not, a separate flood insurance policy may be available from the National Flood Insurance Program (NFIP). See Flood coverage. [*Commercial Property Insurance* V.Q.19 and *Contractual Risk Transfer* IV.P.4]

FMs—See Factory mutuals.

FOB—See Free on board.

FOB destination—See Free on board destination.

follow form—When an umbrella policy provision follows the underlying policy as to how the provision applies. Follow form also identifies an "excess" liability policy that follows the underlying policies for most policy provisions. The policy may stand alone for certain exclusions, conditions, etc., while relating back to the underlying coverage for most provisions. This type of policy form is typically used excess of scheduled underlying insurance and usually contains a requirement that the insured maintain scheduled underlying insurance.

follow form professional liability endorsement—An endorsement in an umbrella liability policy indicating that coverage applies under the same basis as in the underlying professional liability policy. In recent years, however, such endorsements are becoming increasingly difficult to obtain and are very unusual. This is because few umbrella insurers are also willing to assume the types of risks that are covered by professional liability policies. [*Professional Liability Insurance* VII.F.18]

following the fortunes—The clause in a reinsurance contract stating that it is the reinsurer's duty to "follow the fortunes" of the insured as if the reinsurer were a party to the original insurance.

force majeure—An unexpected or uncontrollable event that upsets one's plans or releases one from obligation. A superior force.

force majeure insurance—Provides coverage for financial losses arising out of the inability to bring a project to completion. The coverage encompasses delays as well as total termination of the contract resulting from events totally outside the control of the contractor i.e. fire, earthquake, war, revolution, flood, and epidemics. Types of losses covered by the policy include continued debt servicing, loss of income, ongoing fixed costs, spoilage, and related contingencies. The coverage has a very limited domestic market, but is commonly placed as a political risk coverage for contractors working in foreign countries. [*Commercial Property Insurance* IX.J.27]

foreign insurer—An insurer domiciled in the United States but outside the state in which the insurance is to be written. In effect, it is a domestic insurer doing business outside of the state in which it is domiciled. See Alien insurer. [*Professional Liability Insurance* IV.J.3]

forgery or alteration coverage—Covers loss due to dishonesty in writing, signing, or altering checks, bank drafts, and other financial instruments through Coverage Form B (CR 00 03). [*Commercial Property Insurance* XII.D.14]

form—A document prepared in a prescribed arrangement of words and layout. A rider, policy, endorsement, or application—all of these are forms.

fortuitous event—An event subject to chance without the implication of suddenness.

forum shopping—A term used to describe a search by legal counsel for the best venue or jurisdiction for a particular lawsuit.

FPA—See Free of particular average.

FPAAC—See Free of particular average (American Conditions).

FPAEC—See Free of particular average (English Conditions).

fractional premium—A premium paid over time, e.g., monthly, quarterly, or semiannually during the policy period.

frame construction—Exterior walls of wood, brick veneer, stone veneer, wood ironclad, stucco on wood. This is one of six basic construction types used in categorizing buildings for Insurance Services Office, Inc. (ISO), *Commercial Lines Manual* rating purposes. The other five construction categories are: joisted masonry, noncombustible, masonry noncombustible, modified fire resistive, and fire resistive. [*Commercial Property Insurance IV.F.4*]

franchise deductible—A minimum amount of loss that must be incurred before insurance coverage applies. A franchise deductible differs from an ordinary deductible in that, once it is met, the entire amount of the loss is paid, subject to the policy limit. Franchise deductibles can be stated either as a dollar amount or as a percentage of the policy limit.

franchise insurance—Insurance for groups too small to qualify for true group coverage. Also known as wholesale insurance.

free alongside (FAS)—One of several standard terms of sale for exports and imports. When goods are shipped FAS, the seller's responsibility ends when the merchandise is brought alongside the vessel (e.g., in a barge) or placed on the dock from which it will be loaded onto the vessel. The buyer is responsible for insuring the goods from that point on.

free of capture and seizure (FC&S) warranty—A clause in ocean marine policies which essentially functions to delete war risk coverage from hull insurance. Losses excluded are those due to nuclear weapons, mines, torpedoes, war (including civil war), piracy, and confiscation or nationalization of property.

free of particular average (American conditions) (FPAAC)—An ocean marine policy provision that eliminates coverage for partial loss to cargo unless caused by stranding, sinking, fire, or collision. See Free of particular average; Free of particular average (English conditions); Particular average; With average; and With average 3 percent.

free of particular average (English conditions) (FPAEC)—An ocean marine policy provision that eliminates coverage for partial loss to cargo except in the event of stranding, sinking, fire, or collision (regardless of whether those perils were the proximate cause of the loss). See Free of particular average; Free of particular average (American conditions); Particular average; With average; and With average 3 percent.

free of particular average (FPA)—An ocean marine policy provision that eliminates all coverage for any partial loss of cargo. See Free of articular average (American conditions); Free of particular average (English conditions); Particular average; With average; and With average 3 percent.

free on board destination (FOB destination)—One of several standard terms used in contracts of sale to indicate responsibility for damage to goods during shipment. When goods are shipped FOB destination, the seller's responsibility for the goods continues until they are delivered to the buyer in accordance with the contract terms.

free on board (FOB)—One of several standard terms used in contracts of sale to indicate responsibility for damage to goods during shipment. When goods are shipped FOB, the seller's responsibility ends when a carrier takes possession of them, or, with respect to ocean shipments, when the merchandise is placed safely aboard the vessel or when an on-board bill of lading has been issued. The buyer is responsible for insuring the goods from that point on.

frequency—The likelihood that a loss will occur. Expressed as low frequency (meaning the loss event is possible but the event has not happened in the past and is not likely to occur in the future), moderate frequency (meaning the loss event has happened once in a while and can be expected to occur sometime in the future), or high frequency (meaning the loss event happens regularly and can be expected to occur regularly in the future). Workers compensation losses normally have a high frequency as do automobile collision losses. General liability losses are usually of a moderate frequency, and property losses often have a low frequency. [*Risk Financing I.B.5*]

friable asbestos—Any material containing more than one percent asbestos, and that can be crumbled or reduced to powder by hand pressure.

friendly fire—An intentionally kindled fire that remains within its intended confines, such as in a furnace or fireplace. [*Commercial Property Insurance III.B.1*]

fronting—The use of an insurer to issue paper, i.e., an insurance policy, on behalf of a self-insured organization or captive insurer without the intention of bearing any of the risk. The risk of loss is transferred back to the self-insured or captive insurer with an indemnity or reinsurance agreement. However, the fronting company (insurer) assumes a credit risk since it would be required to honor the obligations imposed by the policy if the self-insurer or captive failed to indemnify it. Fronting companies charge a fee for this service, generally between 5 and 10 percent of the premium being written. Fronting arrangements allow captives and self-insurers to comply with financial responsibility laws imposed by many states that require evidence of coverage written by an admitted insurer, such as for auto and workers compensation insurance. Fronting arrangements must also be used in business contracts with other organizations, such as leases and construction contracts, where evidence of coverage through an admitted insurer is also required. [*Risk Financing* IV. A.19]

FSLIC—See Federal Savings and Loan Insurance Corporation.

full coverage—Any form of insurance that provides for payment in full of all losses caused by the perils insured against.

full preliminary term reserve valuation—A technique in reserving for life insurance in which no reserve is required for the first year of the life of the contract, with this difference being made up over the contract's duration. This is to minimize the heavy first year expenses in writing life insurance.

fully insured status—The highest covered status under the Social Security benefits under the Old Age, Survivors, Disability, and Health Insurance Act (OASDHI), entitling the worker to all types of benefits, including retirement. Before a worker can collect social security benefits under the OASDHI Act, he or she must have credit for a certain amount of covered work. Fully insured status is typically reached after 10 years of employment in a covered occupation.

fully paid policy—A life insurance policy on which all of the premiums necessary to obtain the benefits have been paid.

functional replacement cost provision or endorsement—A property insurance provision changing the valuation basis otherwise applicable (actual cash value or replacement cost value) to valuation at the cost to replace the damaged or destroyed property with property that serves the same function. Used when replacement of damaged property with substantially identical property is either impossible (perhaps due to technological change) or unnecessary. [*Commercial Property Insurance* VI.F.9]

funded—Having sufficient sums of money to meet future liabilities.

funded pension plan—An actuarially sound pension plan whose reserves are adequate at the time benefits become payable.

funding of reserves—An arrangement sometimes used in the case of undamaged reinsurance whereby the ceding company retains funds representing either the unearned premium reserve or outstanding loss reserves, which are applied to the business it cedes to a reinsurer.

fund states coverage—See Competitive state funds and Monopolistic state funds.

furriers block policy—Inland marine insurance covering the inventory of a fur dealer.

furriers customers insurance—Inland marine insurance covering furs that are stored by the insured fur dealer.

G

garagekeepers coverage aka garagekeepers legal liability—Provides coverage to owners of storage garages, parking lots, body and repair shops, etc., for liability as bailees with respect to damage to automobiles left in their custody for safekeeping or repair. Coverage is contingent upon establishing liability on the part of the insured. [*Commercial Auto Insurance* IX.E]

garagekeepers extra legal liability—Extends the garagekeeper's liability policy to provide coverage for damage to customers' automobiles regardless of the legal liability of the insured. The term "extra legal" has been replaced with the term "direct" in modern insurance parlance [*Commercial Auto Insurance* IX.E.2]

garage liability insurance—Insurance covering the legal liability of automobile dealers, garages, repair shops, and service stations for claims of bodily injury and property damage arising out of business operations. Damage to customers' vehicles is excluded from this coverage; however, garagekeepers coverage can be written as a part of the garage policy to cover that exposure. [*Commercial Auto Insurance* IX.D]

garage policy—A commercial auto policy designed to address the needs of auto dealers and other auto-related businesses (e.g., repair shops, service stations, storage garages). Coverages include garage liability, garagekeepers, and auto physical damage; other coverages are available by endorsement. See also garage liability insurance and garagekeepers coverage. [*Commercial Auto Insurance* Section IX]

garment contractors floater—An inland marine policy that protects the insured garment manufacturer against damage to or loss of garments on the manufacturer's premises, in transit, or in the custody of contractors or subcontractors.

general agency system—A life insurance marketing system whereby a general agent is delegated responsibility for a geographic territory. Field agents, agents who sell insurance, report to an agency supervisor. Agency supervisors then report to general agents.

general aggregate limit—Under the standard commercial general liability (CGL) policy, the maximum limit of insurance payable during any given annual policy period for all losses other than those arising from the products and completed operations hazards. [*Commercial Liability Insurance* V.I.1]

general average losses—Maritime partial losses sustained from voluntary sacrifice, such as jettisoning part of the cargo, to save the ship or crew, or from extraordinary expenses incurred by one of the parties for everyone's benefit, such as the cost to tow a disabled vessel. General average losses are proportioned between the shipowner and cargo owners, usually according to the York-Antwerp Rules.

general counsel—Often the highest-ranking lawyer within a corporation. Top in-house attorney often wears this title.

general damages—A subjective monetary award that is designed to compensate an injured person for his pain and suffering.

general exclusions—In workers compensation insurance, operations that are specifically excluded from the basic classifications and are always separately classified unless specifically included in the basic classification wording.

general inclusions—In workers compensation insurance, operations that are to be included in all the basic classifications, even though they may appear to be separate operations. This rule holds true unless the risk operates as a separate business, or is specifically excluded from the classification wording, or the governing business is categorized as a standard exception.

general liability insurance—Insurance protecting commercial insureds from most liability exposures other than automobile and professional liability. [*Commercial Liability Insurance* IV.C.1]

general maritime law—A common law concept whose origin is rooted in historic sea codes and requires the owner of the vessel to provide the entire crew with transportation, wages, room and board (maintenance), and medical services (cure) for the duration of the voyage. This condition applies even if the illness or injury is not job related. Further, the crew member may sue the owner of the ship for additional damages by citing the unseaworthiness of the craft. See Maintenance, cure, and wages. [*IRMI's Workers Comp* VII.B.2 and VII.C.9]

geographical limitations—Contractual provisions limiting coverage to geographical areas within which the insurance is effected. [*Commercial Auto Insurance* VIII.H.17]

GIC—See Guaranteed investment contract.

glass insurance—A property insurance policy covering breakage of building glass (such as windows) regardless of cause. Standard property insurance policies provide very limited coverage for glass breakage. [*Commercial Property Insurance* VII.C.18]

global insurance program—An insurance program with a coverage territory encompassing the entire world, including the country in which the insured is domiciled, that is arranged for a multinational business. Because of the differences in legal climates and regulations, most global programs cover only property, business interruption, and sometimes crime exposures. See Worldwide insurance program.

glovebag—A polyethylene or polyvinyl chloride bag-like enclosure affixed around an asbestos-containing source (most often thermal system insulation) permitting the material to be removed while minimizing release of airborne fibers in the surrounding atmosphere.

good faith settlement—A "blessing" by the court that protects a settling defendant from further claims with respect to the incident alleged in the complaint.

good samaritan statutes—Laws in various states that relieve physicians of any liability for providing treatment in an emergency situation such as an automobile accident, as long as the treatment provided was not grossly negligent, wanton, or reckless, and the physician received no compensation. [*Professional Liability Insurance* XVI.G.16]

governing classification—In workers compensation insurance, the classification that best describes the workers compensation exposure of an employer's business, as determined by payroll.

grace period—A life and health insurance provision allowing the insured 30 or 31 days after the premium due date to make payment if the insurance is to stay in force.

graded commission—A commission schedule based on class of business or quality of business as determined by a claims ratio.

gross earnings coverage—A type of business interruption insurance covering the insured's reduction in gross earnings suffered as a result of a direct damage loss. For a nonmanufacturer, gross earnings is essentially total sales less the cost of goods sold. For a manufacturer, gross earnings is the sales value of production, less cost of raw stock from which the production is derived. Included in this coverage are profits, continuing expenses, management payroll, and ordinary payroll. [*Commercial Property Insurance* V.K.5]

gross line—In reinsurance, the amount of insurance the primary insurer company has written on a risk, including the amount it has reinsured. Gross line is equal to the net line (i.e., the amount of insurance the primary insurer carries on a risk after deducting the amount reinsured) plus reinsurance ceded.

gross negligence—Willful and wanton misconduct.

gross premium—Pure premium adjusted upward to include insurer expenses.

gross profits insurance—A type of business interruption coverage in widespread use in Canada and the United Kingdom. Gross profits insurance differs from gross earnings insurance in two respects: the determination of the loss payment amount and the indemnity period. Loss payment is based on the amount of sales during the same period of time in the year preceding the date of direct damage loss. The indemnity period is the time it takes for the insured's profit to recover, subject to a maximum of 12 months. [*Commercial Property Insurance* II.E.12]

gross receipts or mileage, auto—A method of rating automobile liability insurance using the exposure base of gross receipts or mileage rather than the number of vehicles. This rating basis may be used for rating taxis, buses, and other public automobiles. It is also sometimes used in composite rating of truckers. [*Commercial Auto Insurance* III.G.17]

gross weight—The method of determining the size of a vehicle for insurance purposes. Gross vehicle weight is the maximum loaded weight for which a single vehicle is designed, as specified by the manufacturer. In some states, gross vehicle weight is based on registration receipts. Gross combination weight is the maximum loaded weight for a combination truck-tractor and semitrailer or trailer for which the truck-tractor is designed, as specified by the manufacturer. [*Commercial Auto Insurance* III.G.7]

ground coverage—Aviation insurance for the hull when the airplane is not flying.

group annuity—An annuity issued to an employer or retirement plan trustee to provide benefits for employees under retirement programs.

group certificate—A document provided to each member of a group plan showing the benefits provided under the contract.

group contract—A contract provided to the employer detailing coverage.

group credit insurance—Coverage a creditor may buy on the life or health of debtors to pay the debt in case of disability or death.

group insurance—Insurance provided to groups of people. Group insurance involves the substitution of group selection, the use of experience rating, and the use of a master insurance contract. These aspects of group insurance yield lower administrative costs than would individual policies written for members of the group. Group insurance is commonly used to provide employees and members of associations with life, health, disability, dental, and similar types of coverage.

group of companies—Insurance companies affiliated with others under the same management.

group practice HMO—A type of HMO which consists of various group physician practices including specialists who treat participants of the HMO exclusively. Patients are treated in the offices of the group practices and the physicians are compensated on a per patient basis for specific services. [*IRMI's Workers Comp* XV.F.3]

group property and liability insurance—Group coverage for property and liability exposures.

guaranteed cost—Premiums charged on a prospective basis without adjustment for loss experience during the policy period. A rate is agreed upon at the inception of the policy and is multiplied by the appropriate exposure base (e.g., sales, payroll, number of vehicles, or square footage) to yield the premium. With respect to auditable lines of coverage (e.g., workers compensation and general liability), only a change in the exposure base during the policy period will cause the premium to vary. In other words, if the actual exposure base at the end of the policy period is more or less than the estimate used at policy inception, the premium will be adjusted accordingly. Loss experience during the policy period does not affect the premium for that period. [*Risk Financing* III.B.1]

guaranteed insurability—An optional feature in life and health insurance that guarantees the insured the right to purchase additional insurance without undergoing a medical examination or otherwise providing evidence of good health.

guaranteed investment contract (GIC)—A funding arrangement most often used with profit sharing and savings and thrift plans in which the insurer guarantees the principal and interest rate, assuming that the contract is held to maturity.

guaranteed renewable—A provision in a life or disability policy that requires the insurer to renew the policy on its anniversary. The premium can usually be changed if the change applies to the entire class of insureds covered by the policy.

guardian ad litem—An individual appointed by a court to litigate a matter on behalf of a minor.

Guertin laws—The nonforfeiture laws in life insurance that have been standard in all states since 1948. These laws require that a paid-up nonforfeiture benefit (e.g., paid-up term life insurance) be provided for every whole life policy that lapses because of nonpayment of premium. These laws also require that a cash surrender value be provided if the policy has been in force 3 years or more.

guests' property, premises—See Liability for guests' property—premises, coverage form L.

guests' property, safe deposit box—See Liability for guests' property—safe deposit box, coverage form K.

guest statutes, auto—Legislation governing the rights of guests to sue a host-driver. Some guest statutes prohibit all nonpaying guests from suing for damages arising out of ordinary negligence; other statutes preclude only those guests related to the owner or operator.

H

hangar keepers liability—Provides coverage for damage to or destruction of the aircraft of others while in the insured's custody for storage, repair, or safekeeping and while in or on the scheduled premises.

hazardous ranking system (HRS)—The principle screening tool used by the EPA to evaluate risks to public health and the environment associated with abandoned or uncontrolled hazardous waste sites. The HRS calculates a score based on the potential of hazardous substances spreading from the site through the air, surface water, or groundwater, and on other factors such as density and proximity of human population. This score is the primary factor in deciding if the site should be on the National Priorities List and, if so, what ranking it should have compared to other sites on the list.

hazardous waste—A technical term under the Comprehensive Environmental Response Compensation and Liability Act (CERCLA) for chemical or other products considered to be hazardous or sources of hazardous waste.

health maintenance organization (HMO)—An organization that offers, provides, or arranges for coverage of designated health services needed by plan members under a prepaid per capita or prepaid aggregate fixed-sum basis. Services are provided through contracts and other arrangements into which the HMO enters with health care providers. With limited exceptions, persons enrolled in an HMO must receive health care benefits through these contract providers or no insurance benefit is provided. [*Professional Liability Insurance* XVI.P.2 and *IRMI's Workers Comp* XV.F.2–3]

highly protected risk (HPR) property—Property that is judged to be subject to a much lower than normal probability of loss by virtue of low hazard occupancy or property type, superior construction, special fire protection equipment and procedures, and management commitment to loss prevention. Insurers that specialize in insuring HPR property are referred to as "HPR insurers." [*Commercial Property Insurance* IV.M.1]

high-risk community—A community located within the vicinity of numerous sites of facilities or other potential sources of environmental exposure/health hazards which may result in high levels of exposure to contaminants or pollutants.

hired automobile—An automobile whose exclusive use and control has been temporarily given to another for a consideration. The business auto definition of "hired autos," however, includes autos borrowed except those borrowed from employees or partners. [*Commercial Auto Insurance* VIII.C.10]

hold harmless agreement—A provision in a contract that requires one contracting party to respond to certain legal liabilities of the other party. For example, construction contracts typically require the contractor to indemnify the owner with respect to the owner's liability to members of the public who are injured or whose property is damaged during the course of the contractor's operations. There are a number of types of hold harmless clauses, differentiated by the extent of the liabilities they transfer. The most commonly used types of clauses are the "broad," "intermediate," and "limited" form hold harmless clauses.

- *Limited form*—Where Party A holds Party B harmless for suits arising out of Party A's sole negligence. Party B is thus protected when it is held vicariously responsible for the actions of Party A.

- *Intermediate form*—Where Party A holds Party B harmless for suits alleging sole negligence of Party A or negligence of both parties.

- *Broad form*—Where Party A holds Party B harmless for suits against Party B based on the sole negligence of A, joint negligence of A and B, or the sole negligence of B. Broad form hold harmless agreements are unenforceable in a number of states.

holding power formula—A formula indicating the maximum dollar amount of incurred losses that can be sustained under a specific retro plan without triggering additional premiums at any adjustment period. [*Risk Financing* III.I.5] home foreign—Insurance written in one country on property or risks located in another country. Premiums and losses are usually payable in the country where the insurance is written.

home office—The corporate headquarters of an insurance company.

homeowners modified form 8 (HO-8)—Part of the Insurance Services Office, Inc. (ISO), homeowners portfolio, provides basic named perils coverage for direct damage to property, personal liability coverage, and medical payments to others as respects owner occupied dwellings. This form is quite similar to Form HO-1 except it allows the replacement cost provision to be changed to repair cost and in some instances actual cash value. This policy is often utilized on older homes and those which would not be replaced.

homeowners policy—A multiple line insurance contract providing protection against property and liability exposures for the personal residence exposure.

homeowners policy basic form 1 (HO-1)—Provides basic named perils coverage for direct damage to property, personal liability coverage, and medical payments to others coverage. Originally drafted as part of the Insurance Services Office, Inc. (ISO), homeowners forms portfolio, this basic form has been discontinued in most states because buyers demanded the broader coverages available in the other ISO homeowners forms.

homeowners policy broad form 2 (HO-2)—Part of the Insurance Services Office, Inc. (ISO), homeowners forms portfolio, insures the described dwelling, private structures in connection with the dwelling, unscheduled personal property on and away from the premises, and loss of use. Personal liability coverage and medical payments to others coverage are also provided by the policy. It is a broad named perils form, but the list of covered perils is more extensive than that of HO-1.

homeowners policy contents broad form 4 (HO-4)—Part of the Insurance Services Office, Inc. (ISO), homeowners forms portfolio, insures a tenant for direct damage to unscheduled personal property on a broad named perils basis. Personal liability coverage and medical payments coverage are also provided by this policy.

homeowners policy special form 3 (HO-3)—Part of the Insurance Services Office, Inc. (ISO), homeowners forms portfolio, insures the described owner occupied dwelling, private structures in connection with the dwelling, unscheduled personal property on and away from the premises, and loss of use. Personal liability coverage and medical payments coverage are also provided by this policy. Coverage of the dwelling, related structures, and scheduled personal property is on an all risks basis, while coverage of unscheduled personal property is on a broad named perils basis.

homeowners policy unit owners form 6 (HO-6)—Part of the Insurance Services Office, Inc. (ISO), homeowners forms portfolio, insures a condominium owner for direct damage to unscheduled personal property on a broad named perils basis. Personal liability coverage and medical payments coverage are also provided by this policy. The policy is designed to coordinate with a policy covering the structure and common areas that is purchased by the condominium association.

hospital income insurance—Insurance providing a stated weekly or monthly payment during the hospitalization of the insured. The benefits payable are not based upon the actual expenses incurred.

hostile fire—A fire that is not intentionally kindled or an intentionally kindled fire that does not remain within its intended confines, such as in a fireplace or furnace. [*Commercial Property Insurance* III.B.1]

hostile work environment sexual harassment—A form of sexual harassment occurring when such conduct has the purpose or effect of unreasonably interfering with an individual's work performance or creating an intimidating, hostile, or offensive working environment. Coverage for such claims is covered under employment practices liability policies. [*Professional Liability Insurance* X.J.18]

host liquor liability—Liability for bodily injury or property damage arising out of the serving or distribution of alcoholic beverages by a party not engaged in this activity as a business enterprise. Host liquor liability exposures are insurable under standard general liability policies. [*Commercial Liability Insurance* V.D.5]

HPR property—See Highly protected risk (HPR) property.

HR-10 plan—See Keogh Act plan.

hull coverage—Marine or aviation insurance covering damage sustained to an insured vessel or airplane.

human equivalent dose—A dose which, when administered to humans, produces an effect equal to that produced by a dose in animals.

I

IIADC—See International Association of Drilling Contractors.

IBNER—"Incurred but Not Enough Recorded." This is the portion of IBNR reserves established for additional development on case reserves from currently reported claims. [*Risk Financing* II.B.8]

IBNR—"Incurred but not reported." This denotes: (1) reserve amounts for claims which have been incurred as of a given date but not yet reported to an insurer or self-insured, plus (2) reserves for additional development on case reserves for claims that have been reported. [*Risk Financing* II.B.8]

IBNR losses—See Incurred but not reported (IBNR) losses. (I think we should take this out. It is redundant.)

IBNYR—"Incurred but not yet reported." This is the portion of IBNR reserves established for claims which have been incurred but are not yet reported to an insurer or self-insured. [*Risk Financing* II.B.8]

III—See Insurance Information Institute.

immediate annuity—An annuity purchased with a single premium under which payment to the annuitant begins at the end of the first prescribed payment period. If, for example, payments will be on a monthly basis, the first payment will be made 1 month after the annuity is purchased. If the income period begins at the inception of the first income period, the annuity is an "annuity due." Immediate annuities are most often purchased as a settlement option under a life insurance policy.

immediately dangerous to life and health (IDLH)—The maximum level to which a healthy individual

can be exposed to a chemical for 30 minutes and escape without suffering irreversible health effects or impairing symptoms. Used as a "level of concern."

impaired risk—A risk that is less than the standard required for the risks on which the premium for the cover is based.

impairment capital—The situation in which the surplus account of a stock insurer is threatened by exhaustion, and the insurer invades its capital account to meet liabilities. Some jurisdictions allow this but most do not.

implead—To sue; to prosecute. To bring a new party into an action.

implied warranty—As a point of law, the understanding that a particular product is safe and suitable for a particular use, when the vendor knows at the time of sale the use intended.

improvements and betterments—Permanent additions or changes made by a lessee at his own expense that may not legally be removed. Property policies vary as to whether tenants' improvements and betterments are covered under the building category or under the contents category, so care must be taken to assign these values to the proper category of covered property. [*Commercial Property Insurance* V.F.5]

in camera proceedings—A private hearing with the judge outside of the presence of spectators and the jury.

inchmaree clause—An ocean marine insurance provision adding coverage for damage directly resulting from the bursting of boilers, breakage of shafts, other mechanical failures, latent defects in the ship's equipment or machinery, and faults or errors in the navigation or management of the ship.

incidence of ownership—The rights that might be exercised by the owner of the policy who may or may not be the insured.

incidental malpractice—The liability exposure created by the offering of medical services by an entity not engaged primarily in the offering of such services. A manufacturing business, for example, might have such an exposure by virtue of the fact that it employs an industrial nurse to handle first aid-type claims. Coverage can be provided in a commercial general liability (CGL) policy. [*Commercial Liability Insurance* **V.H.7**]

incident reporting provision—A provision in a liability insurance policy that requires the insured to report incidents, accidents, or occurrences that may lead to claims. Also called an "awareness provision" or a "notice of potential claim provision." [*Commercial Liability Insurance* **V.J.2**]

incontestable clause—A clause in a life or health insurance policy that stipulates a given length of time (usually 2 years) during which the insurer may contest claims. After expiration of this time, claims cannot be contested for any reason other than nonpayment of premium.

increased cost of construction—See Building ordinance coverage.

increased limit factors—Multiplicative factors that are applied to premium amounts for "basic" limits of coverage, to determine premiums for higher limits of coverage.

increased limits table—A table of factors, expressed as percentages, that are used to increase the basic limits rates to the limits of coverage desired by the insured.

incurred but not reported (IBNR) losses—An estimate of the amount of an insurer's (or self-insurer's) liability for claim-generating events that have taken place but have not yet been reported to the insurer or self-insurer. The sum of IBNR losses plus incurred losses provide an estimate of the insurer's eventual liabilities for losses during a given period. [*Risk Financing* **Appendix F.F4**]

incurred expense—Expenses paid plus reserves for expenses to be paid.

incurred losses—The total amount of paid claims and loss reserves associated with a particular period of time, usually a policy year. Incurred losses are customarily computed in accordance with the following formula: losses incurred during the period, plus outstanding losses at the end of the period, less outstanding losses at the beginning of the period. This does not ordinarily include incurred but not reported (IBNR) losses. [*Risk Financing* **III.D.7**]

incurred loss ratio—The ratio of losses paid and reserved (i.e., incurred) to premiums earned.

incurred loss retro—An insurance risk financing plan under which the insured pays a premium based on actual loss experience incurred during the policy period. The premium adjustments made over the life of the plan are based on incurred losses which takes into consideration the outstanding reserves and expenses of the claims in addition to the actual paid indemnity and medical costs. [*IRMI's Workers Comp* **XI.L.1** and *Risk Financing* **III.D.1**]

indemnification—(1) In policies written on an indemnification basis, the insurer reimburses the insured for claims and claim costs already paid by the insured. Technically, the insured must not only suffer a loss but must also pay the loss before being indemnified by the insurer.

(2) The agreement of one party to assume financial responsibility for the liability of another party. Hold harmless agreements are typically used to impose this transfer of risk.

indemnify—To make compensation to an entity, person, or insured for incurred hurt, loss, or damage.

indemnitee—The person or organization who is held harmless in a contract (by the indemnitor).

indemnitor—The person or organization who holds another (the indemnitee) harmless in a contract.

indemnity—Restoration to the victim of a loss up to the amount of the loss.

indemnity bond—A bond indemnifying an obligee against loss that arises as a result of a failure on the part of a principal to perform as required. For example, a lease bond guarantees that a tenant will make his/her rental payments.

indemnity clause—See Hold harmless agreement.

indemnity payments—(1) The losses paid or expected to be paid directly to an insured by an insurer for first-party (e.g., property) coverages or on behalf of an insured for third-party (e.g., liability) coverages.

(2) Payments made by the indemnitor under a hold harmless clause on behalf of the indemnitee.

independent agency system—A system of marketing insurance through independent contractors who sell insurance on a commission or fee basis with one or more insurers. In contrast to the direct marketing system, the independent contractor retains ownership, use, and control of policy records and expiration data.

independent contractor—An individual or company who has signed an agreement with another party to perform some job or function on behalf of that party without the direction or oversight of the party. As respects workers compensation, many states have established criteria which determine whether an individual is functioning as an independent contractor or employee. A worker classified as an independent contractor and not an employee is ineligible to receive benefits under the workers compensation policy of the other party. In spite of the rules established, the delineation of an independent contractor remains in many jurisdictions a legal ambiguity. [*IRMI's Workers Comp* VIII.C.10]

independent director's policies—Directors and officers (D&O) coverage designed for individuals who serve on a number of different corporate boards and are not employees of any individual company. Such policies are becoming increasingly rare because few "professional" directors (or any directors, for that matter) sit on the boards of companies that do not already purchase D&O coverage.

independent medical exam (IME)—A presumably "independent" medical examination, performed on an injured party to assess the nature and extent of his/her injuries.

indirect damage loss—Loss resulting from direct damage to property, e.g., income and expense loss resulting from inability to use damaged property. See Time element insurance.

individual practice association—A type of HMO in which individual practitioners see patients enrolled in the HMO, but also treat their own patients who are not HMO participants. Compensation to the physician is based on either a per patient fee or a discounted fee schedule. [*IRMI's Workers Comp* XV.F.3]

industrial life insurance—See Debit life insurance.

Industrial Risk Insurers (IRI)—An unincorporated association of 40 major insurance companies, formed in 1975 by the merger of the Factory Insurance and Oil Insurance Associations (FIA and OIA). The IRI acts as the highly protected risk (HPR) underwriting arm of its member companies and also provides property insurance and inspection services to the oil industry. [*Commercial Property Insurance* IV.M.4]

inflation factor—The loading factor providing for future increases in either the cost of losses or the size of exposure bases (e.g., payroll, sales) resulting from inflation. It may be applied to historical data of any kind to convert historical data into more current data when making projections. [*Risk Financing* II.B.4]

inflation guard provision—A provision that gradually and continuously increases the limit of insurance by a specified percentage over a specified period of time (such as 3 percent every 3 months). See Inflation guard provision or endorsement. [*Commercial Property Insurance* V.F.56]

informed consent—A duty owed by a medical professional to obtain a patient's consent before performing a procedure or rendering treatment. After fully explaining the treatment, the physician should obtain the patient's consent to allow treatment. There is a presumption of negligence if injury results and the physician did not obtain such consent. [*Professional Liability Insurance* XVI.G.11]

inherent defects insurance (IDI)—First-party property insurance that covers physical damage or imminent collapse of newly constructed property caused by faulty design, engineering, workmanship, or materials in load bearing elements such as foundations, columns, walls, floors, beams, roofs, and land improvements. Available to qualified owners, developers, and contractors for up to a 10-year policy term, IDI provides a mechanism for reducing or avoiding construction defects litigation.

inherent vice—An exclusion found in most property insurance policies eliminating coverage for loss caused by a quality in property that causes it to damage or destroy itself. [*Commercial Property Insurance* V.R.16]

in-house counsel—An attorney employed by the organization for which he or she provides legal services.

initial premium—The amount paid at the inception of an insurance contract.

inland marine coverage—A group of property insurance coverages designed to insure exposures that cannot be conveniently or reasonably confined to a fixed location or insured at a standard rate under a standard form. Includes coverage for: property in transit over land, certain moveable property, property under construction, instrumentalities of transportation and communication (such as bridges, roads, piers, and television and radio towers), legal liability coverage for bailees, and computerized equipment. Many inland marine coverage forms provide coverage without regard to the location of the covered property; these are sometimes called "floater" policies as a result. Inland marine coverage forms are generally broader than property coverage forms due to the relative freedom from rate and form regulation of inland marine insurance as compared with property insurance. [*Commercial Property Insurance* IX.B.1 and *Contractual Risk Transfer* XIV.P.8]

innkeepers legal liability—The legal liability of hotel and motel operators as bailees, for the safekeeping of guest's property. An innkeepers legal liability policy insures against this liability, as imposed by statute in each state, usually with a limit of $1,000 per guest and an appropriate aggregate limit.

in rem endorsement—A workers compensation coverage endorsement extending coverage for suits filed against the value of the ship by an injured crew member seeking for the recovery of damages. The suit must cite the unseaworthy condition of the vessel as proximate cause of the damages. In the absence of this endorsement, an in rem suit could result in an injunction preventing the vessel from leaving port until the suit is settled. In rem coverage is now part of the maritime coverage endorsement rather than a separate endorsement. [*IRMI's Workers Comp* III.C.14]

insolvency clause—(1) A clause holding a reinsurer liable for its share of loss assumed under a treaty, even though the primary company has become insolvent.

(2) A clause in an umbrella liability policy, stipulating that the umbrella will not drop down in the event the primary liability insurer is unable to pay because of insolvency.

inspection bureau—An organization that investigates exposures and establishes rates for property and liability insurers.

inspection reports—A report, by an insurer or one of a number of inspection services available, assessing the moral, financial, and physical aspects of a risk.

installation floater—Inland marine coverage on property (usually equipment) being installed by a contractor. Essentially a specialized type of builders risk coverage that is often written on the same form used to provide builders risk coverage. [*Commercial Property Insurance* IX.J.1]

installment settlement—A settlement other than a lump sum that involves periodic payments. More commonly called a "structured settlement."

insurability—Acceptability to the insurer of an applicant for insurance at a given rate.

insurable interest—An interest by the insured person in the value of the subject of insurance, including any legal or financial relationship. Insurable interest usually results from property rights, contract rights, and potential legal liability.

insurance—A contractual relationship that exists when one party (the insurer) for a consideration (the premium) agrees to reimburse another party (the insured) for loss to a specified subject (the risk) caused by designated contingencies (hazards or perils). The term "assurance," commonly used in England, is considered synonymous with "insurance."

insurance agents errors and omissions coverage—Coverage for financial loss to third parties resulting from the acts, errors, or omissions of insurance agents or brokers. Like most professional liability forms, it is written with a claims-made coverage trigger. Typical exclusions are: fraud/dishonesty, losses due to commingling, and insurer insolvency. The two largest insurance agents associations, the Independent Insurance Agents of America (IIA) and the Professional Insurance Agents (PIA), each sponsor coverage programs that are written by commercial insurers. [*Professional Liability Insurance* XV.B-F]

insurance commissioner—The head of the state's insurance department or regulatory agency.

insurance department—A governmental entity charged with the regulation and administration of insurance laws and other responsibilities associated with insurance.

insurance examiner—A State Insurance Department representative assigned to officially audit and examine insurers.

Insurance Information Institute (III)—An educational, fact-finding, and communications organization for the property and casualty insurance industry. The III is supported by several hundred member insurance companies and serves as the industry's primary public relations organization.

insurance policy—In broad terms, the entire written contract of insurance. More specifically, it is the basic written or printed document, as well as the coverage forms and endorsements added to it.

Insurance Regulatory Information System (IRIS)—Numerical tests consisting of 11 ratios developed and used by the National Association of Insurance Commissioners (NAIC) to determine an insurance company's operating condition and solvency.

Insurance Services Office, Inc. (ISO)—A nonprofit association of insurance companies that collects statistical data, promulgates rating information, develops standard policy forms, and files information with state regulators on behalf of its member companies. ISO is the "bureau" in most states for homeowners, personal auto, commercial auto, commercial general liability, commercial property, commercial crime, and some lines of professional liability insurance. The *Commercial Lines Manual*, which contains classification rules and rating information for these lines of insurance, is published by ISO.

insurance to value—Insurance written in an amount approximating the value of the subject of insurance or which meets coinsurance requirements.

insured—The person(s) protected under an insurance contract.

insured versus insured exclusion—An exclusion found in directors and officers liability policies (and to a lesser extent, in other types of professional liability coverage). The exclusion precludes coverage for claims by one director or officer against another. The purpose of this exclusion is to eliminate coverage for four types of situations: (1) employment practices claims, (2) internal disputes/infighting, (3) claims involving collusion, and (4) claims by organizations against their directors/officers for imprudent business practices. [*Professional Liability Insurance* X.E.23]

insurer—The insurance company that undertakes to indemnify for losses and perform other insurance-related operations.

insuring agreement—That portion of the insurance contract that stipulates the perils insured, persons and property covered, locations, and the period of the contract. [*Commercial Auto Insurance* VIII.D.1]

interchange agreements—An agreement between trucking companies wherein company A has possession of company B's trailer or equipment and agrees to be responsible for loss to such while in A's possession. [*Commercial Auto Insurance* X.E]

interim bill—Any bill for legal services prior to the final one.Waiting until a case is over to get paid would cause substantial cash flow problems for most law firms. Hence, they send interim bills at agreed-on intervals throughout the life of a case or assignment.

interim (permit) status—Period during which treatment, storage, and disposal facilities coming under RCRA in 1980 are temporarily permitted to operate while awaiting a permanent permit. Permits issued under these circumstances are usually called "Part A" or "Part B" permits.

inter-insurance exchange—See Reciprocal company.

intermediary—A reinsurance broker who negotiates contracts of reinsurance on behalf of the reinsured, usually with those reinsurers who recognize brokers and pay them commissions on reinsurance premiums ceded. The intermediary also acts as a conduit through which communications between the insurer and reinsurer are passed, including the payment of premiums by the reinsured to the reinsurer and the collection of losses for the reinsured from the reinsurer. [*Risk Financing* V.A.9]

International Association of Drilling Contractors (IADC)—Promulgator of several standard oil and gas drilling contracts.

international reverse business—An insurance program arranged for a U.S. subsidiary of a foreign-owned parent company. Also known as "reverse flow business."

interrogatory—Written list of questions put to a party—plaintiff or defendant—to a lawsuit. Answers provided are used to prepare questions for depositions or for trial.

interstate experience rating—An experience rating plan for risks operating on a multistate (interstate) basis that utilizes the experience developed within more than one state.

intrafamily immunity—The legal doctrine prohibiting one family member from suing another family member for personal injury.

intrastate experience rating—An experience rating plan that utilizes the experience developed within one state only.

invasion of privacy—Violation of a person's right to be left alone. Invasion of privacy is considered a "traditional" personal injury tort. Coverage for personal injury is excluded in some umbrella and professional liability coverage forms, although it is covered under commercial general liability (CGL) policies and liability policies designed for media firms. [*Commercial Liability Insurance* V.L.28]

investment income—The income of a company derived from its investments as opposed to its operations. The term has special significance in the insurance industry as various factions consider whether such income should be considered in ratemaking.

invitee—A person to whom an express or implied invitation has been given to come onto the premises for the business advantage of the possessor. Under common law, the possessor of the land owes invitee the highest duty of care.

IRI—See Industrial Risk Insurers.

IRIS—See Insurance Regulatory Information System.

irrevocable beneficiary—A beneficiary to a life insurance policy that cannot be changed without his or her consent.

ISO—See Insurance Services Office, Inc.

issued business—Life insurance contracts that have been paid for and written by the insurer but are not yet delivered to or accepted by the insured.

----------------------------- **J** -----------------------------

jettison—The intentional throwing overboard of part of the cargo or some piece of the ship in order to save the ship or its cargo. Virtually all ocean marine policies cover the peril of jettison.

jewelers block insurance—Inland marine insurance designed to provide coverage for loss or damage to jewelry that is the stock of jewelry retailers, wholesalers, manufacturers, and pawnbrokers. [*Commercial Property Insurance* IX.M.1]

joint and several liability—A legal doctrine applying in some states that allows an injured person to sue and recover from any one or more of several wrongdoers at his option, regardless of that wrongdoer's degree of negligence. The injured party cannot receive double compensation but can choose to recover 100 percent of a damages award from any defendant who is found liable to any extent. See Several liability.

joint and survivorship annuity—An annuity issued to two or more persons under which annuity payments continue as long as either annuitant lives.

joint annuity—An annuity issued to two or more persons under which annuity payments cease upon the death of either annuitant.

joint defense—When the defendants in a particular case resolve to present a "united front" in the eyes of plaintiff and the jury.

joint insurance—Life insurance written covering two or more lives with benefits payable when the first of the covered persons dies. This type of policy is most frequently used for key man insurance to allow a surviving partner to purchase a deceased partner's share of the business.

joint venture—A business relationship in which two or more persons combine their labor or property for a single undertaking and share profits and losses equally, or as otherwise agreed. General liability policies normally do not cover liability arising from joint ventures unless they are scheduled as an insured. A manuscript endorsement can sometimes be added to handle this exposure. Otherwise, specific coverage arrangements must be made whenever the insured becomes involved in a joint venture. [*Commercial Liability Insurance* V.H.2]

joisted masonry construction—Exterior walls of masonry material (adobe, brick, concrete, gypsum block, hollow concrete block, stone, tile, or similar materials), with combustible floor and roof. This is one of six basic construction types used in categorizing buildings for Insurance Services Office, Inc. (ISO), *Commercial Lines Manual* rating purposes. The other five construction catego-

ries are: frame, noncombustible, masonry non-combustible, modified fire resistive, and fire resistive. [*Commercial Property Insurance* IV.F.4]

Jones Act—**(Merchant Marine Act of 1920)**—Provides seamen with a negligence remedy for on-the-job injury without having to overcome employer defenses of assumption of the risk or fellow servant liability. Contributory negligence of the employee does not bar recovery; but, recovery is reduced by the proportion of negligence attributable to the employee. Employers can obtain coverage under a standard workers compensation policy by purchasing a maritime coverage endorsement. [*IRMI's Workers Comp* VII.C.2]

judgment rates—Rates that are established by judgment of an underwriter rather than by a rating authority. Judgment rates are used most often for those lines of insurance for which there are not enough similar exposure units to develop statistically credible rates. See "A" rates. [*Risk Financing* III.A.4]

jumping juvenile insurance—A name used for life insurance on children that increases automatically when they reach age 21 without additional premium or proof of insurability.

jurisdiction—A term used to describe which courts have the power or authority to decide a particular matter. Also, the geographical subdivision with respect to which an individual insurance regulatory body (such as a state insurance department) has authority.

K

Kenney ratio—A rule of thumb developed by Roger Kenney that sets a 2 to 1 target ratio of gross premiums written to policyholder surplus. This applies to companies that write strictly property insurance. For companies that also write liability insurance, the ratio is 3 to 1. Such ratios provide a measure of insurers' financial stability and solvency.

Keogh Act Plan—A part of the Individual Tax Requirement Act that enables self-employed individuals to take advantage of formal retirement plans and tax advantages similar to those available for

corporate pension plans which also qualify under the Act.

key man insurance—Life insurance owned by the firm on the life of a key individual that will, in the event of his or her death, offset a loss in earnings and provide the funds necessary to find, hire and develop a replacement. It is designed to offset losses resulting from the death of a key person, such as reduced sales, interruption of a vital research project, flow of production, or an impaired credit standing.

kidnap/ransom insurance—Specialty crime coverage that insures against loss by the surrender of property as a result of a threat of harm to the named insured, an employee, or a relative or guest of the insured or the insured's employees. Available under an Insurance Services Office, Inc. (ISO) crime coverage form G, extortion (CR 00 08). [*Commercial Property Insurance* XII.D.20]

L

large deductible plan—A cash flow workers compensation insurance program that allows the insured to retain a portion of each loss through a substantial deductible and to transfer onto an insurer losses excess of that deductible. The insurer also handles losses falling below the deductible and bills back these costs to the insured. [*IRMI's Workers Comp* XI.P.6 and *Risk Financing* IV.O.1]

lapse—Termination of an insurance policy due to the insured's failure to pay the premium.

lapse ratio—The ratio of the number of policies that lapse during a period to the total number of policies written at the beginning of that period.

laser exclusion—An exclusionary endorsement under a claims-made commercial general liability policy that excludes liability arising from the products, locations, accidents, or work specified in the endorsement. [*Commercial Liability Insurance* VI.N.2]

last injurious exposure—A trigger used to establish which employer and workers compensation insurer are responsible for occupational disease that has manifested in an employee. For the injury to be covered, the last date of the employee's last exposure to the situation causing the illness must be determined to fall in the policy period under which the claim is filed. [*IRMI's Workers Comp* VI.D.3]

lateral hire—Someone who enters the law firm, typically from another firm, at the same level as they were in their old firm. For example, attorney X, who was an associate at one law firm, joins another firm as an associate.

law clerk—Someone who is either in law school and an intern at a law firm or a law school graduate awaiting bar results and employed by a law firm.

law enforcement officers liability—Provides errors and omissions coverage for police departments. Unlike most professional liability coverage, such policies are often written on an occurrence (rather than on a claims-made) basis. Some of the more important covered acts include: false arrest, excessive force, and invasion of privacy. This coverage can sometimes be provided on a limited basis in the general liability policy but must usually be purchased separately. Common exclusions are: criminal/intentional acts, claims for injunctive relief, and motor vehicle operations. [*Professional Liability Insurance* XI.I and XI.G]

law of large numbers—A statistical axiom which states that the larger the number of exposure units independently exposed to loss, the greater the probability that *actual* loss experience will equal *expected* loss experience. In some instances, insurers can virtually eliminate their risk of loss by securing a large enough number of units in an insured group. [*Risk Financing* I.B.6]

lawyers professional liability coverage—Provides attorneys with liability coverage for financial loss suffered by third parties arising from acts, errors, and omissions in providing professional, legal services. Fraud, intentional and criminal acts, bodily injury, and property damage are excluded from coverage. However, most of the policies provide coverage for personal injury perils (i.e., defamation, invasion of privacy) since such acts occur frequently in the legal arena. As is the case with most professional liability forms, lawyers professional liability policies are written with a claims-made coverage trigger. In addition to commercial insurers, lawyers professional liability coverage is also available in many states through bar-sponsored captive insurers. [*Professional Liability Insurance* XIV.A–XIV.F]

layering—The building of a program of insurance coverage using the excess of loss approach. Layered programs involve a series of insurers writing coverage, each one in excess of lower limits written by other insurers. Umbrella liability coverage is frequently structured in this manner, whereby a number of umbrella insurers write coverage at various levels, on an excess of loss basis, ultimately providing an insured with a high total limit of coverage.

LC50/lethal concentration—Median level concentration, a standard measure of toxicity. It tells how much of a substance is needed to kill half of a group of experimental organisms in a given time.

LD50/lethal dose—The dose of a toxicant that will kill 50 percent of the test organisms within a designated period. The lower the LD50, the more toxic the compound.

leasehold interest—Property insurance covering the loss suffered by a tenant due to termination of a favorable lease because of damage to the leased premises by a covered cause. The principal coverage is the net leasehold interest, which is the present value of the difference between the total rent payable over the unexpired portion of the lease and the total estimated rental value of the property during the same period. [*Commercial Property Insurance* VI.C.33]

legal action against insurer—A provision in most standard insurance coverage forms that imposes certain limitations on an insured's right to sue the insurer for enforcement of the policy.Sometimes entitled "Legal Action against Us," such provisions typically require that the insured meet all its own obligations under the policy before bringing suit in contract. Some legal action against insurer clauses in liability policies also attempt to limit the prerogatives of third-party beneficiaries, by stipulating that nothing in the policy gives any third party a right to sue the insurer for damages being sought against an insured.

legal liability coverage form (ISO)—The Insurance Services Office, Inc. (ISO), commercial property coverage form (CP 00 40) that provides coverage for sums the insured is obligated to pay as a result of accidental damage from a covered cause of loss to property of others in the insured's care, custody, or control. Not a suitable means of insuring leased premises because of a contractual liability exclusion that eliminates coverage for contractually assumed liability unless the insured would have been liable in tort regardless of the contract. [*Commercial Property Insurance* VI.C.24]

lender liability—Liability caused by the wrongful acts of a lending institution. Lender liability claims most frequently arise when a debtor challenges the validity of a loan agreement in a counterclaim against a financial institution after the institution has filed a collection action. Such claims typically allege: misrepresentation of repayment terms, fraud, economic duress, and withholding of promised credit by the lender. [*Professional Liability Insurance* X.J.15]

lenders liability coverage—Provides coverage for errors and omissions arising out of the extension of credit by financial institutions. For example, a bank could be held legally liable if it agreed to provide a line of credit for a business firm, failed to honor the agreement, causing the firm to experience financial difficulties. Another instance in which a bank can incur lender liability occurs when, under a loan workout agreement, a bank takes managerial control of a company and as a result of mismanagement causes the company to sustain additional losses. [*Professional Liability Insurance* X.J.3–5]

lessee—The person to whom a lease is granted, the tenant.

lessees of safe deposit boxes coverage form I—Crime form (CR 00 10) that insures against the loss of securities (not money) and property other than money and securities from within a safe deposit box in a vault at a financial institution. [*Commercial Property Insurance* XII.D.21]

lessor—The person granting the lease, the landlord.

letter of credit—A legal commitment issued by a bank or other entity stating that, upon receipt of certain documents, the bank will pay against drafts meeting the terms of the letter of credit. Letters of credit are frequently used for risk financing purposes to collateralize monies owed by an insured under various cash flow programs such as: incurred but not paid losses in paid loss retrospective rating programs, as a means of meeting the capitalization requirements of captives, and to satisfy the security requirements of the excess insurer in "fronted" deductible or retention programs.

liability—Any legally enforceable obligation. Within the context of insurance, the obligation to pay a monetary award for injury or damage caused by one's negligent or statutorily prohibited action. [*Commercial Liability Insurance* V.C.4]

liability for guests' property, premises coverage form L—An Insurance Services Office, Inc. (ISO), crime form covering guests property located anywhere within the insured's premises or outside the premises in the insured's possession. [*Commercial Property Insurance* XII.D.23]

liability for guests' property, safe deposit box coverage form K—Insurance Services Office, Inc. (ISO), crime form (CR 00 12) that covers the insured's legal liability arising out of damage to or loss of property belonging to guests of the insured while the property is in a safe deposit box in the insured's business premises. The ISO form is used primarily to insure businesses that provide lodging facilities, e.g., hotels. A Surety Association of America (SAA) form is typically used to insure financial institutions. [*Commercial Property Insurance* XII.D.23]

liability insurance—Insurance paying or rendering service on behalf of an insured for loss arising out of legal liability to others.

liberalization clause—A provision that extends to persons already insured under a particular policy the broadened coverage features that may be introduced in subsequent editions of that policy form. In umbrella liability insurance, a clause specifying that coverage will be as broad as that provided by the primary liability policies. [*Commercial Auto Insurance* VIII.F.10 and *Commercial Property Insurance* V.C.10]

license—Certification of appropriate authority issued by a regulatory body to allow an entity to operate as an insurer or an insurance agent after certain standards have been met.

license and permit bond—Required by a municipality or other public body as a condition to granting a license or permit to engage in a specified activity, this bond guarantees that the party seeking the license or permit (the obligor) will comply with applicable laws or regulations. These bonds can also be structured to provide indemnity guarantees to third parities who sustain injury or damage as a result of the obligor's activities as described in the license or permit when such a guarantee is required. For example, businesses that hang signs over public sidewalks may be required to provide indemnity guarantees for injuries to pedestrians.

lien—An encumbrance that can be levied by an individual who has an interest in a particular matter.

life expectancy—The average number of years a person of a certain age is expected to live as shown on an annuity table or mortality table.

life insurance trust—An agreement that provides for the placing of life insurance proceeds into a trust fund which is administered by a trustee within the terms of the trust.

Life Office Management Association (LOMA)—An educational organization that focuses on the life insurance business and develops administrative and technical courses.

Life Underwriter Training Council (LUTC)—An organization that prepares and administers life insurance underwriter training programs.

limit of liability—The maximum amount that an insurance company agrees to pay in the case of loss. [*Commercial Auto Insurance* VIII.D.26; *Commercial Liability Insurance* V.I.1; and *Professional Liability Insurance* VII.C.1]

limits under multiple policy years (LUMP)—An approach to structuring limits for insurance programs covering low frequency but high potential severity exposures, such as excess liability (over CGL policies), pollution liability, and directors and officers liability. Under this approach, a single aggregate limit remains in effect for multiple years as opposed to a series of separate policy limits, applicable to single years, as under a traditional approach. Since a single limit applies over several years, the cost is less than the traditional approach, while also offering a higher limit than would typically be purchased in any single policy year.

Line—(1) A class of insurance, such as property, marine, or liability.

(2) In reinsurance, an amount of risk retained by a ceding insurer for its own account. The line varies with the insurer's financial strength and with the nature of the exposure.

line of business—A general classification of insurance industry business, e.g., fire, life, health, liability.

line sheet—Also called a "line guide," this is a schedule showing the maximum limit of liability that can be written by an insurer for different classes of risks.

line slip—See Slip.

liquidity—A measurement of an organization's ability to meet its debt obligations, particularly short-term debt. Cash, accounts receivable, and short-term securities are considered liquid assets since they can be quickly made available to pay debt. Ratios commonly used to measure liquidity include the current ratio, acid-test ratio, number of days' sales in accounts receivable, accounts receivable turnover, total assets turnover, and inventory turnover.

liquor law liability (dramshop)—Common law liability imposed on those selling alcoholic beverages, as well as the statutory liability established in some states, which is excluded in general liability policies. [*Commercial Liability Insurance V.D.5*]

litigation—The process of investigating and adjudicating the facts and law in a particular case. In general usage, the bringing or defense of a lawsuit.

litigation management—The application of management principles to the litigation process and to an organization's use of outside lawyers. Includes components of planning, controlling, organizing, implementing, and monitoring in the context of legal services and costs.

livestock mortality insurance—See Animal mortality insurance.

Lloyd's broker—A client representative sanctioned by the Committee at Lloyd's of London to contact underwriters at Lloyd's and negotiate insurance with them on behalf of their clients. The client is the insured except in the case of U.S. insureds when the client is normally the U.S. broker or agent.

Lloyd's central fund—A fund to protect policyholders in case any underwriting member should be unable to meet their liabilities out of their Syndicate Trust Funds, funds deposited at Lloyd's, their reserves, and personal assets outside of Lloyd's. An annual contribution is made to this fund by every Lloyd's member.

Lloyd's managing agent—A firm or company having complied with the requirements of the Council of Lloyd's for managing a syndicate (and who may also be a members' agent).

Lloyd's members' agent—A firm or company having complied with the requirements of the Council of Lloyd's for conducting an underwriting agency at Lloyd's and who acts for the members except with respect to managing a syndicate.

Lloyd's syndicate—A group of individuals at Lloyd's of London who have entrusted their assets to a team of underwriters who underwrite on behalf of the group.

Lloyd's underwriter—A person that writes business for Lloyd's of London through a Lloyd's association or facility of Lloyd's.

loan participation coverage—See Securities insuring agreement.

locality standard—A common law liability doctrine stating that the standard of care to which a physician is held is a function of the locality in which he/she practices. The rule, however, is rapidly losing favor among most courts and is therefore infrequently invoked as a defense to professional negligence. Given the advanced state of communication and travel, even physicians practicing in relatively isolated, rural areas can avail themselves of the most advanced methods of treatment and technology. [*Professional Liability Insurance III.C.7*]

LOMA—See Life Office Management Association.

London form (BFPD)—Frequently called the London Form B since it covers only property damage liability (no bodily injury coverage is provided), this is a special policy that provides broader coverage for care, custody, or control and workmanship liability exposures than the standard general liability policy. Coverage is usually coordinated with the general liability policy by excluding property damage coverage in the commercial general liability (CGL) policy. An alternative approach involves issuing the policy on a difference-in-conditions basis whereby property damage coverage is not removed from the CGL. The London Form insures property damage not covered by the CGL and would exclude coverage for property damage that would be covered in the standard CGL policy.

Longshore and Harbor Workers Compensation Act (LHWCA)—A federal law that provides no-fault workers compensation benefits to employees other than masters or crew members of a vessel injured in maritime employment—generally, in loading, unloading, repairing, or building a vessel. Employers can obtain coverage under a standard workers compensation policy by purchasing a Longshore and Harbor Workers Compensation Act coverage endorsement. [*IRMI's Workers Comp* VII.D.1]

long-term disability income insurance—LTD insurance replaces earnings lost due to illness or disability occurring on or off the job. Coverage may be purchased on an individual or group basis. Individual policies typically do not pay until the period of the disability exceeds a specified elimination period, usually 30 days or longer. Recovery under group disability income policies is often structured to begin after short-term disability income insurance benefits or uninsured salary continuance payments cease. One of the most important provisions in either group or individual policies is the definition of "disability." The broader the definition, the broader the scope of coverage. Most LTD policies are structured to pay benefits until the insured reaches age 65.

loss—(1) The basis of a claim for damages under the terms of a policy.

(2) Loss of assets resulting from a pure risk. Broadly categorized, the types of losses of concern to risk managers include: personnel loss, property loss, time element loss, and legal liability loss.

loss adjustment expense—The cost of investigating and adjusting losses. Loss adjustment expenses need not be allocated to a particular claim. If they are allocated to a particular claim they are called "allocated loss adjustment expenses" (ALAE); otherwise, they are unallocated loss adjustment expenses.

loss constant—A flat amount added to the premium of a workers compensation policy (after experience rating if applicable) on accounts with premiums of less than $500. It is designed to offset worse-than-average loss experience of the smaller insureds. [*IRMI's Workers Comp* XI.C.5]

loss control—A risk management technique that seeks to reduce the possibility that a loss will occur and/or reduce the severity of those that do occur. Also known as risk control or safety. Driver training programs are loss control programs that seek to reduce the likelihood of accidents occurring. Sprinkler systems are loss control devices that reduce the severity of loss by fire. [*IRMI's Workers Comp* Section XIII]

loss conversion factor—A factor used in the retrospective rating formula that provides a charge to cover unallocated claims and the cost of the insurer's claim services. Since the charge is developed as part of the formula, the amount the insured will pay for unallocated loss expenses is a function of losses. The loss conversion factor and the basic premium factor are inversely related to each other; increasing one decreases the other. [*Risk Financing* III.D.9]

loss costs—Also called "pure premium," the actual or expected cost to an insurer of indemnity payments and allocated loss adjustment expenses. Loss costs do not include overhead costs or profit loadings. Historical loss costs reflect only the costs and allocated loss adjustment expenses associated with past claims. Prospective loss costs are estimates of future loss costs, which are derived by trending and developing historical loss costs. Rating bureaus have begun to develop and publish loss costs instead of insurance rates. Insurers add their own expense and profit loadings to these loss costs to develop rates which are then filed with regulators. [*IRMI's Workers Comp* XI.C.3]

loss development—The difference between the original loss as initially reserved by an insurer and its subsequent evaluation at a later date or at the time of its final disposal. Loss development occurs because of: (1) inflation—both "social inflation" and inflation in the consumer price index—during the time period in which losses are reported and ultimately settled; and (2) time lags between the occurrence of claims and the time they are actually reported to an insurer. To account for these increases, a "loss development factor" or multiplier is usually applied to a claim or group of claims in an effort to more accurately project the ultimate amount for which they will be closed. [*Risk Financing* II.B]

losses incurred—The total amount of losses that are: (1) paid, and (2) unpaid but reserved, that are sustained during a given period. [*Risk Financing* III.D.7] loss forecasting—Predicting future losses through an analysis of past losses. Past loss data must usually span a sufficient number of years (5 or more) to achieve some degree of credibility. The time span is important because the most recent years' losses most closely approximate current exposure, yet the earlier years' losses have had more time to develop. The law of large numbers, exposure data, any anticipated changes in company operations or structure, inflation, workers compensation benefit changes, and any other relevant factors must be considered when forecasting losses. [*Risk Financing* II.A–H]

loss limitation—An optional feature of a retrospective rating plan that limits or "caps" the amount of loss (usually at the $100,000 level, or more) that would otherwise be applied to the calculation of premium. An additional premium is charged for this feature by means of an "excess loss premium factor." [*Risk Financing* III.D.4]

loss loading (multiplier)—A factor applied to pure loss cost or expected losses to produce a premium rate or rate for reinsurance coverage. The multiplier is applied to account for: insurer overhead, profit, and contingencies, that are in addition to anticipated loss amounts.

loss of consortium suits—A legal action often brought by the spouse of the injured worker that alleges the loss of spousal services including but not limited to companionship, help with household duties, and sexual relations. Suits of this type can also be brought by parents or children of the injured worker claiming the loss of services, typically companionship. Many jurisdictions have allowed these type of actions to be heard even when the worker is already receiving workers compensation benefits. Coverage for a lawsuit of this type is provided by the employers liability section of the workers compensation policy. [*IRMI's Workers Comp* VI.D.5]

loss of income coverage—A type of business interruption coverage that does not include a coinsurance clause but limits recovery to loss incurred during a specified period of time (typically 120 days) after the direct damage loss. Approximated by the maximum period of indemnity coverage option of the Insurance Services Office, Inc. (ISO), business income coverage forms (CP 00 30 and CP 00 32). [*Commercial Property Insurance* II.E.9]

loss payable clause—An insurance provision authorizing payment in the event of loss to a person or entity other than the named insured having an insurable interest in the covered property. [*Commercial Property Insurance* VI.I.2; *Commercial Auto Insurance* XIII.N.41; and *Contractual Risk Transfer* XIV.D.3 and XIV.P.5]

loss portfolio transfer—A financial reinsurance transaction in which loss obligations that are already incurred and will ultimately be paid are ceded to a reinsurer. In determining the premium paid to the reinsurer, the time value of money is considered, and the premium is therefore less than the ultimate amount expected to be paid. The cedant's statutory surplus increases by the difference between the premium and the amount that had been reserved. An insurer seeking to withdraw from writing workers compensation coverage in a given state could, for example, use a loss portfolio transfer to meet its obligations under policies it has written, without the need to continue the day-to-day management of the claims resolution function. [*Risk Financing* V.D]

loss prevention—See Loss control.

loss rating—A term applied to a rating technique often used for larger insureds in which that insured's past loss history is used to establish a prospective rate. The past losses are developed and trended, as appropriate, and divided by the amount of a selected exposure base to determine a relationship between the exposure and loss experience. Assuming that the historical data is credible, the resultant factor (loss rate) divided by the insurer's acceptable, or permissible, loss ratio becomes the prospective rate. In some cases, the loss rate is modified to account for possible variations between expected and actual losses before it is converted into the prospective rate. [*Risk Financing* III.A.32]

loss ratio—Proportionate relationship of incurred losses to earned premiums expressed as a percentage. If, for example, a firm pays $100,000 of premium for workers compensation insurance in a given year, and its insurer pays and reserves $50,000 in claims, the firm's loss ratio is 50 percent ($50,000 incurred losses/$100,000 earned premiums). [*Risk Financing* III.A.2]

loss report—A listing of reported claims providing such information as the date of occurrence, type of claim, amount paid and amount reserved for each as of the report's valuation date.

loss reserve—An estimate of the value of a claim or group of claims not yet paid. A case reserve is an estimate of the amount for which a particular claim will ultimately be settled or adjudicated. Insurers will also set reserves for their entire books of business to estimate their future liabilities.

loss trending—Adjusting historical losses to account for inflationary trends so that their value is in *current* dollar amounts. Historical loss amounts are multiplied by "trending factors" to convert historical loss amounts to current dollar amounts. [*Risk Financing* II.B.3]

lost policy release—A statement signed by the named insured releasing the insurer from all liability under a lost or mislaid contract of insurance in cases in which the insured wishes to cancel the policy. At one time many insurance policies required that the original policy be returned to the insurer to effect cancellation, and a lost policy release served in place of the original policy.

lower explosive limit (LEL)—The concentration of a compound in air below which the mixture will not catch on fire.

lowest achievable emission rate—Under the Clean Air Act, the rate of emissions that reflects: (1) the most stringent emission limitation in the implementation plan of any state for such source unless the owner or operator demonstrates such limitations are not achievable; or (2) the most stringent emissions limitation achieved in practice, whichever is more stringent. A proposed new or modified source may not emit pollutants in excess of existing new source standards.

LUTC—See Life Underwriter Training Council.

M

---

maintenance, cure, and wages—A concept within general maritime law that spells out the duties owed by the owner of a vessel to the crew. The terms are defined as follows.

Maintenance—The proper rehabilitation and working environment that should be available to the seaman including but not limited to the provision of lodging and food over the course of recovery.

Cure—Medical treatment toward recovery, at least as far as medical science is able to provide. Also termed "maximum medical cure," this obligation is owed a seaman for accidents as well as sickness, such as appendicitis, which generally do not fall within the provisions of state compensation acts. Medical care is provided free of charge, or at low cost, in those areas where the public health service has facilities.

Wages—A sailor's usual wages during illness, but not extending beyond the end of the voyage. On ships operating year-round, on inland waterways, wages may not extend beyond: a period of a year, the end of the contract, or the period of illness, whichever is shortest. For impairment of future earnings, the seaman must bring suit. See also General maritime law. [*IRMI's Workers Comp* VII.B.2 and VII.C.9]

major medical insurance—Health insurance that provides benefits up to very high limits, subject to a very large deductible. There may also be internal limits and a participation clause, sometimes called the "coinsurance clause."

malpractice—A professional error, omission, or act of negligence in performing a professional act. Also, a term used to denote the type of professional liability insurance coverage written to cover physicians, surgeons, accountants, lawyers, architects and engineers, among others. [*Professional Liability Insurance* III.H.1]

malpractice insurance—Insurance for a professional practitioner that will defend professional liability suits and pay damages up to a maximum limit. Also known as "professional liability insurance." [*Professional Liability Insurance* VII.B.1]

managed care—A process by which the delivery of healthcare is structured and monitored with the goal of providing medical services that are both appropriate and economically reasonable. [*IRMI's Workers Comp* XV.F.1]

managed care liability insurance—A form of liability coverage written to cover organizations engaged in delivering medical services on a managed-care basis, such as health maintenance organizations (HMOs). Representative types of claims covered by the policies include allegations of: negligent provider selection, direct professional liability, and wrongful denial of treatment. [*Professional Liability Insurance* XVI.P.1]

managed care organization (MCO)—A health care provider whose goal it is to provide appropriate, cost-effective medical treatment. Two types of these providers are the health maintenance organization (HMO) and the preferred provider organization (PPO). [*IRMI's Workers Comp* XV.F.1]

management advisory services—Consulting services provided by accounting firms, the bulk of which involve computer software and hardware. Other areas falling under the heading of management advisory services include: business or asset valuation, mergers and acquisitions, investments, capital budgeting, business strategy and marketing, organizational structure, business operations, real estate, and litigation support. This is one of the more severe exposures covered by accountants professional liability policies. [*Professional Liability Insurance* XIII.C.10–11]

managing general agent (MGA)—A wholesale insurance intermediary with the authority to accept placements from (and often to appoint) retail agents on behalf of an insurer. Managing general agents generally provide underwriting and administrative services, such as policy issuance, on behalf of the insurers they represent. These arrangements are most common in the surplus lines marketplace. Typically, MGAs market more unusual coverage, such as professional liability, for which specialized expertise is required to underwrite policies. MGAs benefit insurers because such expertise is not always available within the company and would be more costly to develop on an in-house basis. [*Professional Liability Insurance* XV.C.5]

mandatory securities valuation reserve—A reserve required of life insurers by state laws to offset declines in valuations of securities held as admitted assets. The reserve requirement recognizes

the fact that life insurance contracts span long periods of time and fluctuations in the values of insurers' investments could negatively impact loss reserves.

manifestation theory—A legal theory in latent injury cases which holds that injury occurs when the injury becomes known, manifests itself to the injured party, is diagnosed by a physician, etc.

manual rates—Rates as promulgated by a rating bureau, such as Insurance Services Office, Inc. (general liability, automobile) and the National Council on Compensation Insurance (workers compensation) before application of any credits or deviations. Such rates are referred to as "manual rates" because they are published in a rating manual. [*Risk Financing* III.A.1]

manufacturers and contractors (M&C) insurance—Now obsolete, prior to the 1986 revision of the commercial general liability (CGL)policy, this form was used as a means of providing premises and operations coverage to manufacturers and certain types of contractors, primarily construction and installation contractors. Today, if an insurer wishes to exclude the products-completed operations hazard, it can do so by attaching the products-completed operations hazard exclusion endorsement. The insured can then purchase separate products and completed operations coverage. [*Commercial Liability Insurance* VI.T.1]

manufacturer's output policy (MOP)—A special policy for manufacturers designed to provide all-risk insurance for inventory and other personal property on or away from premises. This policy may be written either on a reporting or a nonreporting form. [*Commercial Property Insurance* IX.Q.1]

manufacturers penalty insurance—Coverage in the event of late delivery of a product for an agreed amount based on the contract between the insured manufacturer and a purchaser. Designed for manufacturers who are compelled to enter into contracts under which they assume responsibility for delay in completion of a product. The policy generally covers 90 percent of the penalty loss sustained, but does not extend to strikes or labor disputes.

manufacturer's selling price endorsement—See Selling price clause or endorsement.

marine insurance—A type of insurance designed to provide coverage for the transportation of goods either on the ocean or by land as well as damage to the waterborne instrument of conveyance and to the liability for third parties arising out of the process. The two branches of marine insurance are ocean marine (primarily water based exposures) and inland marine (primarily land based exposures).

market value clause—A property insurance endorsement or provision establishing market value (rather than actual cash value or replacement cost value) as the valuation basis for covered property. Usually used in connection with agricultural products and other commodities whose value fluctuates in accordance with a commodities exchange. Also occasionally used as the valuation basis for a building. [*Commercial Property Insurance* IV.D.2]

masonry noncombustible construction—Exterior walls of masonry material (adobe, brick, concrete, gypsum block, hollow concrete block, stone, tile, or similar materials), with floor and roof of metal or other noncombustible materials. This is one of six basic construction types used in categorizing buildings for Insurance Services Office, Inc. (ISO), *Commercial Lines Manual* rating purposes. The other five construction categories are: frame, joisted masonry, noncombustible, modified fire resistive, and fire resistive. [*Commercial Property Insurance* IV.F.2]

master policy—In property and liability coverage, the combining of several locations or operations under a single policy for the same insured or insureds. The term may also be used in the case of construction wrap-ups. In either case, underlying policies or certificates of insurance are issued to insureds under the policy as evidence of coverage under the master policy.

material safety data sheet (MSDS)—Under the Hazard Communication Standard promulgated by OSHA in 1983, chemical manufactures and importers are required to distribute these forms with the initial shipment of a hazardous chemical to a given employer. The forms must describe the chemical's properties, identify potential hazards, and provide safe use and handling procedures. Employers must maintain a file, accessible to employees, of MSDSs for all chemicals they use in their business.

mature—Used to describe a life insurance policy whose face amount has become payable.

mature claims-made—A claims-made commercial general liability (CGL) policy in at least its fifth consecutive claims-made year without advancement of the retroactive date. No premium discounts (claims-made multipliers) are applied in rating mature claims-made policies. [*Commercial Liability Insurance* VIII.C.7]

maturity—The span of time, usually expressed in months, since the beginning of an occurrence year. This measures the age of development of a body of losses.

maturity date—The date at which the face amount of a life insurance policy becomes payable either by death or other contract stipulation.

M&C insurance—See Manufacturers and contractors insurance.

McCarran-Ferguson Act (Public Law 15)—Congressional action exempting insurance from federal regulation as a form of interstate commerce, to the degree effective regulation is undertaken by the individual states.

MDRT—See Million Dollar Round Table.

media liability coverage—A type of errors and omissions liability insurance designed for publishers, broadcasters, and other media-related firms. The policies are typically written on a named perils basis and cover the following broad areas: defamation, invasion of privacy, infringement of copyright, and plagiarism. [*Professional Liability Insurance* XVIII.B–F]

mediation—The act of a third person in assisting two adverse parties adjust or settle their dispute.

Medicaid—The U.S. government welfare system administered by the states and subsidized by the federal government covering various medical expenses for those of low income, below limits set by state laws.

medical fee schedule—A provision of most state workers compensation laws that establishes the maximum amount a health care provider may collect for injuries treatable under the act. [*IRMI's Workers Comp* VIII.C.28]

medical malpractice insurance—Coverage for the acts, errors, and omissions of physicians and surgeons, encompassing physicians professional liability insurance, hospital professional liability insurance, and allied health care (e.g., nurses) professional liability insurance. Although the majority of policies are written with a claims-made coverage trigger, such coverage is sometimes available on an occurrence basis. Typical exclusions are for: intentional/criminal acts, punitive damages, sexual misconduct, and specialized procedures (e.g., radial keratotomy) for which coverage may be "bought back" in return for additional premium. In addition to commercial insurers, medical malpractice coverage is also available in most states through physician-owned insurance companies known as "bedpan mutuals." [*Professional Liability Insurance* XVI.G–J]

medical payments, auto—Optional coverage under an auto policy to pay for medical expenses for an insured who sustains bodily injury caused by an auto accident, without regard to fault. Coverage for persons other than the named insured and his or her family members is typically restricted to circumstances when they are occupants of the insured auto. [*Commercial Auto Insurance* XIII.N.1]

medical payments, general liability—A general liability coverage that reimburses others, without regard to the insured's liability, for medical or funeral expenses incurred by such persons as a result of bodily injury or death sustained by accident under the conditions specified in the policy. [*Commercial Liability Insurance* V.F.1]

Medicare—The U.S. government program providing medical expense benefits for persons over the age of 65 or who are disabled if they qualify for benefits under Social Security.

members of Lloyd's of London—Persons who have pledged their entire financial estate against the acceptance of risk underwritten by them or their underwriting representatives (underwriters) at Lloyd's. These individuals, also known as "names," are usually organized into groups called "syndicates."

mercantile open stock—An obsolete crime coverage form. Coverage for loss of property, other than money and securities, stolen from within the insured's premises or taken from a guard inside the premises, is available under an Insurance

Services Office, Inc. (ISO), crime form E, premises burglary (CR 00 06). [*Commercial Property Insurance* XII.D.18]

mercantile robbery—An obsolete crime coverage form. Coverage for robbery of money and securities is available under an Insurance Services Office, Inc. (ISO), coverage form Q, robbery and safe burglary—money and securities (CR 00 18). Coverage for robbery of property other than money and securities is available under an ISO coverage form D, robbery and safe burglary—property other than money and securities (CR 00 05). [*Commercial Property Insurance* XII.D.17]

mercantile safe burglary—An obsolete crime coverage form. Coverage for loss of money and securities by safe burglary is available under an Insurance Services Office, Inc. (ISO), coverage form Q, robbery and safe burglary—money and securities (CR 00 18). [*Commercial Property Insurance* XII.D.26] Coverage for safe burglary loss of property other than money and securities is available under an ISO coverage form D, robbery and safe burglary—property other than money and securities (CR 00 05). [*Commercial Property Insurance* XII.D.17]

Mexico coverage—(1) The coverage provided under certain nonstandard automobile policies issued by U.S. insurers for operation of an insured motor vehicle within Mexico, usually limited to a stated number of miles from the U.S. border.

(2) Coverage purchased from a Mexican insurance company for the operation of a motor vehicle within Mexico. In the event of incurred automobile liability, Mexican law recognizes only coverage written by Mexican insurance companies as proof of financial responsibility. [*Commercial Auto Insurance* VIII.F.17]

midi-tail—A term used for an extended reporting period longer than 60 days but not unlimited. The standard Insurance Services Office, Inc. (ISO), claims-made commercial general liability (CGL) policy midi-tail is for 5 years. The CGL's midi-tail applies only for known and reported circumstances in most cases. [*Commercial Liability Insurance* V.K.4]

Migrant and Seasonal Agricultural Worker Protection Act (MSAWPA)—Establishes a private right of action for actual or statutory damages (as well as criminal and administrative sanctions) against employers and contractors of migrant or seasonal agricultural workers who violate the Act's housing and motor vehicle safety requirements, motor vehicle liability insurance requirements, and job information disclosure requirements. [*IRMI's Workers Comp* VII.I and *Contractual Risk Transfer* XIV.E.4]

mill construction—A strong, durable, slow-burning type of joisted masonry construction, also called "heavy timber construction,"characterized by heavy floors and thick wooden columns or beams. The walls of such a building generally are assigned a fire-resistive rating of at least 2 hours. The lack of floor joists in this form of construction contributes to its fire-resistance since the corresponding air pockets are eliminated.

Million Dollar Round Table (MDRT)—An association of life insurance agents who qualify by selling $1 million or more on a face value in a calendar year. Applicants must be members of the National Association of Life Underwriters (NALU).

minimum deposit policy—A cash value life insurance policy having a first-year loan value available for borrowing immediately upon payment of the first year premium. It is generally held that the life insurance must be in force for 4 years before borrowing can occur.

minimum premium—The least amount of premium to be charged for providing a particular insurance coverage. The minimum premium may apply in any number of ways such as per location, per type of coverage, or per policy.

mini-tail—An extended reporting period with a very short (i.e., 60 days) duration. The Insurance Services Office, Inc. (ISO), commercial general liability policy's mini-tail is part of the basic extended reporting period. It runs concurrently with the midi-tail and covers claims associated with occurrences previously unknown to the insured.

mini-trial—Can be a mock trial, designed to allow the presentation of a case before a panel to ferret out strengths and weaknesses in a case—a dry run. This can also be the term for an actual short version of a trial in which each side presents its case before a judge or a mediator for the purpose of settlement.

minor's compromise—An approval by the court that a claim settled on behalf of a minor is fair and that the monies provided on behalf of the minor are deposited in an appropriate account.

miscellaneous liability coverage—A form of errors and omissions coverage provided for a variety of professionals and quasi-professionals, including stock brokers, process servers, detective agencies, auctioneers, customs house brokers, franchisors, etc., for which no standard policy form is available (as for the "traditional" professions such as physicians, accountants, and attorneys). To tailor such policies to the particular profession involved, insurers generally append manuscript coverage provisions and exclusions. [*Professional Liability Insurance* XIX.B–F]

misrepresentation—A false or misleading statement that, if intentional and material, can allow the insurer to void the insurance contract. Some insurance policies and state laws that govern insurance contract provisions vary on the exact details of the conditions under which coverage may be voided; these variations are usually denoted in state amendatory endorsements. See also Warranty and Representation [*Commercial Auto Insurance* VIII.F.9 and *Commercial Property Insurance* V.C.7]

misstatement of age provision—A provision in a life insurance policy that adjusts the amount of insurance when the insured's age was misstated on the application to the amount which the premium would have purchased at the correct age based on the insurer's rates at the date of policy issuance.

mobile equipment—A term that is defined in both the CGL and commercial auto policies, it refers to equipment such as earthmovers, tractors, diggers, farm machinery, forklifts, etc., that, even though self-propelled, are not considered as automobiles for insurance purposes. Liability arising from mobile equipment is covered in the general liability policy. Physical damage coverage is usually provided by an "equipment floater." Also see Automobile. [*Commercial Auto Insurance* VIII.G.11 and *Commercial Liability Insurance* V.L.20]

modified fire-resistive construction—Characterized by exterior walls, floors, and roof of masonry or fire-resistive material with a fire-resistance rating of at least 1 hour but less than 2 hours. One of six basic construction categories used by Insurance Services Office, Inc. (ISO), for rating property insurance. The other categories are frame, noncombustible, masonry noncombustible, modified fire-resistive, and fire-resistive construction. [*Commercial Property Insurance* IV.F.4]

money and securities broad form policy—An obsolete crime coverage form. Coverage for loss of money and securities from within the insured's premises or from the insured's bank or safe depository is available under an Insurance Services Office, Inc. (ISO), coverage form C, theft, disappearance and destruction (CR 00 04). [*Commercial Property Insurance* XII.D.15]

money orders and counterfeit paper currency insurance—Covers loss due to acceptance of money order that was issued (or is purported to have been issued) by a post office or express company and loss due to acceptance of counterfeit paper currency of the United States or Canada. [*Commercial Property Insurance* XII.L.9]

monopolistic state funds—Jurisdictions where employers must obtain workers compensation insurance from compulsory state funds or qualify as a self-insurer as is allowed in four of the states. Such insurance is not subject to any of the procedures or programs of the National Council on Compensation Insurance (NCCI). The following states/jurisdictions are monopolistic fund states: Nevada, North Dakota, Ohio, Washington, West Virginia, Wyoming, Puerto Rico, and the U.S. Virgin Islands. Also see Competitive state funds. [*IRMI's Workers Comp* V.C.1]

MOP—See Manufacturer's output policy.

morale hazard—A term used to describe a subjective hazard that tends to increase the probable frequency or severity of loss due to an insured peril. Morale hazard, as contrasted with moral hazard, does not imply a propensity to cause a loss, but implies a certain indifference to loss simply because of the existence of insurance. For example, an insured's attitude may be indifferent if a loss occurs because they have insurance.

moral hazard—A term used to describe a subjective hazard that tends to increase the probable frequency or severity of loss due to an insured peril. Moral hazard is measured by the character of the insured and the circumstances surrounding the subject of the insurance, especially the extent of potential loss or gain to the insured in case of loss. For example, insurance on a thriving business is not subject to a moral hazard to as great an extent as insurance on an unprofitable business. On the other hand, an insured with high moral standards may pose less of a moral hazard even with an unprofitable business than an insured with low moral standards. Moral hazards are considered when underwriting insurance, particularly fire insurance, and are also addressed by certain policy exclusions. For example, underwriters are hesitant to insure vacant and unoccupied buildings because of the possibility that an insured will be tempted to intentionally start a fire in order to obtain an insurance recovery.

morbidity—The relative incidence of disease.

mortality—The relative incidence of death.

mortality table—A table showing mortality rates for each age. Mortality rates shown in such a table are based on actuarial analysis and depict the probability that a person of the age for which a rate applies will die during the following year. Mortality tables are used by insurers to determine premium rates and establish loss reserves.

mortgage holders errors and omissions coverage—A policy providing four specialty coverages for financial institutions: (1) coverage for loss to the insured's interest as a mortgage holder due to error or omission in requiring or arranging insurance on mortgaged property; (2) coverage for the insured's liability as trustee with respect to loss due to error or omission in maintaining insurance on property held in trust; (3) coverage for damages for which the insured is legally liable as a result of error or omission in maintaining insurance on mortgaged property for the benefit of the mortgagor; and (4) coverage for damages for which the insured is legally liable as a result of error or omission in paying real estate taxes on behalf of the mortgagor.

mortgage insurance—A life or health insurance policy intended to pay off the balance of a mortgage upon death or to meet payments on the mortgage in case of disability. Also known as "mortgage redemption insurance."

mortgage (mortgagee) clause—A property insurance provision granting special protection for the interest of a mortgagee named in the policy. It establishes that loss to mortgaged property is payable to the mortgagee named in the policy, grants continuing coverage for the benefit of the mortgagee in the event that the policy is voided by some act of the insured, and promises advance written notice to the mortgagee of policy cancellation. [*Commercial Property Insurance* V.F.52 and *Contractual Risk Transfer* XIV.P.5]

motion—An application made to a court or judge for the purpose of obtaining a rule or order directing some act to be done in favor of the applicant.

motion *in limine*—A written motion that is usually made before or in the beginning of a jury trial for a protective order against prejudicial questions and statements. This avoids introduction of testimony into trial that is irrelevant, inadmissible, and prejudicial.

motion practice—Habitual application to the court for the purpose of obtaining a favorable ruling in lieu of informally reaching agreement between the parties.

motion to dismiss—A motion introduced before trial to attack the action on the basis of insufficiency of the pleading, of process, venue, joinder, etc.

motor carrier policy—A commercial auto policy introduced by Insurance Services Office, Inc. (ISO) in 1993 to address the needs of the motor carrier (i.e., trucking) industry. Coverages available include auto liability, trailer interchange, and auto physical damage; other coverages are available by endorsement. The policy was developed as an alternative to the truckers policy because of the changes taking place in the industry. That is, the truckers policy is applicable only for "for-hire" motor carriers, whereas the motor carrier policy is appropriate for all types of motor carriers-for-hire, private, or a combination of both types of operations. [*Commercial Auto Insurance* Section XI]

motor truck cargo—An inland marine form covering loss of property in the course of transit, either by common carrier or on the insured's own vehicles, depending on the form used. [*Commercial Property Insurance* IX.E.14]

multiple coordinated policies—In an effort by insurance regulators to make certain that employees involved in a leasing arrangement are provided coverage without gaps or overlaps, multiple coordinated endorsements must be placed on policies written in state assigned risk pools. This is achieved by requiring that the leasing company

and each of its clients purchase separate policies that have a common expiration and are written by a single assigned risk insurer. Then the multiple coordinated policy endorsement is added to each policy which specifies which leased employees are covered by that policy. [*IRMI's Workers Comp* VI.L.30]

multiple indemnity—A life insurance policy provision that specifies the payment of some multiple of the face value, e.g., 100 or 200 percent, when the insured's death is caused by certain types of accidents.

multiple protection insurance—A combination of whole life and term insurance paying some multiple of the amount of protection.

multiyear single limit (MYSL)—See Limits under multiple policy years (LUMP).

mutual benefit association—An organization offering benefits to members for no fixed premiums, but assessments are levied to meet specific losses as they occur.

mutual company—A corporation owned and operated by and for its insureds. Every owner of the company is an insured; every insured is an owner.

mutual fund—An investment company that raises capital by selling its own stock and then buying other securities as an investment with the proceeds generated.

mutualization—The process of converting a stock insurer into a mutual insurer.

mutual law enforcement agreements—A formal agreement between neighboring municipalities to provide law enforcement assistance in emergency situations when a local police department requires additional personnel. Frequently such agreements contain hold harmless provisions. Although law enforcement liability policies normally exclude contractual assumptions of liability, the policies typically contain exceptions to such exclusions so that liability assumed under mutual law enforcement agreements is usually covered. [*Professional Liability Insurance* XI.I.12–13]

N

name—An underwriting member who participates in any syndicate at Lloyd's of London. Also see Members of Lloyd's of London.

named insured—Any person, firm, or organization, or any of its members specifically designated by name as an insured(s) in an insurance policy, as distinguished from others who, although unnamed, fall within the policy definition of an "insured." [*Commercial Liability Insurance* V.C.2; *Contractual Risk Transfer* XI.C.1]

named perils coverage—A property insurance term referring to policies that provide coverage only for loss caused by the perils specifically listed as covered. It contrasts with all-risks coverage, which applies to loss from all causes not specifically listed as excluded. [*Commercial Property Insurance* VIII.C.2 and *Contractual Risk Transfer* XIV.P.1]

name partner—A principal of the firm whose name appears in the firm's legal name.

National Council on Compensation Insurance (NCCI)—A voluntary nonprofit unincorporated association formed in 1915. Its duties are the promulgation and administration of workers compensation rates. Its membership is composed of stock and mutual insurers, reciprocals, and state funds. The NCCI is a filing agency and rating organization in 32 jurisdictions, and it serves as an advisory or service organization in many states where independent or state bureaus exist.

National Flood Insurance Program (NFIP)—A federally funded program established in 1968 to make flood insurance available at a reasonable cost for properties located in participating communities. NFIP flood insurance is available only for direct damage to buildings and contents; there is no time element coverage. [*Commercial Property Insurance* IV.N.1]

nationalization—Conversion of privately held assets to government ownership and control. Nationalization of a business's overseas property by a foreign government is a loss exposure that can be covered through political risk insurance.

National Priorities List (NPL)—The Environmental Protection Agency's (EPA's) list of the most serious uncontrolled or abandoned hazardous waste sites identified for possible long-term remedial action under Superfund. The EPA is required to update the NPL at least once a year. A site must be on the NPL to receive money from the Trust Fund for remedial action.

National Response Center—The federal operations center that receives notifications of all releases of oil and hazardous substances into the environment. Open 24 hours a day, it is operated by the U.S. Coast Guard, which evaluates all reports and notifies the appropriate agency.

National Response Team (NRT)—Representatives of 13 federal agencies that, as a team, coordinate federal responses to nationally significant incidents of pollution (an oil spill, a major chemical release, or a Superfund response action) and provide advice and technical assistance to the responding agency(ies) before and during a response action.

National Safety Council—Set up by Congress in 1913, a nonprofit organization made up of industry members nationwide for the purpose of dissemination of safety educational materials.

natural death—Death by means other than accident.

NCCI—See National Council on Compensation Insurance.

negligence—The failure to use that degree of care considered to be reasonable under the given circumstances. Acts of either omission or commission, or both, may constitute negligence.

negligence per se—Conduct that violates standards of care as established by statute or law.

net interest earned—The amount of interest earned by an insurance company on its investments, after deducting investment expenses but before federal income taxes.

net level premium—The pure mortality cost of a life insurance policy from age of entry to maturity date.

net line—The amount of coverage a company retains on a specific risk after deducting reinsurance.

net loss—The amount of loss sustained by an insurer after deducting collectible reinsurance, salvage, and subrogation recovery.

net retention—See Net line.

new for old—A historic provision in marine insurance contracts stipulating that when repairs are made and new parts are supplied in place of old ones that have been lost or damaged, there shall be an agreed discount to represent the depreciation. Modern marine policies however, generally provide for the repairs without a deduction for depreciation.

newsgathering torts—Torts committed by news personnel during the course of obtaining and covering news events. Examples of such torts include: intrusion on seclusion, private facts made public, and false light in public eye. Media liability insurance is designed to cover these kinds of exposures. [*Professional Liability Insurance* XVIII.C.4]

New Source Performance Standards (NSPS)—Uniform national Environmental Protection Agency air emission and water effluent standards that limit the amount of pollution allowed from new sources or from modified existing sources.

NFC mortality rate—Mortality table prepared for fraternal insurers in 1898.

NFIP—See National Flood Insurance Program.

no-fault—See Personal injury protection.

no further remedial action planned—Determination made by EPA following a preliminary assessment that a site does not pose a significant risk and so requires no further activity under the Comprehensive Environmental Response Compensation and Liability Act (CERCLA).

nonadmitted insurance (international insurance)—Insurance written by a company that is neither licensed nor registered to do business in the country where the property or risk is located. Some countries allow nonadmitted insurance, others do not.

nonadmitted insurer—An insurance company not licensed to do business in a certain state. Such insurers can nevertheless write coverage through an excess and surplus lines broker that is licensed in these jurisdictions. [*Professional Liability Insurance* IV.J.1]

nonadmitted reinsurance—Reinsurance purchased from a company not licensed or authorized to transact business in a particular jurisdiction. Nonadmitted reinsurance may not be treated as an asset against reinsured losses or unearned premium reserves for insurance company accounting and statement purposes.

Nonappropriated Fund Instrumentalities Act—A federal act that extends the benefits of the Longshore and Harbor Workers Act to civilians working for the U.S. military. As a result, the Act essentially provides no-fault workers compensation benefits to this employee segment. [*IRMI's Workers Comp* VI.D.11 and VII.H.1]

nonassessable—The term refers to an insurance policy under which the insurer (e.g., a stock company) does not have the right to assess policyholders for additional amounts to make up shortfalls in the cost of operating the company. Such a policy is the opposite of one issued by an assessment company.

nonassignable—A policy that cannot be assigned by the owner to a third party.

noncombustible construction—Exterior walls, floor, and supports made of metal, asbestos, gypsum, or other noncombustible materials. This is one of six basic construction types used in categorizing buildings for Insurance Services Office, Inc. (ISO), *Commercial Lines Manual* for rating purposes. The other five construction categories are: frame, joisted masonry, masonry noncombustible, modified fire-resistive, and fire-resistive. [*Commercial Property Insurance* IV.F.2]

nonconcurrency—The condition created by two or more policies covering the same loss exposure that do not have identical inception and expiration dates. Nonconcurrency of an insured's umbrella policies and the liability policies required by the umbrella as underlying insurance is a problem because the nonconcurrent policy terms make it possible for a loss under an underlying policy's annual aggregate limit to use up part of the limit required by the umbrella and thus violate its underlying limits requirement. [**Commercial Liability Insurance XI.B.21**]

nonconcurrency of coverage triggers—A situation in which the coverage triggers in a primary policy differ from those in an excess or umbrella policy. Typically this takes place when an umbrella policy is written on a claims-made basis and a primary policy is written on an occurrence basis.

noncontributory insurance—A plan of insurance for which the employer pays the entire premium and the employee does not contribute to premium payment.

noncumulation of limits provisions—Provisions within professional liability insurance policies stating that if more than one claim results from a single wrongful act, and if claims are made during more than one policy period, the insured is entitled to the limit applicable when the *first* claim was made rather than the sum of the limits that were applicable to the policy periods during which *all* claims were made. [**Professional Liability Insurance VII.C.2**]

nonderivative suits—A lawsuit alleging that the acts of directors and officers of a corporation caused damage to the individual(s) bringing the suit. This is in contrast to derivative suits, which are brought by one or more stockholders on behalf of the organization, alleging financial loss to the organization. [**Professional Liability Insurance X.C.2**]

nonduplication of benefits—A provision in a health insurance or disability policy designed to eliminate the possibility of an insured receiving benefits greater than the economic loss suffered. Most long-term disability income policies offset the benefits paid in accordance with other benefits to which the disabled claimant is entitled. Similarly, most health insurance policies contain provisions to avoid duplication of benefits when more than one policy applies.

noneconomic damages—An award to an injured person that is not based on actual monetary loss but on other forms of injury, e.g., pain and suffering awards.

nonforfeiture values—In whole life insurance policies, benefits that accrue to the insured when the policy lapses from nonpayment of premium. These benefits are usually either an amount of paid-up term life insurance or a cash surrender value. All states have enacted nonforfeiture laws that require that whole life insurance policies specify the nonforfeiture values in a schedule in the policy.

noninsurable risk—A risk that cannot be measured actuarially or in which the chance of loss is so high that insurance cannot be written on it.

noninsurance—The thoughtful and intentional abstention from the use of insurance to cover an exposure to loss. If risk identification is thorough, the uninsured risks are known, and insurance has been considered. Uninsured losses are absorbed as a direct expense. Also see Self-insurance.

noninsurance risk transfer—The transfer of risk from one party to another party other than an insurance company. This risk management technique usually involves risk transfers by way of hold harmless, indemnity, and insurance provisions in contracts and is also called "contractual risk transfer." [**Contractual Risk Transfer III.C.1**]

nonledger assets—Assets that are not entered on the books of an insurer but instead, are recorded directly in Exhibit 1 of the Annual Statement by way of a single-entry bookkeeping system. The two most important nonledger assets are "Interest, Dividends, and Real Estate Income Due and Accrued" and the excess of market or amortized value over the book value of certain invested assets.

nonmedical—Life or health insurance coverage written without a medical exam. However, the insured completes a detailed questionnaire concerning his or her health. This information becomes a warranty so that any misstatements could potentially void the policy.

nonowned automobile—Described in commercial auto policies as an auto that is used in connection with the named insured's business but that is neither owned, leased, hired, rented, or borrowed by the named insured. As used in the business auto policy, the term specifically applies to vehicles owned by employees and used for company business; as used in the truckers policy, it applies only if such autos are private passenger type autos. [*Commercial Auto Insurance* **VIII.C.11 and X.C.10**]

nonparticipating (non-par)—Life insurance contracts in which no policy dividends are paid.

nonparticipation settlement clause—Provisions in professional liability policies that give the insurer the right to settle claims against insureds—for any amount the insurer deems appropriate—without first consulting the insured. Such provisions are unfavorable, and only a minority of insurers use this approach. In contrast, most professional liability insurers' forms reserve for the insured the right to approve settlement amounts to claimants. [*Professional Liability Insurance* **VII.B.22**]

nonprofit directors and officers liability insurance—Errors and omissions liability insurance covering the directors and officers (D&O) of nonprofit organizations. Such policies, while resembling the D&O forms covering for-profit firms, generally offer broader protection by providing: entity coverage, employment practices liability insurance, and substantially lower retention levels. [*Professional Liability Insurance* **XI.Q.1**]

nonprofit insurers—Insurers that do not operate for profit, such as the "Blue plans."

nonratable elements—A type of charge, especially in workers compensation rating, that is based on a catastrophic type exposure and is thus excluded from ordinary rate-making and is also not subject to experience rating and retrospective rating. An example of a nonratable element is an aircraft seat surcharge. [*Risk Financing* **III.D.8**]

nonresident agent—An agent who is licensed in a state in which` he or she does not reside.

nonsubscription—An option available in Texas permitting employers to opt out of the workers compensation system. However, such firms, if proven negligent in causing a worker's injury, can be held liable in tort, since nonsubscribing employers waive the traditional common law defenses available to employers subject to workers compensation laws. Two special types of insurance policies can be purchased by these firms: occupational accident insurance and employers excess indemnity insurance. [*Risk Financing* **IV.J.1**]

nonsuit—A judgment issued by the court, before the defense presents its case, based on the plaintiff's failure to produce sufficient evidence.

nontransferability provisions—Clauses indicating that an insured cannot transfer coverage to a noninsured without the insurer's approval. For example, attorney A who sells his practice to B cannot transfer coverage under his professional liability policy to B without the assent of his insurer. This is because insurance is a "personal" contract. Also see Assignment.

noon clause—A provision in an insurance policy providing that the starting time of the coverage is noon on the date of coverage inception. The noon clause has been replaced in most policies with a time shown of 12:01 a.m.

normal loss—A noncatastrophic level of loss within the working layer. It is the predictable loss and encompasses expected loss.

notice—The knowledge of facts that would lead a reasonably prudent person to take action.

notice of cancellation/nonrenewal clauses—Provisions in policies mandating that insurers are to provide advance notice of cancellation or nonrenewal of a policy. Most commonly, the required cancellation notice period is 30 days, although state amendatory endorsements frequently extend this period to 60 days. However, only a small handful of policies require that the insurer provide advance notice of nonrenewal. [*Commercial Auto Insurance* **XII.B.1**; *Professional Liability Insurance* **VII.D.1**; *Commercial Liability Insurance* **V.M.2**; and *Commercial Property Insurance* **II.D.23**]

notice of claim provision—A provision in a liability insurance policy requiring the insured to promptly notify the insurer in the event that a claim is made against the insured. Also called "awareness provision." See also Discovery period. [*Professional Liability Insurance* **VII.D.9** and *Commercial Liability Insurance* **V.J.1**]

notice of occurrence—One of the insured's specified duties under a general liability policy. Notice to the insurer of an occurrence must include the time, place, and circumstances of the occurrence, a description of any resulting injury or damage, and the names and addresses of injured persons and witnesses. [*Commercial Liability Insurance* **V.J.3**]

notice to the company—Written notice to the insurer as to an occurrence upon which a claim is to be based.

nuclear exclusion—(1) A provision or endorsement found in or attached to virtually all commercial property policies (other than the specialty policies designed to cover loss as a result of nuclear radiation). Eliminates coverage for loss or damage from nuclear reaction or radiation or radioactive contamination, except that ensuing fire is explicitly covered.

(2) A provision or endorsement found in or attached to virtually all commercial lines liability policies. The standard broad form nuclear energy exclusion most often attached to liability policies (IL 00 21) precludes coverage only for liability insured under a nuclear energy liability policy or for which indemnity is available from the U.S. government. The exclusion does not normally apply to liability arising from radioactive isotopes, the most common commercially used nuclear materials. [*Commercial Property Insurance* V.Q.15; *Commercial Liability Insurance* V.M.6; and *Commercial Auto Insurance* XII.C.1]

O

object—A boiler and machinery insurance term for equipment or machinery. Boiler and machinery coverage applies to loss or damage resulting from an accident (such as a breakdown or explosion) to a covered object. [*Commercial Property Insurance* XI.D.8]

obligatory treaty—A reinsurance treaty between an insurer and a reinsurer (usually involving pro-rata reinsurance), in which the insurer agrees to automatically cede all business that falls within the terms of the treaty. The reinsurer, in turn, is obligated to accept such business. "Automatic treaty" is another term for obligatory treaty. [*Risk Financing* V.A.6]

obligee—A person or organization to whom another party (the "obligor") owes an obligation. In a bonding situation, this is the party that requires and receives the protection of the bond. For example, under a performance bond, the obligee is the project owner for whom the bonded contractor is required to perform the specified work.

obligor—A person or organization that is bound by an obligation to another. In a bonding situation, this party, commonly called the "principal," purchases a bond to protect the party to whom it owes an obligation. For example, under a performance bond, the obligor is the contractor that is required to perform the specified work for the project owner.

occupational accident insurance—A type of coverage purchased by firms that have chosen to opt-out of the Texas workers compensation system. The policies allow an employer to provide benefits similar to those afforded under workers compensation laws. [*Risk Financing* IV.J.6]

occupational classification—In workers compensation, the assembling of like occupations together for classification and premium rating purposes. The rationale for the grouping is that certain occupations share common exposures and hazards. [*IRMI's Workers Comp* XI.C.2]

occupational disease—Any abnormal condition or disorder, other than one resulting from an occupational injury, that is caused by, or alleged to be caused by, exposure to environmental factors associated with employment, including acute and chronic illnesses or diseases that may be caused by inhalation, absorption, ingestion, or direct contact. State workers compensation laws vary as to whether coverage is afforded for occupational disease. [*IRMI's Workers Comp* XIV.R.1]

occupational injury—An injury arising in the course and scope of employment that is caused by factors associated with the work undertaken. [*IRMI's Workers Comp* III.C.5]

occupational manual—A manual listing occupational classifications for different types of work.

occurrence—In a commercial general liability coverage form, an accident, including continuous or repeated exposure to substantially the same general harmful conditions. General liability policies insure liability for bodily injury or property damage that is caused by an occurrence. [*Commercial Liability Insurance* V.L.25]

occurrence year—The time period defined by a body of losses composed of all claims occurring during a particular year.

ocean marine coverage—Insurance covering the transportation of goods and/or merchandise by vessels crossing both foreign and domestic waters including any inland or aviation transit associated with the shipment. This type of marine insurance also encompasses coverage for damage to the vessels involved in shipments and any legal liability arising in the course of shipment.

OCP—See Owners and contractors protective liability.

OCSLA—See Outer Continental Shelf Lands Act (OCSLA).

OEE—See Operators extra expense.

of counsel—Can mean many things: someone who is neither an associate nor a partner; someone who is not on the partner track but whom the law firm nevertheless desires to retain; may be an interim limbo position; or an attorney retained by a law firm to provide services and to be available as needed.

off-duty coverage—Coverage for police officers' personal liability exposure while moonlighting or otherwise off-duty. This exposure is typically excluded in most law enforcement liability policies. However, coverage can usually be added by endorsement for an additional premium. [*Professional Liability Insurance* XI.I.3]

offer—The terms of an insurance contract as proposed by one party (the potential insured) to another party (the potential insurer).

office burglary and robbery—Commercial crime coverage plan 5 of the Insurance Services Office, Inc., portfolio. The following coverage forms are mandatory for the plan: robbery and safe burglary—other than money and securities (D)(CR 00 05) [*Commercial Property Insurance* XII.D.17]; robbery and safe burglary—money and securities (Q)(CR 00 018) [*Commercial Property Insurance* XII.D.26]; and premises theft and robbery outside the premises—other than money and securi-

ties (H)(CR 00 09). [*Commercial Property Insurance* XII.D.26]

off-premises power coverage—See Utility service interruption coverage.

OL&T liability policy—See Owners, landlords, and tenants liability policy.

omnibus clause—A provision in standard automobile liability policies that embraces within the definition of "insured" certain persons without the necessity of naming them or designating them specifically. [*Commercial Auto Insurance* VIII.D.4]

on-demand bonds, bank guarantees—An unconditional bond or bank guarantee required of many contractors and sellers by overseas buyers to guarantee the tender (the actual form of money exchanged), as security against the value of advance payments under a contract, or to guarantee performance of the contract. Payable "on-demand," these bonds and guarantees may be called even when the contract has not been breached or when the breach is caused by circumstances outside the contractor's or seller's control, such as a trading embargo.

open rating—A pricing regulation approach associated with workers compensation premium costs in which state regulators allow insurers to issue policies using rates other than those established by the managing rating bureau. Types of variances include the use of rate deviations and the promulgation of rates by the insurers. [*IRMI's Workers Comp* III.E.4]

open perils—Sometimes used as a substitute for the term "all risks" in describing property insurance that insures against loss to covered property from all causes except those that are specifically excluded.

open stock burglary policy—Coverage insuring merchandise, furniture, fixtures, and equipment against loss by burglary or robbery while the premises are not open for business.

operators extra expense (OEE)—A specialized policy available to oil or gas well operators that covers the cost of regaining control of a wild well. Coverage for pollution, stuck drill stem, evacuation expense, and care, custody, or control exposures can be added by endorsement.

optionally renewable—A provision in a health policy, for example, that gives the insurer to right to renew the contract or not at its option on the policy's anniversary date; midterm cancellation is not permissible.

ordinance or law coverage—See Building ordinance coverage.

ordinary construction—Characterized by noncombustible exterior bearing walls (i.e., brick, concrete, or masonry) and combustible floors, roofs, and interior walls. Less sturdy than mill construction, this type of joisted masonry construction the exterior walls generally receive a fire-resistive rating of an hour.

ordinary life—A type of whole life insurance contract arranged so that the premiums are payable as long as the insured lives. The contract is not paid up and does not mature until the named insured reaches age 100 or dies, whichever event comes first.

ordinary payroll limitation or exclusion endorsement—An endorsement to a property business interruption policy limiting to a specified number of days (such as 90 days), or eliminating altogether, coverage for payroll expense of employees other than executives, department managers, employees under contract, and other "important" employees. In the absence of such an endorsement, virtually all property business interruption policies cover ordinary payroll. However, the reverse is true of boiler and machinery business interruption coverage forms, which exclude ordinary payroll unless coverage is added back by endorsement. [*Commercial Property Insurance* IV.D.12]

other insurance clause—A provision found in both property and liability insurance policies establishing how loss is to be apportioned among insurers when more than one policy covers the same loss. These provisions vary: some policies provide no coverage when other insurance is in place, some pay a pro-rata share, and others apply in excess. They are included to comply with the principle of indemnity which states that an insured should not profit from an insured loss. [*Commercial Property Insurance* V.C.11; *Commercial Liability Insurance* V.J.9; *Commercial Auto Insurance* VIII.F.11; *Professional Liability Insurance* VII.D.6; and *Contractual Risk Transfer* XI.C.10]

other states coverage—Workers compensation and employers liability insurance coverage for an insured's employees traveling through or temporarily working in states other than the insured's home state, as specifically listed in item 3.C of the information page of the policy. The endorsement expands the policy so that an injured employee can receive compensation benefits as prescribed by the other states listed on the endorsement. However, coverage only applies to states so listed, and coverage cannot be extended in this manner to monopolistic fund states. [*IRMI's Workers Comp* VI.E.1]

outcomes measurement—The process by which the ability of a physician to treat an injured worker competently, efficiently, and cost effectively is gauged. The evaluation of the doctor is based on the successful performance of the employee after returning to work and the financial costs associated with the treatment. [*IRMI's Workers Comp* XV.F.10]

outer continental shelf—Generally defined as all submerged lands that lie beyond the coastal states' territorial boundaries, to a water depth of 200 meters or where exploration is feasible. The state territorial boundaries normally extend 3 nautical miles, except in Florida and Texas where seaward boundaries extend 10 nautical miles. [*IRMI's Workers Comp* VII.D.2]

Outer Continental Shelf Lands Act (OCSLA)—Extends the benefits of the Longshore and Harbor Workers Compensation Act (LHWCA) to workers injured or killed upon fixed structures, e.g., oil well platforms, that are permanently attached to the outer continental shelf for the purpose of natural resource exploration or development. [*IRMI's Workers Comp* VII.D.1]

outstanding losses—Losses that have been reported to the insurer but are still in the process of settlement. Paid losses plus outstanding losses equal incurred losses. [*Risk Financing* III.D.7]

outstanding premiums—Premiums due but not yet collected by the insurer.

overinsurance—Insurance in an amount that is in excess of the insured object's fair or reasonable value.

overlapping insurance—Coverage from two or more policies or insurers that duplicates coverage for certain hazards in whole or in part.

over-line—An amount of insurance or reinsurance that exceeds an insurer's or reinsurer's normal capacity.

overriding commission—In insurance, a commission paid by an insurer to an agent or managing general agent for premium volume produced by other agents in a given geographic territory. In reinsurance, a commission paid to an intermediary in return for placing a retrocession of reinsurance.

overtime surcharge—Extra pay for overtime hours worked by employees. When an employee works overtime, many firms pay them time and a half or double time for the overage worked. States govern how the additional payroll charge is handled for the computation of workers compensation premium. Normally, the only payroll that goes into a workers compensation premium calculation is the basic rate of pay per hour. Any additional compensation for overtime worked in excess of the regular hourly rate, subject to state specific exceptions, are deleted from the payroll when computing workers compensation premiums. [*IRMI's Workers Comp* XI.C.2]

owner controlled insurance program (OCIP)—See Consolidated insurance program.

owners and contractors protective (OCP) liability coverage—Covers bodily injury and property damage liability arising out of an independent contractor's operations for another party. Although the contractor purchases the policy, the named insured is the party for whom it is performing operations. The OCP policy also responds to liability arising out of the acts or omissions of the insured in connection with the general supervision of the contractor's operations. [*Commercial Liability Insurance* VI.Q.1 and *Contractual Risk Transfer* XII.C.1]

ownership clause—In life insurance, the provision or endorsement that designates the owner of the policy when such owner is someone other than an insured, e.g., a beneficiary. This clause vests ownership rights (e.g., the right to designate the beneficiary) to the specified person or entity.

owners, landlords, and tenants (OL&T) liability policy—A now obsolete liability insurance coverage form designed for businesses whose liability loss exposure (other than automobile and workers compensation) derives principally from the business premises. Manufacturers and contractors, whose principal liability loss exposure derives from the business operations, products, or completed operations, commonly purchased a manufacturers and contractors liability policy (M&C) policy. Now both types of businesses are customarily insured under a commercial general liability policy.

P

package policies—A combination policy providing several different coverages. Usually refers to a policy providing both general liability insurance and property insurance. Premium discounts are usually allowed to reflect cost efficiencies. [*Commercial Property Insurance* XIII.B.1]

paid-in capital—Capital acquired by a corporation from sources other than its business operations. The most common source of paid-in capital is the sale of the corporation's own common and preferred stock. The amount of paid-in capital becomes part of the stockholders' equity shown in a balance sheet.

paid loss retrospective rating plan—An insurance cash flow plan that allows the insured to hold loss reserves until they are paid out in claims. Used most frequently with workers compensation and general liability lines.

paid up—Life insurance for which premiums have been paid but the policy has not yet matured.

paid-up additions—Single premium life insurance coverage bought in addition to the face amount of the policy by using policy dividends.

pain and suffering—A term for physical discomfort, emotional trauma and other nonquantifiable ills for which a claimant may collect from a negligent party in addition to the actual damages awarded.

PAP—See Personal auto policy.

par—See Participating.

paralegal—Someone who is trained and certified to perform any function of assistance to a lawyer. Can perform summaries, research, investigation, and the retrieval of records.

parameter risk—This describes the uncertainty in estimating the exact nature of the loss process in which statistical models are used to describe the randomness of the loss process. The choice and specification of these models are themselves exposed to potential errors in estimation.

parcel post coverage—Inland marine coverage on packages shipped by registered or unregistered mail or parcel post against all risks of transportation, from the time property is placed in custody of the U.S. Postal Service.

parent company—Where property and casualty insurers constitute a group of companies, the "flagship" or senior company. The use of multiple corporate entities allows additional flexibility in working with varying state regulations. For example, an insurance company group might consist of one or more admitted insurers and one or more nonadmitted insurers operating in various states. The entire group is often referred to by the parent company's name.

Part A permit, Part B permit—See Interim (permit) status.

partial disability—Disability that is not total. The definition of "partial disability" varies from policy to policy, but it is often defined as "the inability of the insured to perform one or more of the important duties of his or her occupation." When a disability income policy covers partial disability, the benefit is usually equal to a specified percentage, e.g., 50 percent, of the total disability benefit for a limited period of time, e.g., 3, 6, or 9 months).

partial loss—A property insurance term referring to a loss that does not completely destroy or render useless the insured property or does not completely exhaust the applicable insurance limit.

participating (par)—An insurance policy that pays dividends.

participating reinsurance—A generic form of reinsurance under which the reinsurer and primary insurer share losses in the same proportion as they share premiums and policy limits. Quota share reinsurance and surplus share reinsurance are the two types of participating reinsurance. Pro-rata reinsurance is another term often used to describe participating reinsurance. [*Risk Financing* **V.A.9**]

particular average—In ocean marine insurance, a partial loss sustained by a specified cargo or vessel. Ocean marine policies do not necessarily cover partial loss (referred to as "average" loss); but those that are covered must be the result of a covered peril. Such cargo losses are usually subject to separate particular average coverage provisions. See Free of particular average (American conditions); Free of particular average (English conditions); With average; and With average 3 percent.

partner—A member of a partnership or firm; one who has united with others to form a partnership in business and who participates fully in the profits, losses, and management of the partnership and is personally liable for its debts. Partners in a named insured partnership under a commercial general liability policy automatically qualify as insureds also. [*Commercial Liability Insurance* **V.H.2**]

partner-track—A term used in law firms to describe and evaluate an associate's potential for partnership. An associate who is progressing appropriately is deemed "on track."

party—Any person or entity named as a plaintiff, defendant, cross-complainant, or cross-defendant in a lawsuit.

patent infringement—An encroachment on a right granted by a government to an inventor assuring the sole right to make, use, and sell an invention for a certain period of time. Coverage for this exposure is normally not provided by liability policies.

Paul v Virginia—An 1869 U.S. Supreme Court decision holding that insurance is not commerce and is therefore not subject to regulation by the federal government. The ruling was overturned in 1944 by another Supreme Court decision, *United States v South-Eastern Underwriters Association*.

payor benefit—A provision under which premiums are waived if the person paying the premiums becomes disabled or dies. This option is often used when the insured is the child or spouse of the policyholder.

payout profile—A schedule illustrating the percentage of loss dollars actually paid in settlement of claims over time. For example, less than 25 percent of the total loss dollars for workers compensation claims are paid during the first year of coverage. The final claim costs are usually not completely settled until year 10. General liability losses have a payout that is even slower than workers compensation. As a result, many insureds choose insurance options that allow them to retain control of loss reserves and therefore the income accrued on the reserves while waiting for the claim to be paid. [*IRMI's Workers Comp* XI.T.3 and *Risk Financing* VII.C.3]

payroll—The premium basis used to calculate premium in workers compensation insurance and for some classifications, in general liability insurance. Also known as "remuneration." [*IRMI's Workers Comp* XI.C and *Commercial Liability Insurance* VIII.C.2]

payroll audit—A review of an insured's payroll records by a representative of the insurer to determine the earned premium on a policy such as workers compensation. [*IRMI's Workers Comp* VI.G.7]

payroll limitation—Involves a limitation on the amount of payroll for certain classifications that is used for the development of premium. In workers compensation insurance, payroll limitations typically apply only to sole proprietors, executive officers, partners, and certain noted classifications. In general liability, payroll limitations typically apply to executive officers, sole proprietors, and partners. The limitation varies by state. [*Commercial Liability Insurance* VIII.F.1]

penalty—The limit of liability under a surety bond.

per capita—Literally, per head or person.

percentage participation—A provision in a health insurance contract stipulating that the insurer and insured will share covered losses in agreed proportions. For example, the insurer may be required to pay 80 percent of the insured's hospital costs with the insured responsible for the remainder. Also called a "copayment" or "coinsurance" provision.

per diem business interruption coverage—A form of business interruption insurance in which the insured is entitled to recover a stipulated amount for each day of fully interrupted operations. Also referred to as "valued business interruption coverage." [*Commercial Property Insurance* II.E.2]

peril—A property insurance term referring to a cause of loss insured against in a property insurance policy, e.g., fire, windstorm, explosion, etc. [*Commercial Property Insurance* II.D.7 and *Contractual Risk Transfer* XIV.P.1]

permanent life insurance—Life insurance that has no expiration date and which provides for the payment of the face value upon death of the insured, regardless of when it may occur. This contrasts with term insurance, which pays benefits only if death takes place during the limited term (e.g., 1, 3, 5, or 10 years) of the policy. Under permanent life insurance policies, the insured pays a level premium rate all of his or her life. This approach results in an overpayment of premiums in the early years of the policy and an underpayment in the latter years—which is intended to average out over the life of the insured. Most types of permanent life insurance (e.g., whole life, universal life, and variable life insurance) accumulate a cash value that may be borrowed or otherwise used by the insured.

permanent partial disability—A workers compensation disability level in which the injured employee is still able to work but not with the skill and efficiency demonstrated prior to the injury. As a result, the earning capability of the worker is affected. Most workers compensation statutes provide for scheduled benefits based on the percentage of disability. [*IRMI's Workers Comp* III.C.7]

permanent total disability—A class of workers compensation disability in which the injured employee is incapable of ever working again at any employment. Under most statutes, the employee will receive weekly wages for life. [*IRMI's Workers Comp* III.C.7]

per risk excess reinsurance—A form of reinsurance under which both the retention and limit of coverage apply on a "per risk" basis rather than on a per accident or annual aggregate basis.

personal articles floater—A personal lines inland marine policy that is used to cover scheduled personal property on an all-risks basis. The policy is particularly appropriate for property that receives limited coverage under the homeowners forms, such as furs, jewelry, fine arts, silverware, cameras, musical instruments, stamp and coin collections, and similar property. Standard forms have been developed by both Insurance Services Office, Inc., and American Association of Insurance Services, Inc. Coverage is also sometimes afforded in homeowners policies by endorsement.

personal auto policy (PAP)—A standard form promulgated by Insurance Services Office, Inc., for insuring private-passenger-type autos owned by individuals. The policy may be structured to provide a combination of liability, personal injury protection, medical payments, uninsured and underinsured motorists, and physical damage coverages.

personal injury—(1) Under general liability coverage, a category of insurable offenses that produce harm other than bodily injury. As covered by the 1986 commercial general liability (CGL) policy, personal injury includes: false arrest, detention, or imprisonment; malicious prosecution; wrongful eviction; slander; libel; and invasion of privacy.

(2) Under umbrella liability insurance, a broad category of insurable offenses that includes both bodily injury and the offenses defined as "personal injury" in CGL policies. [*Commercial Liability Insurance* **V.L.27 and XI.B.1**]

personal injury protection (PIP)/no-fault—A type of auto insurance coverage mandated by statute in some jurisdictions. The statutes typically require insurers to provide or offer to provide first-party benefits for medical expenses, loss of income, funeral expenses, and similar expenses without regard to fault. Coverages, limits, and each party's responsibilities vary from state to state, as provided by law. [*Commercial Auto Insurance* **IV.I**]

personal property—All tangible property not classified as real property. See Real property. [*Commercial Property Insurance* **V.F.4**]

personnel risk—One of several categories of loss exposures facing organizations that may be treated with the risk management process. This expo-

sure encompasses losses arising from the death, injury, disability, or departure of employees. Examples include costs to replace a key employee who has died or becomes disabled and benefits mandated under workers compensation laws. Other categories of loss exposures include direct and indirect property risks and liability risks.

per stirpes—Literally, by branches. Provides for distribution of property by stipulating that in the event one beneficiary predeceases the insured, his or her heirs shall have his or her full share to distribute among themselves.

physical hazard—The material, structural, or operational features of a business that may create or increase the opportunity for injury or damage. [*Commercial Property Insurance* **III.B.1**]

P&I insurance—See Protection and indemnity insurance.

PIP—See Personal injury protection/no-fault.

plaintiff—In a civil action, the party bringing suit and seeking damages from the defendant.

plate glass insurance—See Glass insurance.

pleadings—The formal allegations of the respective claims and defenses by the parties to a lawsuit, consisting of a complaint, an answer, a reply to a counterclaim, an answer to a cross-claim, a third-party complaint, and answer to a third-party complaint.

PML—See Probable maximum loss.

point-of-entry treatment device—A treatment device applied to the drinking water in a house or building to reduce the contaminants in the water.

point-of-use treatment device—A treatment device applied to a single tap to reduce contaminants in the drinking water at the one faucet.

police professional liability insurance—Provides liability coverage for police officers and police departments, in conjunction with acts, errors, and omissions while performing their professional duties. The policies cover such perils as false arrest and civil rights violations. Unlike most professional liability insurance, the policies are sometimes written with occurrence triggers. [*Professional Liability Insurance* **XI.G.1**]

policy anniversary—See Anniversary date.

policy date—See Effective date.

policy dividend—See Dividends.

policy fee—A one-time charge or flat per policy charge that does not change with the size of the policy.

policyholder—Person in actual possession of insurance policy; policy owner. See Insured.

policyholder surplus—The difference between an insurer's admitted assets and liabilities, i.e., its net worth. This figure is used in determining the insurer's financial strength and capacity to write new business.

policy loan—A loan from the insurer to a life insurance policy owner using the cash value as security for the loan.

policy owner—The person who has ownership rights in an insurance policy, usually the policyholder or insured.

policy period—The term of duration of the policy. The policy period encompasses the time between the exact hour and date of policy inception and the hour and date of expiration.

policy reserve—See Unearned premium.

policy territory—Specifies the geographic area in which the property must be damaged (inland marine policies) or where injury or damage must occur (liability policies) for coverage to apply.

policy writing agent—An agent empowered to write and issue policies on behalf of his or her insurer.

policy year—The period between anniversary dates.

policy year experience—To determine policy-year experience for an individual insurance policy, include each premium or loss transaction that relates to that particular policy. Then, an aggregate for the book of business is calculated by including the individual experience of all policies that became effective during that year. For example, 1992 policy year data would include the experience of all policies effective between January 1, 1992, and December 31, 1992, regardless of the date on which losses or other events associated with those policies occur. This approach provides a clear match between losses and premiums. See Accident year data.

political risk insurance—Specialized insurance for companies doing business or conducting operations in foreign countries. The insurance addresses the business exposures to loss faced by these companies as a result of governmental action either foreign or domestic. Types of exposures that can be covered under political risk policies include confiscation, expropriation, deprivation, nationalization, political violence, currency inconvertibility, contract frustration, and export credit.

pollutant—As defined in standard liability insurance policies, an irritant or contaminant, whether in solid, liquid, or gaseous form, including—when they can be regarded as an irritant or contaminant—smoke, vapor, soot, fumes, acids, alkalis, chemicals and waste. [*Commercial Liability Insurance* V.D.23]

pollutant standard index (PSI)—Measure of adverse health effects of air pollution levels in major cities.

pollution—The contamination of an environment by substances regarded as pollutants. Liability from pollution is normally excluded to some degree by the general, auto, and umbrella liability policies. In recent years, insurers have attempted to introduce strict exclusionary language into these policies, making it necessary for insureds to seek coverage under separate "environmental impairment liability" policies. [*Commercial Liability Insurance* V.D.13]

pool—(1) A group of insurers or reinsurers through which particular types of risks (often of a substandard nature) are underwritten, with premiums, losses, and expenses shared in agreed ratios.

(2) A group of organizations that form a shared risk pool. Pooling is an attractive alternative for insureds who are not large enough to legally or feasibly self-insure but who desire more control over their loss exposures as well as an opportunity to reduce their cost of risk, compared to a program written by a commercial insurer. [*Risk Financing* IV.D.1]

portfolio reinsurance—A transaction in which an entire line of insurance, class of business, territory, or book of business of an insurer is reinsured. Under portfolio reinsurance, the reinsurer assumes all of the primary insurer's liability. It is typically arranged when an insurer wishes to discontinue operations in a specific state or territory. [*Risk Financing* V.A.5]

portfolio return—The return of unearned reinsurance premium to the ceding company when a reinsurance treaty is terminated. It is the opposite of a portfolio run-off.

portfolio run-off—A practice under which a reinsurance portfolio is allowed to continue until all ceded premium is earned or all losses are closed, or both. It is the opposite of a portfolio return.

post-mortem dividend—A policy dividend paid after the death of the insured. Sometimes called "mortuary dividend."

potentially responsible party (PRP)—Any individual or organization—including owners, operators, transporters or generators—potentially responsible for, or contributing to, a spill or other contamination at a Superfund site. Whenever possible, through administrative and legal actions, the EPA requires PRPs to clean up hazardous sites they have contaminated.

power of attorney—Authority given one person or organization to act on behalf of and obligate another.

preauthorized check plan—A plan under which an insured authorizes an insurer to periodically debit his bank account for the purposes of making premium payments.

precedent—A case that provides guidance or authority.

predecessor firm coverage—A provision found in professional liability policies written mainly for lawyers or accountants which affords coverage for the acts of the firm that preceded the current insured organization. For example, assume that two accountants, "A" and "B," form a partnership. After 5 years, they merge their practice with an existing partnership consisting of accountants "C," "D," and "E." The predecessor firm provision in the professional liability policy purchased by this new combination would provide coverage for errors and omissions committed during the AB partnership even if claims arising

from those errors or omissions are not made until after the merger of the two firms. [*Professional Liability Insurance* VII.B.8]

preexisting condition—A health or physical condition that existed prior to the effective date of a medical insurance policy. Some health and disability policies contain provisions that preclude coverage for loss arising from preexisting conditions.

preferred provider organization (PPO)—A group of doctors and hospitals who join together to dispense medical services to specified user groups at discounted costs. This type of organization differs from a health maintenance organization (HMO) in that the medical care providers are not economically tied to one another but rather to fee schedules. [*IRMI's Workers Comp* XV.F.4]

preferred risk—Any risk considered to be a better or preferred risk (i.e., one having lower potential loss frequency and severity) than the standard or "average" risk upon which premium rates are calculated.

prejudgment interest—Interest accruing on the amount of a legal award from the time of the injury or damage to the time the judgment is entered by the court. Prejudgment interest, when awarded as part of a judgment against the insured, is covered by the Supplementary Payments provision of standard general liability policies. [*Commercial Liability Insurance* V.G.2]

premises—(1) In a property insurance policy, the location where coverage applies. Usually described in the policy with a legal address.

(2) Building or land occupied or owned by an insured. See Premises-operations. [*Commercial Property Insurance* II.D.5]

premises burglary coverage—The Insurance Services Office, Inc. (ISO), crime form E, CR 00 06. Covers loss of property, other than money and securities, stolen from within the insured's premises or taken from a watch guard inside the premises. [*Commercial Property Insurance* XII.D.18]

premises-operations—One of the categories of hazards ordinarily insured by a general liability policy. Composed of those exposures to loss that fall outside the defined "products-completed operations hazard," it includes liability for injury or damage arising out of the insured's premises or out of the insured's business operations while in progress.

premises theft and outside robbery coverage form H—Insurance Services Office, Inc., crime form (CR 00 09) that covers property other than money and securities for theft from inside the premises and robbery of a messenger away from the premises. [*Commercial Property Insurance* **XII.D.21**]

premium—The amount of money an insurance company charges to provide the coverage described in the policy or bond.

premium, advance—The premium charged at the inception of the policy in cases where the final premium of the policy is not determined until the policy has expired; for example, where the policy premium is determined on an exposure base such as payroll that is subject to final audit adjustment. This is also referred to as a "provisional" or "deposit" premium.

premium basis—See Exposure base.

premium deposit—See Deposit premium and Premium, advance.

premium discount—A volume discount applied to premiums which acknowledges the administrative cost savings associated with larger premiums. Mostly used in workers compensation insurance, it is available in states where rates are approved and published (insurers in loss cost states are already free to discount the expense factor of their premium). After experience rating, the premium discount is applied to premiums in excess of $5,000 on a graduated rate increasing with the premium. Premium discount is not available when a retrospective plan applies. [*IRMI's Workers Comp* **XI.C.6**]

premium loan—A loan against the cash value of a life insurance policy to pay the policy premium.

premium notice—Notice from the insurer that the premium is or will soon be due.

premium prepayment—The payment by the insured of future premiums.

premium, pure—See Loss costs.

premium reserve—Insurers earn the premium paid for an insurance policy over the life of the policy. In other words, one-twelfth of an annual premium is earned each month. An unearned premium reserve is maintained on an insurer's balance sheet to reflect the unearned premiums that would be returned to policyholders if all policies were canceled on the date the balance sheet was prepared.

prepaid legal plans—An employee benefit plan that provides free or low cost legal services to employees.

preponderance of evidence—An amount of evidence in support of a cause that, on the whole, is more convincing than the evidence offered in opposition to it. A preponderance of the evidence is the burden of proof that must be met to prevail in a civil case.

present value—The value today of a future payment, or payments, discounted at an appropriate interest rate. Given the time value of money, the present value of $1 today is greater than the present value of $1 a year from today. Due to the earning power of funds on hand compared to funds received in the future, delaying loss and/or premium payments generates cash flow and increases the present value of funds held. Present value analysis can be used for a variety of purposes including: (1) calculating loss funding needs for risk retention programs and (2) comparing risk financing alternatives having different loss and premium payment streams. [*Risk Financing* **II.M.3**]

PRIMA—See Public Risk Management Association.

primary beneficiary—The beneficiary named as being first to receive proceeds or benefits when they come due or are payable. If the primary beneficiary is not living at the time the proceeds are payable, the benefits are paid to the secondary beneficiary.

primary cover—The policy that responds first to an insured loss, either on a first-dollar basis or after allowing for a deductible. When the primary coverage limits are paid, any remaining loss is covered by whatever excess layer of insurance may be in place. [*Commercial Liability Insurance* **XI.B.19**]

primary liability—As respects professional liability coverage for contractors, primary liability refers to the direct performance of design and other professional services conducted by in-house employees. This is in contrast to design services that are subcontracted to third parties for which the design firm has contingent liability. [*Professional Liability Insurance* XVII.E.33]

principal—In a surety bond, the entity whose performance is being guaranteed, i.e., the obligor.

principal sum—The amount payable in one sum in the event of accidental death and, in some cases, accidental dismemberment.

prior acts coverage—A feature of claims-made policies that have either no retroactive date or a retroactive date earlier than the inception date of the policy. Such a policy covers claims during the policy period arising out of events that precede the policy period. Without such a feature, the policy's retroactive date would preclude coverage with respect to these "prior acts." [*Commercial Liability Insurance* II.C.7]

privileged communication—Communication during "special" relationships that is protected from disclosure to third parties. The most common protected relationships are those of attorney/client, cleric/penitents, and husband/wife.

privity of contract—The relationship that exists between two parties by virtue of their having entered into a contract. This concept incorporates the legal principle that a contract may not impose duties on a noncontracting party, nor may a noncontracting party claim any right or benefit as being guaranteed by the contract.

probability—A numerical measure of the chance or likelihood that a particular event will occur. Probabilities are generally assigned on a scale from 0 to 1. A probability near 0 indicates an outcome that is unlikely to occur, while a probability near 1 indicates an outcome that is likely to occur. [*Risk Financing* II.F.7]

probable maximum loss (PML)—A property loss control term referring to the maximum loss expected at a given location in the event of a fire at that location, expressed in dollars or as a percentage of total values.

probationary period—A provision in some disability income policies stipulating that benefits will not be payable for sickness commencing during a specified period of time, e.g., 15–30 days, after inception of the policy. The purpose is to clarify that the policy is not intended to cover disability resulting from preexisting disease.

proceeds—See Principal sum.

process risk—This describes the uncertainty in outcomes that is inherent in the loss process due to its random nature.

process wastewater—Any water that comes into contact with any raw material, product, byproduct, or waste.

producer—A term commonly used for an agent, broker, or other insurance representative who has responsibility for selling insurance.

product—The subject of product liability insurance; defined in the standard Insurance Services Office, Inc. (ISO), commercial general liability policies to include property—other than real property—manufactured, sold, handled, distributed, or disposed of by the named insured or others involved with the named insured in the stream of commerce. The definition of "product" includes containers, parts and equipment, product warranties, and provision of or failure to provide instructions and warnings. [*Commercial Liability Insurance* V.L.40]

production of documents—To be compelled to produce, or bring forward, show, or exhibit documents deemed to be relevant to the case.

product liability—The liability for bodily injury or property damage incurred by a merchant or manufacturer as a consequence of some defect in the product sold or manufactured. [*Commercial Liability Insurance* V.D.37, V.D.43, and V.L.30]

product liability exclusion—An exclusion of liability arising from products found in some law enforcement policies. This could include alleged misuse of weapons or other law enforcement aids. It is preferable to delete this exclusion if contained in the policy.

product recall—Insurance coverage for the cost of getting a defective product back under the control of the manufacturer or merchandiser who would be responsible for possible bodily injury or property damage from its continued use or existence. Standard product liability insurance does not cover this exposure due to the "sistership liability exclusion." [*Commercial Liability Insurance* **V.D.43**]

products-completed operations—One of the hazards ordinarily insured by a general liability policy. It comprises liability arising out of the insured's products or business operations conducted away from the insured's premises once those operations have been completed or abandoned. [*Commercial Liability Insurance* **V.L.30**]

products guarantee legal liability—Specialty insurance coverage that insures the liability of a manufacturer for damage to the product resulting from the product. Normally, the product failure must result from a mistake or deficiency in design, plan, or specifications for coverage to apply.

products tampering insurance—Insurance to indemnify the insured for loss of net profit, chemical analysis, recall, examination, transportation, destruction, and extra expenses incurred to regain marketshare following a malicious product tampering incident.

professional liability—Coverage designed to protect traditional professionals (e.g., physicians) and quasi-professionals (e.g., real estate brokers) against liability incurred as a result of errors and omissions in performing professional services. Although there are a few exceptions, most professional liability policies cover economic losses suffered by third parties, as opposed to bodily injury and property damage (which is typically covered under commercial general liability policies). The vast majority of professional liability policies are written with claims-made coverage triggers. [*Professional Liability Insurance* **III.C.1**]

professional reinsurer—A term used to designate a company whose business is confined solely to reinsurance and the peripheral services offered by a reinsurer to its customers. This is in contrast to primary insurers who exchange reinsurance or operate reinsurance departments as adjuncts to their basic business of primary insurance.

profit sharing plan—A defined contribution benefit plan that does not promise a set amount at retirement. Up to 15 percent of employee compensation can be contributed on behalf of any employee annually.

prohibited risk—Any class of business excluded by underwriters of an insurance company that will not be insured under any condition.

prohibition of voluntary payments provision—A clause found in some liability policies barring coverage in the event that an insured makes a payment to a third party and then seeks reimbursement from the insurer. In the standard commercial general liability coverage form, such a prohibition is included as one of the insured's "Duties in the Event of Occurrence, Claim or Suit." [*Commercial Liability Insurance* **V.J.7**]

pro hoc vice—Latin for, "for this time only." A lawyer from New York who is not licensed to practice in Texas may, for a Texas trial, be admitted *pro hoc vice.*

project liability insurance—A form of architects and engineers liability coverage in which coverage applies only to an insured's work on a single project rather than to the entire scope of an insured's practice. Such policies are advantageous because they provide coverage for all members of a project's design team, reduce the incidence of disputes in the event of a claim, assure coverage continuity following completion of work, and facilitate the availability of high limits needed on large projects. [*Professional Liability Insurance* **XVII.E.28**]

promissory note—A financial instrument used to provide an insurer with financial security necessary to implement a collateralized cash flow program, such as retrospectively rated insurance plan. Promissory notes provide an insurer with status as a senior creditor rather than a general creditor.

proof of loss—A formal statement made by the insured to the insurer regarding a claim, especially in property insurance, so that the insurer may determine its liability under the policy.

property damage—As defined in the general liability policy, physical injury to tangible property including resulting loss of use and loss of use of tangible property that has not been physically injured.

property insurance—First-party insurance that indemnifies the owner or user of property for its loss, or the loss of its income-producing ability, when the loss or damage is caused by a covered peril, such as fire or explosion. In this sense, property insurance encompasses inland marine, boiler and machinery, and crime insurance, as well as what was once known as fire insurance, now simply called property insurance: insurance on buildings and their contents. [*Commercial Property Insurance* II.D.1]

proposal bond—See Bid bond.

pro rata—Proportionately.

pro rata cancellation—The cancellation of an insurance policy or bond with the return premium credit being the full proportion of premium for the unexpired term of the policy or bond, without penalty for interim cancellation. See also Short-rate cancellation.

pro rata distribution clause—A seldom used property insurance provision that essentially converts a single blanket limit, applying over several locations, to specific limits.

pro rata reinsurance—A term describing all forms of "proportional" reinsurance. Under pro-rata reinsurance, the reinsurer shares losses in the same proportion as it shares premiums and policy amounts. Quota share and surplus share are the two major types of pro rata reinsurance.

proration—The adjustment of policy benefits due to a change of exposure or existence of "other insurance."

pro se—Also known as "*in propria persona*," refers to a plaintiff who does not (or cannot) hire an attorney and who represents himself.

prospect—The potential buyer of insurance.

prospecting—The act of looking for potential buyers of insurance.

prospective aggregate contract—A form of finite risk insurance applying to losses that have not yet occurred. They operate as prefunding mechanisms in which the insured pays a premium at the inception of the contract and then begins receiving reimbursement once aggregate losses reach a specified level. [*Risk Financing* V.D.7]

prospective loss costs—See Loss costs.

prospective rating—A method used in arriving at an insurance or reinsurance rate and premium for a policy period based on the loss experience of a prior period. Schedule credits, experience modification, and individual risk rating modifications are factors used in prospective rating, whereas losses incurred during the policy period have no effect on final premium. Guaranteed cost plans, with or without a dividend, are examples of prospectively rated insurance plans. [*Risk Financing* I.B.3]

protection and indemnity (P&I) insurance—Liability insurance for practically all maritime liability associated with the operation of a vessel, other than that covered under a workers compensation policy and under the collision clause in a hull policy.

protection classes—The 10 categories used by Insurance Services Office, Inc. (ISO), to rank cities and towns according to the availability of water, e.g., fire hydrants and water pressure, and the quality of firefighting, e.g., training of personnel and paid versus volunteer. Protection class 1 indicates the best available protection; class 10 indicates a rural area without fire hydrants or fire departments. [*Commercial Property Insurance* IV.F.5]

protective liability insurance—A general term describing a type of liability insurance that is purchased by an indemnitor, such as a contractor, for its indemnitee, such as the person for whom the contractor is performing operations, to protect that party against liability for bodily injury or property damages arising out of the indemnitor's operations. See also Owners and contractors protective liability insurance and Railroad protective liability insurance. [*Contractual Risk Transfer* XII.B.1]

protective order—Any order or decree of a court whose purpose is to protect a party from harassment or further discovery.

protective safeguards endorsement—A property insurance endorsement that makes it a condition of coverage that the protective safeguards cited in the endorsement (such as an automatic sprinkler system or night watch guard) be in operation at all times except when the insurer has been notified of the impairment in protection. Failure to maintain the protective safeguards in good working order or failure to notify the insurer of even a temporary impairment in protection suspends coverage until the protection is re-

stored.   [*Commercial   Property   Insurance*
VI.C.47]

proximate cause—A legal concept often applied by
courts in determining whether property damage
has been caused by an insured peril. A number
of different definitions have been used, including:
the primary cause of loss or damage; the cause
without which a given result would not have occurred; the cause that sets other causes in motion.

public employee dishonesty coverage—Insurance
for governmental entities, e.g., cities, towns,
counties, etc., covering loss resulting from employee dishonesty. Limits can be written to apply
per loss (ISO coverage form O, CR 00 16) or per
employee (coverage form P, CR 00 17). [*Commercial Property Insurance* XII.D.25–26]

Public Law 15 (McCarran Act)—A congressional act
of 1945 exempting insurance from federal antitrust laws to the extent that the individual states
regulate the industry. The legislation was made
necessary by the U.S. Supreme Court decision in
*United States v South-Eastern Underwriters As-
sociation.*

public liability insurance—Insurance covering an insured's liability to third parties for causing bodily
injury or property damage.

public officials bond—A bond under which the surety guarantees that the specified public official
will faithfully perform his or her official duties,
including accounting for all funds entrusted to
his or her care.

public officials liability—The liability exposure faced
by public officials from "wrongful acts," usually
defined under public officials liability insurance
policies as: actual or alleged errors, omissions,
misstatements, negligence, or breach of duty, in
their capacity as a public official or employee of
the public entity. [*Professional Liability Insurance* XI.C.1]

public officials liability insurance—Provides liability
coverage for the errors and omissions of public
officials. In effect, such policies serve the same
function for elected/appointed officials of state
and local government as directors and officers
(D&O) insurance serves for the directors and officers of corporations.

However, one major difference is that under public officials liability forms, employees and the
public entity itself are insureds, whereas this is
not the case with D&O policies.Exclusions under
this policy include losses due to fraud or dishonesty, bodily injury or property damage, false arrest, assault and battery, defamation, and fiduciary liability. [*Professional Liability Insurance*
XI.E.1]

Public Risk Management Association (PRIMA)—An
association of governmental risk managers that
publishes a monthly magazine, sponsors seminars and an annual conference, and provides
other services to its members.

publishers liability—Liability of a book, periodical, or
other type of publisher arising from acts such as
plagiarism, libel, or copyright infringement. Publishers of medical, engineering, and technical
works may also face an errors and omissions exposure from damage or injury arising from incorrect information that they provide. Coverage for
these exposures is available in specialized policies, known as media liability insurance. [*Professional Liability Insurance* XVIII.C.1]

punitive damages—Damages in excess of those required to compensate the plaintiff for the wrong
done, which are imposed in order to punish the
defendant because of the particularly wanton or
willful nature of his wrongdoing. Also called "exemplary damages." Although the standard commercial general liability and business auto policies contain no punitive damage exclusion, many
umbrella and excess liability policies contain
such an exclusion. [*Commercial Liability Insurance* XI.D.27]

purchasing group—Authorized by the Liability Risk
Retention Act of 1986, this group was formed to
obtain liability coverage for its members, all of
whom must have similar or related exposures.
The Act required a purchasing group to be domiciled in a specific state. In contrast to risk retention groups, purchasing groups are not risk-bear-
ing entities. [*Risk Financing* IV.M.13]

pure endowment—An endowment payable at the
end of the policy period if the insured is alive. If
the insured has died, there is nothing paid in the
form of benefits.

pure loss cost—Under a reinsurance agreement, the
ratio of reinsured losses to the ceding company's

earned, subject premium for that agreement, the less expense loading. Also known as "burning cost."

pure premium—See Loss costs.

pure risk—The risk involved in situations that present the opportunity for loss but no opportunity for gain. Pure risks are generally insurable, whereas speculative risks (which also present the opportunity for gain) generally are not. See Speculative risk.

Q

qualified plan—An employee benefit plan the Internal Revenue Service has approved as meeting the requirements of Section 401(a) of the Internal Revenue Code. Such plans receive favorable tax advantages.

qualitative claim auditing—The comprehensive review of claim files that seeks to discover whether the claims are being appropriately managed. Some of the criteria used to measure the quality of the claim handling being delivered include: adequacy of reserves, timeliness with which the files are handled, experience and skill level of the adjusters, and the effectiveness of the internal communications system. [*IRMI's Workers Comp* XIV.N.2]

quantitative claim auditing—A type of audit in which claim files are reviewed to determine if file reserves and the number of claims match a computer generated loss run. This type of audit places the emphasis on accuracy rather than if the claims are being handled adequately. [*IRMI's Workers Comp* XIV.N.2]

quantity discount—A premium discount given to purchasers of large face amount life insurance policies.

quasi-contract—A legal doctrine invoked by courts that imposes an obligation not actually established in a contract. Most frequent insurance application is in matters relating to preservation of salvage.

quick assets—Highly liquid assets, consisting of: (1) cash, (2) marketable securities, and (3) net receivables.

quid pro quo—Latin for "this for that." Pertains to the exchange of values by both parties in order to form a valid contract. In workers compensation, employees trade their right to sue their employers in exchange for no-fault benefits. This is considered the quid pro quo in workers compensation.

quid pro quo sexual harassment—A form of sexual harassment, such as unwelcome sexual advances or requests for sexual favors when (1) submission to such conduct is made a condition of an individual's employment, and (2) submission to or rejection of such conduct is used as a basis for employment decisions affecting these individuals. Claims alleging quid pro quo sexual harassment are afforded coverage under employment practices liability policies. [*Professional Liability Insurance* X.J.17]

quota share reinsurance—A form of reinsurance in which the ceding insurer cedes an agreed on percentage of every risk it insures that falls within a class or classes of business subject to a reinsurance treaty. [*Risk Financing* V.A.9]

R

Racketeer Influenced and Corrupt Organizations (RICO) Act of 1970—A law providing for treble damages against those engaged in "a pattern of racketeering activity." A number of liability policies exclude coverage for suits alleging RICO Act violations against insureds, despite the fact that such claims have been increasing in recent years.

radius class—The customary distance traveled by commercial vehicles as measured in a straight line from the place of garaging to the destination. There are three radius classes: local (not over 50 miles); intermediate (between 50 and 200 miles); and long distance (over 200 miles). [*Commercial Auto Insurance* III.G.6]

radius of operations—The area or areas where a company conducts its business. See also Radius class. [*Commercial Auto Insurance* III.G.6]

railroad protective liability—Insurance coverage protecting a railroad from liability it incurs because of the work of contractors on or near the railroad right-of-way. [*Commercial Liability Insurance* VI.R.1 and *Contractual Risk Transfer* XII.D.1]

railroad sidetrack agreement—An agreement between a railroad and a business in which the railroad agrees to build a siding on the property of the business, and the business will hold the railroad harmless for certain liability arising out of the use of the sidetrack. Sidetrack agreements are "insured contracts" under the provisions of standard contractual liability insurance coverage. [*Commercial Liability Insurance* V.L.12]

rainmaker—One who markets the law firm and attempts to generate new business, particularly one who is very adept at bringing in new accounts.

rate—A unit of cost that is multiplied by an exposure base to determine an insurance premium. An insurance rate is the amount of money necessary to cover losses, expenses, and provide a profit to the insurer for a single unit of exposure. Rates, as contrasted with loss costs, include provision for the insurer's profit and expenses. [*Commercial Auto Insurance* III.G.1]

rate basis—See Exposure base.

rate discrimination—Using different rates for exposures of the same risk type and classification. This is illegal in most states.

rate manual—A book containing classifications and rates for a given line of insurance.

rate of natural change—Birth rate minus death rate. In the absence of migration, this would be the change in the population.

rating bureau—An organization that collects necessary statistical data (e.g., premiums, exposure units, and losses) to compute suggested rates to be used by insurers. Rating bureaus are usually nonprofit associations owned by numerous insurers. The use of bureaus allows data from many different insurers to be combined which enhances the credibility of the actuarial analysis. Bureaus also perform other functions, such as the development of standard policy forms, inspection of insured properties, and communication with regulators on behalf of their members. The best known bureaus are Insurance Services Office, Inc. (ISO), National Council on Compensation Insurance (NCCI), Surety Association of America (SAA), and American Association of Insurance Services (AAIS). [*Commercial Property Insurance* II.R.1; *IRMI's Workers Comp* III.E.2; and *Risk Financing* III.A.7]

rating class—The classification for rating purposes of an individual exposure.

RCRA—See Resource Conservation and Recovery Act (RCRA).

readjustment income—In life insurance, an amount of money to provide for readjustment expenses after the death or disability of the breadwinner.

real estate errors and omissions—Professional liability for persons engaged in buying, selling, leasing, or otherwise dealing in real estate on behalf of others. Depending on the scope of such policies, coverage may also apply to persons engaged in: property management, real estate appraisal, real estate consulting, or other related aspects of the business. As is the case with most professional liability policy forms, coverage is written on a claims-made basis. [*Professional Liability Insurance* XX.F.1]

real property—Land and most things attached to the land, such as buildings and vegetation. Growing crops, since they are physically attached to the soil, are generally considered to be real property. The definition of "land" includes not only the surface of the earth, but also everything above and beneath it. Thus, the ownership of a tract of land theoretically includes both the airspace above it and the soil from its surface to the center of the earth. [*Commercial Property Insurance* II.D.2]

reasonably available control technology (RACT)—Pollution control technology that is reasonably available and both technologically and economically feasible. Usually applied to existing sources in nonattainment areas; in most cases is less stringent than new source performance standards.

rebate—The sharing of the agent's or broker's commission with the insured.

recapture—The process by which a ceding company takes back a risk or risks that previously were ceded to a reinsurer.

reciprocal company—An unincorporated group of persons or organizations that exchange risks. Each member of a reciprocal is both an insured and an insurer of the other members. While reciprocals may allow for limited assessments of their members, each member's liability is limited. A member cannot be called on to pay the obligation of another member.

reciprocity—The exchanging of reinsurance between two reinsurers, frequently in equal amounts. The purpose of such transactions is to balance underwriting results for both companies.

recision—Repudiation of a contract for cause or by consent of the contracting parties.

recurrent disability—A period of disability resulting from the same or a related cause of a prior disability.

recurring clause—A health insurance policy provision setting the time that must elapse between periods of disability for the recurrence to be considered a new benefit period.

redact—To erase. If a pharmaceutical manufacturer is required to produce records of prior drug reactions reported, the drug firm might "redact" patient names from the reports to preserve patient privacy and prevent plaintiff's counsel from trolling for more lawsuits.

reduced paid-up insurance—A life insurance nonforfeiture benefit that provides paid-up insurance for a lesser amount than the cash value of a policy that has lapsed because of premium nonpayment.

refund annuity—A form of periodic payment that provides for refund to a beneficiary in the event the annuitant dies before the total compensation has been paid.

registered mail coverage—Coverage for items, including money and securities, that are lost when sent through registered mail. Usually written on a reporting form and purchased by businesses such as bank trust departments that frequently send valuable items through the mail.

regression analysis—A statistical tool for predicting one variable (known as the dependent variable) based on its relationship with one or more other variables (known as independent variables). For example, the dependent variable of workers compensation losses are often predicted on the basis of the independent variable of workers compensation payroll. [*Risk Financing* II.F.16]

regulated asbestos-containing material (RACM)—Friable asbestos material or nonfriable asbestos-containing material (ACM) that will be or has been subjected to sanding, grinding, cutting, or abrading or has crumbled, or been pulverized, or reduced to powder in the course of demolition or renovation operations.

regulated medical waste—Under the Medical Waste Tracking Act of 1988, any solid waste generated in the diagnosis, treatment, or immunization of human beings or animals, in research pertaining thereto, or in the production or testing of biologicals. Included are cultures and stocks of infectious agents; human blood and blood products; human pathological body wastes from surgery and autopsy; contaminated animal carcasses from medical research; waste from patients with communicable diseases; and all used sharp implements, such as needles and scalpels, etc., and certain unused sharps.

regulatory agency exclusion—An exclusion found in directors and officers liability policies that precludes coverage for suits by national and state banking authorities against directors and officers. The exclusion came into use during the mid-1980s when, in the wake of widespread financial institution insolvencies, regulators such as the FDIC took control of failed banks. In their attempts to recover lost assets, regulators frequently initiated lawsuits against former directors and officers, recognizing that D&O policy proceeds would be available. [*Professional Liability Insurance* X.E.23] reinstatement—Under many forms of reinsurance and insurance, the payment of a claim reduces an aggregate limit by the amount of the claim. Provision is sometimes made for reinstating the policy limit to its original amount when the original limit has been exhausted. Depending on policy conditions, it may be done automatically, either with or without premium consideration, i.e., a reinstatement premium, or it may be done only at the request of the insured, in return for an additional premium.

reinstatement premium—A prorated insurance or reinsurance premium charged for the reinstatement of the amount of a primary policy or reinsurance coverage limit that have been reduced or exhausted by loss payments under such coverages.

reinsurance—A transaction in which one party, the "reinsurer," in consideration of a premium paid to it, agrees to indemnify another party, the "reinsured," for part or all of the liability assumed by the reinsured under a policy or policies of insurance that it has issued. The reinsured may also be referred to as the "original" or "primary" insurer, or the "ceding company." [*Risk Financing* V.A.1]

reinsurance assumed—That portion of a risk that a reinsurer accepts from an original insurer (also known as a "primary" insurer) in return for a stated premium.

reinsurance ceded—That portion of a risk that an original insurer (also known as a "primary" insurer) transfers to a reinsurer in return for a stated premium.

reinsurance credit—Credit taken in an annual statement by a ceding insurer for reinsurance premiums ceded and for reinsurance losses recoverable.

reinsurance intermediaries—Brokers who act as intermediaries between reinsurers and ceding companies. For the reinsurer, intermediaries operate as an outside sales force. They also act as advisers to ceding companies in assessing and locating markets that meet their reinsurance needs. [*Risk Financing* V.A.19]

reinsurance premium—The premium paid by the ceding company to the reinsurer in consideration for the liability assumed by the reinsurer. [*Risk Financing* V.A.2]

reinsured—An insurer that contracts with a reinsurer to share all or a portion of its losses under insurance contracts it has issued in return for a stated premium. Also called the "ceding company." [*Risk Financing* V.A.2]

reinsurer—An insurer that accepts all or part of the liabilities of the ceding company in return for a stated premium. [*Risk Financing* V.A.2]

related product liability exclusion—An exclusion of liability found in some architects & engineers professional liability policies precluding coverage of claims involving products that are manufactured or designed by the insured. The rationale for the exclusion is that if a third party suffers bodily injury or property damage from the insured's products, the insured's commercial general liability policy should cover the loss. [*Professional Liability Insurance* XVII.E.19]

release—The document relinquishing a claim. A plaintiff or claimant signs a release in exchange for monetary payment, thereby giving up the right to pursue further indemnity in connection with the claim.

relief well coverage—Coverage for the cost of drilling a new well for the purpose of releasing underground pressure to assist in bringing a wild oil or gas well under control. It is an optional operators extra expense policy coverage.

remedial action (RA)—The actual construction or implementation phase of a Superfund site cleanup that follows remedial design. [*Commercial Liability Insurance* VI.W.10]

remedial design—A phase of remedial action that follows the remedial investigation/feasibility study and includes development of engineering drawings and specifications for a site cleanup.

remedial investigation—An in-depth study designed to gather data needed to determine the nature and extent of contamination at a Superfund site, establish site cleanup criteria, identify preliminary alternatives for remedial action, and support technical and cost analyses of alternatives. The remedial investigation is usually done with the feasibility study. Together they are usually referred to as the "RI/FS."

remedial project manager (RPM)—The Environmental Protection Agency (EPA) or state official responsible for overseeing on-site remedial action.

remedial response—Long-term action that stops or substantially reduces a release or threat of a release of hazardous substances that is serious but not an immediate threat to public health.

remediation—(1) Cleanup or other methods used to remove or contain a toxic spill or hazardous materials from a Superfund site.

(2) For the Asbestos Hazard Emergency Response program, abatement methods including evaluation, repair, enclosure, encapsulation, or removal of greater than 3 linear feet or square feet of asbestos-containing materials from a building.

renewable term—Term life insurance that may be renewed periodically without evidence of insurability but often at a higher premium.

renewal certificate—A very limited method of policy renewal by issuing a certificate rather than by issuing a new policy. The certificate refers to the original policy but does not enumerate all of its terms.

renewal policy—An insurance policy issued to replace an expiring policy.

rent-a-captive—An arrangement in which a captive insurer "rents" its facilities to an outside organization, thereby providing the benefits that captives offer without the financial commitments that captives require. In return for a fee (usually a percentage of the premium paid by the renter), certain captives agree to provide underwriting, rating, claims management, accounting, reinsurance, and financial expertise to unrelated organizations. [*Risk Financing* IV.K.42]

rental cost reimbursement (cost of hire) endorsement—A contractors equipment coverage endorsement that adds coverage for the cost of renting temporary replacement equipment in the event of covered damage to covered equipment.

rental value insurance—Time element insurance that reimburses the owner occupant of a building for the expense of renting another location in the event the insured's property becomes unusable as a result of damage by an insured peril. [*Commercial Property Insurance* II.E.10]

rents or rental value insurance—Time element insurance that reimburses the owner of a building for loss of rents due to damage by an insured peril. Coverage is also provided for the fair rental value of the premises occupied by the insured. Under the current Insurance Services Office, Inc. (ISO), commercial property program, there is no separate rental value coverage form. Instead this coverage is available under the business income coverage form. [*Commercial Property Insurance* II.E.10]

repatriation—Bringing back to one's homeland, generally referring to transportation of an injured or ill employee back to his home country. This coverage is sometimes added to the workers compensation policy by a manuscript foreign voluntary compensation endorsement. [*IRMI's Workers Comp* VI.L.11]

repatriation of dividends insurance—Political risk insurance that indemnifies the insured for financial loss incurred because of the inability to repatriate funds resulting from currency export restrictions.

replacement cost coverage endorsement/option—A property insurance provision that changes the valuation of covered property from actual cash value to replacement cost value: the cost to replace it today with property of like kind and quality without deduction for depreciation. [*Commercial Property Insurance* V.F.57 and *Contractual Risk Transfer* XIV.P.1]

reportable quantity (RQ)—The quantity of a hazardous substance that triggers reports under the Comprehensive Environmental Response Compensation and Liability Act (CERCLA). If a substance exceeds its RQ, the release must be reported to the National Response Center, the State Emergency Planning Commission (SERC), and community emergency coordinators for areas likely to be affected.

reporting form coverage—Property insurance that allows an insured with fluctuating inventory values to establish a limit of insurance adequate to cover the highest possible exposed value, but to pay a premium based on the actual values exposed. Initial provisional premium is adjusted on the basis of required periodic, e.g., monthly or quarterly, reports of actual property values. The insured is penalized for late or inaccurate reports. [*Commercial Property Insurance* II.D.19]

reporting lag—This denotes the span of time between the occurrence of a claim and the date it is first reported to the insurer.

repossessed autos endorsement—An automobile policy endorsement providing coverage for autos that have become the property of the financing institution because of the failure of the purchaser to comply with the terms of the financing agreement. [*Commercial Auto Insurance* XIII.H.37]

representation—A statement made in the application for insurance that the prospective insured represents as being correct to the best of his or her knowledge. If the insurer relies on a representation in entering into the insurance contract and if it proves to be false at the time it was made, the insurer may have legal grounds to avoid the contract. See also Warranty and Misrepresentation.

request for proposal (RFP)—A document used to secure proposals for insurance or risk management services.

reserve—An amount of money earmarked for a specific purpose. Insurers establish unearned premium reserves and loss reserves indicated on their balance sheets. Unearned premium reserves show the aggregate amount of premiums that would be returned to policyholders if all policies were canceled on the date the balance sheet was prepared. Loss reserves are estimates of outstanding losses, loss adjustment expenses, and other related items. Self-insured organizations also maintain loss reserves.

resident agent—An agent domiciled in the state in which he or she conducts his or her business activities. [*Professional Liability Insurance* IV.J.13]

residual market—Insurance market systems for various lines of coverage (most often workers compensation, personal automobile liability, and property insurance). They serve as a coverage source of last resort for firms and individuals that have been rejected by voluntary market insurers. Residual markets require insurers writing specific coverage lines in a given state to assume the profits or losses accruing from insuring that state's residual risks in proportion to their share of the total voluntary market premiums written in that state. [*IRMI's Workers Comp* XII.J.6 and *Risk Financing* III.A.47]

residual market load—A factor applied to workers compensation policies by insurers to recover costs assessed them by states for deficits in the residual markets. It is left to the individual insurer to determine how and if this cost will be passed onto its policyholders. The most common application is as a cost component included in a retrospective rating plan. [*IRMI's Workers Comp* XI.E.1 and *Risk Financing* Appendix G.6]

residual market loading—A multiplicative factor applied to retrospectively rated workers compensation plans. Their purpose is to compensate insurers for the losses sustained when writing workers compensation risks in the residual market. [*Risk Financing* III.A.55]

residual value insurance—Guarantees the owner of leased personal property, e.g., autos or equipment, a particular value at a specified future date, usually the termination of the lease. Covers the difference between the actual liquidated value of property returned to the insured lessor and the expected value of the property specified in the policy.

res ipsa loquitor—A Latin term meaning "the thing speaks for itself." This is a legal doctrine used to assess liability (often against professionals) when there is no evidence as to how an injury took place. For instance, if a sponge is inadvertently left in a patient's stomach, the doctrine of *res ipsa loquitor* is typically invoked to establish liability because such an event is presumed not to occur in the absence of negligence.

res judicata—A final judgment between parties that is conclusive as to that issue in later suits between those same parties.

Resource Conservation and Recovery Act (RCRA)—A federal act regulating the handling of hazardous waste from its generation to disposal. The Act defines "hazardous waste" and establishes standards and permit programs for waste generating, treatment, storage, and disposal. It implements detailed recordkeeping requirements and imposes civil and criminal penalties for noncompliance.

respondeat superior—A legal doctrine under which an employer can be held liable for the actions of employees. [*Contractual Risk Transfer* III.E.1]

response action—(1) Generic term for actions taken in response to actual or potential health-threatening environmental events such as spills, sudden releases, and asbestos abatement/management problems.

(2) An action authorized by the Comprehensive Environmental Response Compensation and Liability Act (CERCLA) involving either a short-term removal action or a long-term removal response. This may include but is not limited to: removing hazardous materials from a site to an Environmental Protection Agency approved hazardous waste facility for treatment; containment or treating the waste on-site; identifying and removing the sources of groundwater contamination; and halting further migration of contaminants.

(3) Any of the following actions taken in school buildings in response to AHERA to reduce the risk of exposure to asbestos: removal, encapsulation, enclosure, repair, and operations and maintenance.

retaliatory law—A state law providing that another state will be treated in the same terms that the home state is treated by the foreign state in dealings with insurance. If, for example, another state requires that all nonresident agents writing insurance or risks in that state obtain a license from that state, a state with a retaliatory law will impose the same requirement on that other state's agents.

retaliatory suits—Claims against professionals, filed by their clients, that allege negligence. Retaliatory suits are normally in response to the professional's attempt to collect fees for services performed. Retaliatory suits are typically covered by all forms of professional liability insurance. [*Professional Liability Insurance* III.C.22–23]

retention—(1) Assumption of risk of loss by means of noninsurance, self-insurance, or deductibles. Retention can be intentional or, when exposures are not identified, unintentional.

(2) In reinsurance, the net amount of risk the ceding company keeps for its own account. See Self-insured retention. [*Risk Financing* V.A.2]

retention plan—A type of dividend plan most often used only in connection with workers compensation insurance. This plan provides that the net cost to the insured is equal to a retention factor (insurance company expenses) plus actual incurred losses, subject to a maximum equal to standard premium less premium discount. Can be used for other lines of insurance. [*Risk Financing* III.B.12]

retirement annuity—A form of deferred annuity that provides for retirement income.

retirement income policy—A life insurance policy providing for income during retirement age based on a percentage of the face amount for monthly income. This type of policy will have a cash value in excess of the face amount in later policy years so as to provide high death benefits or adequate retirement income.

retraction provisions—Clauses contained in media professional liability policies state that if an insured is sued (or threatened with suit) as a result of information that has been published but is untrue or incorrect, the insured is required to publish a timely retraction of these misstatements. [*Professional Liability Insurance* XVIII.E.18]

retroactive conversion—The conversion of term life insurance into whole life insurance at the original age rather than attained age.

retroactive date—A provision found in many claims-made policies that eliminates coverage for injuries or damage that occurred prior to a specified date even if the claim is first made during the policy period. [*Commercial Liability Insurance* II.C.5]

retroactive insurance—Insurance purchased to cover a loss after it has occurred. For example, such insurance may cover incurred but not reported (IBNR) claims for companies that were once self-insured.

retrocedent—The ceding reinsurer in a retrocession. [*Risk Financing* V.A.2]

retrocession—A transaction in which a reinsurer transfers risks it has reinsured to another reinsurer. [*Risk Financing* V.A.2]

retrocessionaire—A reinsurer of a reinsurer. [*Risk Financing* V.A.2]

retrospective aggregate contract—A type of finite risk contract applying to losses that have already occurred at the inception of the contract. Such contracts insure against the possibility that the ultimate magnitude of such loses is higher than expected and/or they are paid out more quickly than anticipated. [*Risk Financing* V.D.4]

retrospective rating—A rating plan that adjusts the premium, subject to a certain minimum and maximum, to reflect the current loss experience of the insured. Retrospective rating combines actual losses with graded expenses to produce a premium which more accurately reflects the current experience of the insured. Adjustments are performed periodically, after the policy has expired. [*Risk Financing* III.D.1]

return of premium (or cash value)—A form of life insurance that provides for the return of premium as well as payment of the face upon death of the insured. This is usually accomplished with increasing term insurance.

return premium—The amount due the insured if the actual cost of a policy is less than what the insured has previously paid, e.g., if the limits are reduced, the estimated exposure at inception is greater than the audited exposure, or the policy is canceled.

return-to-work program—A post-injury program that returns injured employees to some type of work as soon as medically possible. Even if the injured workers are impaired, temporary or modified duties can be assigned that take into consideration the impairments. The end result is the reduction of indemnity costs associated with the claims. [*IRMI's Workers Comp* XVI.E.1]

reverse flow business—See International reverse business.

reversionary—A contract providing benefits only if the beneficiary is living at the time of death of the insured.

RICO—See Racketeer Influenced and Corrupt Organizations Act of 1970.

rider—An attachment to a policy that adds some extra benefit, right, or feature to the policy. Sometimes used synonymously with the term "endorsement," riders generally do not change the existing policy provisions, whereas endorsements generally do. Because they tend to add extra value to the policy, most riders are premium-bearing.

RIMS—See Risk and Insurance Management Society.

risk—(1) Uncertainty arising from the possible occurrence of given events.

(2) The insured or the property to which an insurance policy relates.

Risk and Insurance Management Society (RIMS)—An industry association of risk managers that publishes several periodicals, lobbies, sponsors seminars, and conducts an annual conference.

risk assumption—See Risk retention.

risk-based capital (RBC) requirements—A set of formulas developed by the National Association of Insurance Commissioners (NAIC) that calculate the amount of capital an insurer should hold as a function of the types of risks it has assumed. The individual components of the formula are designed to assess an insurer's risk exposure in four areas: asset risk, underwriting risk, credit risk, and off-balance-sheet risk. Insurers whose capital falls below prespecified percentages of its RBC requirement will have various types of actions taken against it, depending on the degree of undercapitalization. [*Risk Financing* X.A.21]

risk control—A synonym for loss control. The technique of minimizing the frequency or severity of losses with training, safety, and security measures.

risk financing—Achievement of the least-cost coverage of an organization's loss exposures, while assuring post-loss financial resource availability. The risk financing process consists of 5 steps: identifying and analyzing exposures, analyzing alternative risk financing techniques, selecting the best risk financing technique(s), implementing the selected technique(s), and monitoring the selected technique(s). Risk financing programs can involve insurance rating plans, such as retrospective rating, self-insurance programs, or captive insurers. [*Risk Financing* I.A.2]

risk management—The practice of identifying and analyzing loss exposures other than business risks (i.e., possible loss by fortuitous or accidental means) and taking steps to minimize the financial impact of those risks. See Risk management process.

risk management information system (RMIS)—A very flexible computerized management information system that allows the manipulation of claims, loss control, and other data to assist in risk management decision making.

risk management process—A system for treating pure risk: identification and analysis of exposures, selection of appropriate risk management techniques to handle exposures, implementation of chosen techniques, and monitoring of the results.

risk management techniques—Methods for treating pure risks. Includes retention, contractual or non-insurance transfer, loss control, avoidance, and insurance transfer.

risk purchasing group—A group formed in compliance with the Risk Retention Act of 1986 authorizing a group of insureds engaged in similar businesses or activities to purchase insurance coverage from a commercial insurer. This is in contrast to a risk retention group, which actually bears the group's risks rather than obtaining coverage on behalf of group members. [*Risk Financing* **IV.M.13**]

risk quantification—Forecasting of loss frequency and severity in order to make risk financing decisions. Dependable estimates of the likelihood and dollar amount of loss-causing events allow an organization to take appropriate steps now and in the future to minimize their financial impact. [*Risk Financing* **II.A.1**]

risk retention—Planned acceptance of losses by deductibles, deliberate noninsurance, and loss-sensitive plans where some, but not all, risk is consciously retained rather than transferred.

Risk Retention Act—Federal legislation passed in 1986 that authorized the formation of purchasing groups and group self-insurance programs for certain types of liability exposures. According to the Act, members of risk purchasing and risk retention groups must be engaged in similar or related businesses or activities. [*Risk Financing* **IV.M.2**]

risk retention group—A group self-insurance plan or group captive insurer operating under the auspices of the Risk Retention Act of 1986 retention group can cover all the liability exposures, other than workers compensation exposures, of its owners. They are not subject to the individual state laws that would otherwise prohibit the formation of group captives or make it difficult to form or operate them. [*Risk Financing* **IV.M.5**]

RMIS—See Risk management information system.

robbery—Theft during which force is used or threatened.

robbery and safe burglary coverage, money and securities form Q—Insurance Services Office, Inc., crime form (CR 00 18) that insures against the loss of money and securities by robbery or safe burglary. Prior to October 1990, the robbery and safe burglary form (form D) was endorsed to provide this coverage. A separate coverage part is now available. [*Commercial Property Insurance* **XII.D.26**]

robbery and safe burglary coverage, other than money and securities form D—Insurance Services Office, Inc., crime form (CR 00 05) that insures against the loss of property, other than money and securities, by robbery or safe burglary. [*Commercial Property Insurance* **XII.D.17**]

Rule 11 sanctions—Sanctions (court-ordered fines) imposed for abuse of process. The attempt to prevent frivolous, unfounded lawsuits.

running down clause—An ocean marine hull policy clause adding legal liability coverage for damage done to another ship or its cargo resulting from a collision with and caused by the insured vessel.

run off—A provision in a reinsurance contract stating that the reinsurer remains liable for losses under reinsured policies in force on the termination date, that result from occurrences taking place after the termination date.

S

safe burglary insurance—Coverage for loss of property caused by forcible entry into a safe or vault or by theft of the entire safe. Coverage for property other than money and securities is available under an Insurance Services Office, Inc. (ISO), coverage form D (robbery and safe burglary—property other than money and securities, CR 00 05) [*Commercial Property Insurance* XII.D.17]; coverage for money and securities is available under an ISO coverage form Q (robbery and safe burglary—money and securities, CR 00 18). [*Commercial Property Insurance* XII.D.26]

safe deposit box coverage—See Safe depository coverage.

safe depository coverage—Commercial crime coverage plan 8 of the Insurance Services Office, Inc., portfolio. Provides coverage for any loss to property located in any safe or box leased to a customer of the insured, other than a financial institution, within the safe deposit vaults located within any of the insured's offices. There are two optional coverage forms. Coverage form M (CR 00 14) [*Commercial Property Insurance* XII.D.24] applies only to the extent the insured is legally liable. Coverage form N (CR 00 15) [*Commercial Property Insurance* XII.D.24] covers loss of customers' property regardless of liability. Financial institutions can obtain this coverage through the combined safe depository policy promulgated by the Surety Association of America (Form CSD–1). [*Commercial Property Insurance* XII.L.6]

sale bond—A real estate transaction bond used as a guaranty when a fiduciary makes a sale.

salesmen's samples coverage—Inland marine insurance covering samples carried by salespersons. [*Commercial Property Insurance* V.F.23]

saline substances contamination endorsement—An Insurance Services Office, Inc. (ISO), general liability endorsement (CG 22 47) excluding coverage for liability associated with saline substances used in oil and gas drilling operations. The term "saline substances" refers to drilling "mud" or fluid and saltwater pumped into a well to stimulate oil recovery.

salvage—(1) Property after it has been partially damaged by an insured peril such as a fire.

(2) As a verb, to save endangered property and to protect damaged property from further loss.

schedule bond—A fidelity bond in which covered persons (usually employees) are listed by name, with a corresponding coverage limit for each individual listed.

scheduled limits—Separate property insurance limits applicable to each type of covered property interest (building, personal property, business interruption, etc.) at each covered location. Contrasts with blanket limits that apply over more than one covered property interest or more than one location or both. Also called "specific limits." [*Commercial Property Insurance* II.D.16]

Schedule P reserve—A liability loss reserve relating to the business written by a property-casualty insurer that must be shown on Schedule P of the convention blanks required by the National Association of Insurance Commissioners (NAIC). The purpose of the reserve is to allow for an evaluation of the financial strength of the insurer over a period of time as losses develop relative to earned premium.

schedule rating—Modification of manual rates either upward (debits) or downward (credits) to reflect the individual risk characteristics of the subject of insurance. [*Risk Financing* III.A.4]

school board liability—A type of directors and officers liability policy that protects school board members and, if so arranged, employees, against claims alleging errors and omissions in the performing their duties. It is also known as school leaders errors and omissions coverage. [*Professional Liability Insurance* XI.T.1]

seasonal risk—A business that operates during only part of the year (such as a ski resort) or experiences seasonal peaks production or income (such as a toy manufacturer). [*Commercial Property Insurance* IV.D.13 and VI.I.3]

secondary beneficiary—The person named to receive benefits if the primary beneficiary is not alive upon the death of the insured or if the primary beneficiary does not collect all benefits before his or her own death.

secondary classification—special industry class—In commercial auto insurance rating, the classification based on the specific industry for which the vehicle is being used. The secondary classification is a tool for gathering statistical data for assessment of factors other than the primary classification factors of size of vehicle, radius of operations, and business use. [*Commercial Auto Insurance* III.G.12]

second surplus reinsurance—A reinsurance treaty that is supplementary to a first surplus treaty. It is the amount that exceeds the total of the reinsured's original insurer's net retention plus the full limit of the first surplus treaty.

securities deposited with others coverage form J—Insurance Services Office, Inc., crime form (CR 00 11) that insures against theft, disappearance, or destruction of securities deposited with stockbrokers, financial institutions, or others. [*Commercial Property Insurance* XII.D.22]

securities insuring agreement—A provision of the SAA Financial Institution Bond No. 24 that provides coverage to banks and other financial institutions for loss resulting from alteration or forgery of a signature on specified types of securities (such as typically accepted as collateral for loans), from counterfeit securities of specified types, and from guaranteeing or witnessing signature of certain types of securities and financial documents. This coverage may be removed from the bond by rider. [*Commercial Property Insurance* XII.L.8]

securities valuation reserve—A reserve required of life insurers to reduce the risks associated with market declines in the values of investments. The reserve is built through annual accruals out of income.

selection—The process of determining whether or not to insure a particular entity. Selection is usually done by an underwriter.

self-insurance—A system whereby a firm sets aside an amount of its monies to provide for any losses that occur—losses that could ordinarily be covered under an insurance program. The monies that would normally be used for premium payments are added to this special fund for payment of losses incurred. Self-insurance is a means of capturing the cash flow benefits of unpaid loss reserves and also offers the possibility of reducing expenses typically incorporated within a premium under a traditional insurance program. It involves a formal decision to retain risk rather than insure it and is distinguished from noninsurance or retention of risks through deductibles, by a formalized plan or system to pay losses as they occur. [*Risk Financing* IV.E.1]

self-insured retention (SIR)—A dollar amount specified in an insurance policy (usually a liability insurance policy) that must be paid by the insured before the insurance policy will respond to a loss. SIRs typically apply to both the amount of the loss and related costs, e.g., defense costs, but some apply only to amounts payable in damages, e.g., settlements, awards, and judgments. An SIR differs from a true deductible in at least two important ways. Most importantly, a liability policy's limit stacks on top of an SIR while the amount of a liability insurance deductible is subtracted from the policy's limit. As contrasted with its responsibility under a deductible, the insurer is not obligated to pay the SIR amount and then seek reimbursement from the insured; the insured pays the SIR directly to the claimant. While these are the theoretical differences between SIRs and deductibles, they are not well understood, and the actual policy provisions should be reviewed to ascertain the actual operation of specific provisions. [*Professional Liability Insurance* VII.C.4]

self rating—Prospective or retrospective rating whereby the rate depends on the experience of the insured. The term implies that the insured's exposure and loss experience is of a large enough size and time period so as to be statistically credible.

selling price clause or endorsement—A property insurance provision or endorsement valuing finished goods at their selling price, rather than their actual cash value or replacement cost, so as to cover the profit portion of the price in addition to the replacement cost. [*Commercial Property Insurance* V.K.18]

separate account—A fund held by a life insurance company that is maintained separately from the insurer's general assets. It is generally used for investing pension assets or variable annuity holdings in common stocks. In the event of insolvency of the insurer, separate accounts may be protected from claims by creditors and other insureds.

servicing contractors rider—An endorsement to the financial institution bond that extends coverage for fraud losses perpetrated by an outside contractor retained to service real property mortgages. [*Commercial Property Insurance* XII.O.3]

settlement lag—This denotes the span of time between the first report of a claim and the date of its ultimate settlement.

settlement options—In life insurance, how proceeds are paid to the designated beneficiaries. Most life insurance policies provide for payment in a lump sum. The four most common alternative settlement approaches are: the interest option, under which the insurer holds the proceeds and pays interest to the beneficiary until such time as the beneficiary withdraws the principal; the fixed period option, under which the future value of the proceeds is calculated and paid in installments for a specified number of years; the fixed amount option, under which a fixed dollar amount is paid in periodic installments until such time as the principal and interest are exhausted; and the life income option, under which a stipulated amount is paid periodically to the beneficiary throughout his or her life.

severability of interests clause—A policy provision clarifying that, except with respect to the coverage limits, insurance applies to each insured as though a separate policy were issued to each. Thus, a policy containing such a clause will cover a claim made by one insured against another insured. [*Commercial Liability Insurance* V.J.16 and *Contractual Risk Transfer* XIV.B.6]

several liability—Liability that may be assigned or apportioned separately to each of a number of liable parties. Distinguishable from, but often paired with, joint liability.

severity—The amount of damage that is (or that may be) inflicted by a loss or catastrophe. Sometimes quantified as a severity rate, which is a ratio relating the amount of loss to values exposed to loss during a specified period of time.

share reinsurance—See Pro rata reinsurance.

short-term cancellation—Refers to the cancellation of an insurance policy prior to the expiration date. Short rate cancellation generally results in a penalty in the form of a less than a full pro-rata premium refund. [*Risk Financing* Appendix F.23]

sidetrack agreement—See Railroad sidetrack agreement.

single interest insurance—Property insurance protecting the interest of only one of the parties having an insurable interest in the property. Usually refers to insurance protecting a mortgagee or other lending institution but not the owner-borrower. See also Vendors single interest insurance.

single premium insurance—An insurance policy or annuity bought with one premium with no further premiums due during the term of the contract.

SIR—See Self-insured retention.

sistership liability exclusion—A general liability exclusion applicable to damages claimed for the withdrawal, inspection, repair, replacement, or loss of use of the named insured's product or work completed by or for the named insured or of any property of which such products or work form a part. Commonly referred to as a "product recall" exclusion. [*Commercial Liability Insurance* V.D.43]

size class—In commercial automobile insurance, the type and weight of the automobile, i.e., gross vehicle weight (GVW) for trucks, gross combined weight (GCW) for trucks-tractors, and load capacity for trailers. Automobiles are classified by vehicle size, with higher rates applying to larger vehicles. [*Commercial Auto Insurance* III.G.7]

sliding scale—(1) A type of dividend plan used with workers compensation insurance under which the amount of the dividend is a function of the insured's loss experience. The lower the insured's losses, the higher the dividend. [*IRMI's Workers Comp* XI.M.1 and *Risk Financing* III.B.2]

(2) A predetermined formula under which the commission payable by a reinsurer to the ceding company varies inversely with the actual loss experience.

sliding scale dividend—A rating plan that pays a dividend to the insured on a loss-sensitive basis. Dividends are not guaranteed and are paid based on the ratio the final audited premium bears to the total incurred losses of the insured for the specific policy period. Since losses stay open for several years after policy expiration, periodic dividend adjustments are made after the initial reconciliation. [*IRMI's Workers Comp* XI.M.1 and *Risk Financing* III.B.2]

slip—The piece of paper containing all the pertinent information regarding the risk and the insurance terms and conditions that is submitted by the broker to the underwriter at Lloyd's of London. Should the underwriter decide to participate on the risk, the percentage and pricing is recorded in addition to the underwriter's signature. The process is then repeated until the slip is completely filled. The slip forms the basis for the insurance coverage contract and in the event of a difference in wording between the slip and the policy issued from it, the slip supersedes the policy as the binding insurance document.

small quantity generator—An enterprise that produces 220–2,200 pounds per month of hazardous waste; such operations are required to keep more records than conditionally exempt generators. The largest category of hazardous waste generators, small quantity generators (SQGs) include automotive shops, dry cleaners, photographic developers, and a host of other small businesses.

soft costs coverage—Time element coverage for property under construction, also commonly referred to as delayed opening coverage. Covers income loss or specified additional expenses resulting from delay in project completion when the delay is caused by damage to the project from an insured peril. [*Commercial Property Insurance* IX.J.20]

solicitor—A representative of an agent appointed and authorized by that agent to solicit and receive applications for insurance.

source revelation provisions—A provision in media liability policies indicating that in the event of a claim against the insured, the insured is not compelled to reveal to the insurer defending the claim, the source of the material that is the subject of a claim. [*Professional Liability Insurance* XVIII.E.19]

special acceptance—An agreement by a reinsurer to include under a reinsurance contract, coverage for a risk that was not automatically included under the terms of the contract.

special causes of loss form (ISO)—One of the four Insurance Services Office, Inc. (ISO), causes of loss forms; an ISO commercial property policy must include one or more causes of loss forms. This form (CP 10 30) provides what is commonly referred to as "all risks" coverage: coverage for loss from all causes not specifically excluded. See Causes of loss forms. [*Commercial Property Insurance* VI.G.5 and *Contractual Risk Transfer* XIV.P.3]

special damages—Objectively assessed monies awarded to an injured party for tangible losses, such as wage loss, loss of use, nursing care, and medical expenses.

special risk—A term used to denote those accounts whose premium size, unique exposures, or other characteristics are such that require specialized handling by an underwriting operation specifically set up for that purpose. What constitutes a "special risk" varies by insurer.

special waiver—Operations conducted under a special permit or waiver required by the Federal Aviation Administration (FAA). These could include maintenance flights and ferry flights of damaged aircraft or the carrying of hazardous materials. Some aircraft policies exclude flights conducted under this waiver.

specific excess insurance—Provides coverage once claims arising out of a single occurrence exceed the retention specified in the policy declarations.

specific rating—An Insurance Services Office, Inc. (ISO), property insurance rating method based on rates applicable only to individual properties, determined by physical inspection of the property. [*Commercial Property Insurance* IV.F.22]

specified causes of loss coverage—An auto physical damage coverage that is an alternative to comprehensive coverage. The coverage applies only for losses caused by the perils listed, as compared to the "all-risk" nature of comprehensive coverage. [*Commercial Auto Insurance* VIII.E.3]

specified perils coverage—An obsolete auto physical damage term; see Specified cause of loss coverage.

speculative risk—Uncertainty about an event under consideration that could produce either a profit or a loss, such as a business venture or a gambling transaction. A pure risk is insurable while speculative risk is not.

split dollar plans—A form of life insurance co-ownership that allows one party, often the employer, to help another person carry life insurance protection. Generally the insured pays the portion of the premium attributable to the life insurance protection while the other party pays the portion attributable to the cash value build-up. At the insured's death, an amount of the proceeds equal to the cash value is paid to the other party with the remaining amount paid to the insured's beneficiaries. This approach provides protection in a permanent life insurance contract at a very low cost to the insured.

spread loss reinsurance—A form of excess of loss property reinsurance under which there is a periodic adjustment of the reinsurance premium rate given the reinsured's loss experience for the previous years (typically 5), plus a loading for the reinsurer's expenses, catastrophe losses, and profit.

spread of risk—Consideration of the number of independent exposures to loss in a given time period. As the number of units exposed independently to loss increases, the spread of risk expands and the likelihood that all units will suffer loss diminishes. Predictive ability increases as the spread of risk increases. This is often called the "law of large numbers."

sprinkler leakage coverage—Coverage for property damage caused by the accidental discharge or leakage of water or other substances from automatic sprinkler systems. This coverage is included in most property insurance policies. [*Commercial Property Insurance* V.Q.6]

staff model HMO—Provides medical care to subscribers on an exclusive basis in a centralized medical operation. Medical services that cannot be provided internally are referred to outside providers with the HMO picking up the costs. Physicians on staff of the HMO are compensated through a salary and bonus plan. [*IRMI's Workers Comp* XV.F.3]

stamp duty—A form of premium tax in overseas insurance.

standard exceptions—Certain classes of employees in workers compensation insurance who are common to many types of business and are separately rated unless included specifically in the wording of the governing occupational classification. Some of these exceptions include clerical employees, drivers, and salespersons.

standard policy—A policy whose provisions are identical in all jurisdictions, regardless of the insurer issuing the policy.

standard premium—The premium developed by multiplying the appropriate rate by the proper exposure unit. This figure is then modified by experience rating, if applicable. If the risk is not subject to experience rating, the premium at manual rate is the standard premium. [*Risk Financing* III.F.2]

standard property policy (ISO)—A restrictive Insurance Services Office, Inc. (ISO), commercial property policy (CP 00 99) intended for use when, for underwriting reasons, coverage would otherwise be unavailable. Combines in one form many of the provisions of the common policy conditions, commercial property conditions, building and personal property coverage, and basic causes of loss forms. However, there are significant coverage restrictions in the following areas: covered causes of loss, cancellation, vacancy, coverage territory, and coverage options. [*Commercial Property Insurance* VI.C.42]

State Emergency Response Commission (SERC)—Commission appointed by each state governor according to the requirements of Superfund Amendments and Reauthorization Act of 1986 (SARA) Title III. The SERCs designate emergency planning districts, appoint local emergency planning committees, and supervise and coordinate their activities.

state funds—State-owned and operated organizations that write workers compensation insurance. Some states have monopolistic funds, which are the only market for workers compensation insurance in those states. Other states have competitive funds that compete with insurers in that state only. The monopolistic fund states are: Nevada, North Dakota, Ohio, Washington, West Virginia, and Wyoming. Puerto Rico and the U.S.

Virgin Islands also have monopolistic funds. Currently, 19 other states offer the option of purchasing workers compensation insurance from a competitive state fund. [*IRMI's Workers Comp* **V.B.1**]

State Implementation Plans (SIP)—Environmental Protection Agency-approved state plans for the establishment, regulation, and enforcement of air pollution standards.

statute of limitations—A law prescribing the period within which certain types of causes of action must be brought. This time period usually begins to run when the injury or damage occurs or is discovered. The statute may run from 1 to 6 years. In the case of a minor, the statute begins to run from the date he or she reaches legal age. See Statute of repose.

statute of repose—A law that cuts off a right of action after a specified period of time has elapsed, regardless of when the cause of action accrues. For example, such a statute might dictate that a manufacturer cannot be held liable for injury caused by a product that was sold more than 12 years in the past. Relatively few states have these statutes, and those that do typically provide for exceptions in extenuating circumstances. This is different from a statute of limitation in that the time periods specified in statutes of limitations usually do not begin to run until the injury actually occurs, irrespective of when the product was sold.

statutory accounting—The rules of accounting prescribed by state law for use by insurance companies. These rules focus on the balance sheet and solvency analysis, and differ from the generally accepted accounting principals (GAAP) used for other types of businesses. For example, statutory accounting rules do not allow the inclusion of certain nonadmitted assets on the balance sheet; require that certain loss reserves be set by conservative formulas instead of the insurer's estimates; require the insurer to immediately recognize the expenses associated with writing new business instead of amortizing them over the policy period; and do not allow premiums for reinsurance placed with unauthorized reinsurers to be recognized as an asset.

stay of proceedings—A temporary suspension by direction of the court, generally related to an appellate or procedural issue.

stipulation—An informal "agreement" reached between the parties.

stock company—An insurance company that has, in addition to surplus and reserve funds, a capital fund paid in by stockholders, as distinguished from mutual or cooperative companies which have no stockholders. Shares of stock companies are usually traded on one of the organized stock exchanges.

stop gap endorsement—An endorsement that provides employers liability coverage for work-related injuries arising out of incidental operations or exposure in monopolistic fund states (fund workers compensation policies do not provide employers liability coverage). If the employer has operations in nonmonopolistic states, the endorsement is attached to the workers compensation policy providing coverage in those states. For employers operating exclusively in a monopolistic fund state, the endorsement is attached to the employer's general liability policy. Also see State funds. [*IRMI's Workers Comp* **VI.L.5** and *Commercial Liability Insurance* **VII.C.7**]

stop loss—A form of reinsurance also known as "aggregate excess of loss reinsurance" under which a reinsurer is liable for all losses, regardless of size, that occur after a specified loss ratio or total dollar amount of losses has been reached. [*Risk Financing* **V.A.13**]

storekeepers broad form—Commercial crime coverage plan 3 of the Insurance Services Office, Inc., portfolio. The following coverage forms are mandatory for the plan: employee dishonesty (A) (CR 00 01 and CR 00 02) [*Commercial Property Insurance* **XII.D.6**]; forgery (B) (CR 00 03) [*Commercial Property Insurance* **XII.D.14**]; theft, disappearance, and destruction of money and securities (C) (CR 00 04) [*Commercial Property Insurance* **XII.D.15**]; robbery and safe burglary—other than money and securities (D) (CR 00 05) [*Commercial Property Insurance* **XII.D.17**]; and premises burglary (E) (CR 00 06) [*Commercial Property Insurance* **XII.D.18**].

storekeepers burglary and robbery policy—The Insurance Services Office, Inc. (ISO), commercial crime coverage plan No. 4, composed of coverage form D, robbery and safe burglary—property other than money and securities (CR 00 05) [*Commercial Property Insurance* **XII.D.17**]; and coverage form E, premises burglary (CR 00 06)

[*Commercial Property Insurance* **XII.D.18**]. Covers loss of property other than money and securities by robbery and burglary.

straight life policy—An ordinary life policy or whole life policy.

strict liability—A legal doctrine under which liability is imposed with respect to injury or damage arising from certain types of hazardous activities. For example, under strict liability standards, the manufacturer or distributor of a defective product is liable to a person who is injured by the product, regardless of the degree of care exercised by the manufacturer or distributor in the production or sale of the product.

strike coverage—Specialty business interruption insurance covering loss resulting from interrupted operations caused by a labor strike.

strikes, riots, and civil commotions (SR&CC) warranty—An ocean marine coverage provision that excludes damage from strikes, riots, civil commotions, lockouts, vandalism, and sabotage, including terrorist acts and any other acts carried out for political or ideological purposes. Coverage can be added back with an SR&CC endorsement.

strike through clause—A reinsurance contract provision requiring a reinsurer to pay its share of a loss directly to the insured, in the event that the ceding insurer becomes insolvent.

structured settlement—A settlement under which the plaintiff agrees to accept a stream of payments in lieu of a lump sum. Structured settlements can be tailored to the individual's need to provide for inflation, anticipated future medical expenses, education costs for children, etc. Annuities are usually used as funding mechanisms.

subbroker—A second intermediary from whom a first reinsurance intermediary obtains reinsurance business to be placed.

subject premium—(1) In conjunction with retrospective rating, the portion of the premium applied to the retro formula.

(2) In reinsurance, the reinsurance rate is applied to the subject premium to produce the reinsurance premium. Subject premium is also known as the "base premium" or "underlying premium."

submission—A proposal for insurance submitted to an underwriter, the term implies more than simply a completed application unless the application contains all the information needed by the underwriter.

subpoena—A command to appear at a certain time and place to give testimony.

subpoena duces tecum—A form of subpoena requiring not only the appearance of the subpoenaed party but also the production of books, papers, and other items.

subrogation—The assignment to an insurer by terms of the policy or by law, after payment of a loss, of the rights of the insured to recover the amount of the loss from one legally liable for it. [*Contractual Risk Transfer* **V.C.1**]

subrogation release—A release taken by the insurer upon paying the insured a claim that enables the insurer to subrogate against the negligent third party.

subrogation waiver—An agreement between two parties in which one party agrees to waive subrogation rights against another in the event of a loss. Generally, insurance policies do not bar coverage if an insured waives subrogation against a third party before a loss. However, coverage is excluded from many policies if subrogation is waived after a loss because to do so would violate the principle of indemnity. [*Contractual Risk Transfer* **V.B.1**]

substandard—Less than standard. For example, substandard auto insurance is insurance written for drivers with poor driving records. For obvious reasons, substandard insurance premiums are typically higher and coverage terms more restrictive than insurance written on standard risks.

substitute physician coverage endorsement—An endorsement sometimes attached to physicians professional liability insurance policies, providing coverage for a substitute physician—who treats the insured physician's patients—in the insured's absence. While there is no generally accepted time period in which they apply, substitute physician endorsements are usually written only for periods of prolonged physician absence. [*Professional Liability Insurance* **XVI.I.5**]

sue and labor clause—A property and marine insurance provision (originating in ocean marine insurance) requiring the insured to protect damaged property from further loss once a loss has occurred. Current standard property forms call this provision "preservation of property," but ocean and inland marine policies still use the title "sue and labor." [*Commercial Property Insurance V.F.34*]

summary judgment—A court judgment based on the judge's conclusion that the litigation involves only a question of law, with no associated questions of fact. Disputes as to the meaning of insurance policy provisions, when they involve only the interpretation of the policy itself and not the determination the circumstances of the loss, are often the subject of a summary judgment.

summons—Instrument used to commence a civil action or special proceeding and is a means of acquiring jurisdiction over a party. Process directed to a sheriff or other officer, requiring the sheriff to notify a person named that an action has been commenced against him or her. A general liability insured is required by the standard commercial general liability policy to provide the insurer immediately with copies of any summons received in connection with a claim or suit. [*Commercial Liability Insurance V.J.5*]

Superfund—The program operated under the legislative authority of Comprehensive Environmental Response Compensation and Liability Act (CERCLA) and Superfund Amendments and Reauthorization Act of 1986 (SARA) that funds and carries out Environmental Protection Agency (EPA) solid waste emergency and long-term removal and remedial activities. These activities include establishing the National Priorities List, investigating sites for inclusion on the list, determining their priority, and conducting and/or supervising the cleanup and other remedial actions.

Superintendent of Insurance—See Commissioner.

superseded surety rider—A provision or endorsement on a bond under which the surety company assumes liability for claims that cannot be recovered from a prior bond because of the lapse of the discovery period.

supervision coverage—For construction management risks, coverage for supervision may be purchased from underwriters for an additional premium. Purchasing supervision coverage avoids the exclusion in design/build professional liability policies for liability arising from "services rendered in connection with the approval, reviewing, supervising, surveying, or the failure to review, inspect, supervise, or survey any construction or demolition operation or procedure" contained in a few policies. It is possible, however, to amend the exclusion in some instances.

supplemental extended reporting period—The optional extended reporting period (of unlimited duration) under the standard claims-made commercial general liability (CGL) policy. The insured must request and pay for this coverage in order to activate it. [*Commercial Liability Insurance II.C.11 and V.K.5*]

surety—A party that guarantees the performance of another. The contract through which the guarantee is executed is called a surety bond.

surety bond—A contract under which one party (the surety) guarantees the performance of certain obligations of a second party (the principal) to a third party (the obligee). For example, most construction contractors must provide the party for which they are performing operations with a bond guaranteeing that it will complete the project by the date specified in the construction contract in accordance with all plans and specifications.

surplus—The amount by which an insurer's assets exceeds its liabilities. It is the equivalent of "owners' equity" in standard accounting terms. The ratio of an insurer's premiums written to its surplus is one of the key measures of its solvency.

surplus line—Risks placed with non-admitted insurers. [*Professional Liability Insurance IV.J.1*]

surplus lines insurance—Refers to coverage lines that need not be filed with state insurance departments as a condition of being able to offer coverage. The types of risks typically insured in the surplus lines insurance markets can usually be categorized as risks with adverse loss experience, unusual risks, and those for which there is a shortage of capacity within the standard market. [*Professional Liability Insurance IV.J.1*]

surplus reinsurance—Reinsurance of amounts that exceed a ceding company's retention. In surplus reinsurance, the reinsurer contributes to the payment of losses in proportion to its share of the total limit of coverage. [*Risk Financing* **V.A.10**]

surplus relief—An insurer's purchase of reinsurance to offset unusual drains against the insurer's surplus. The use of reinsurance for surplus relief purposes is most common when an insurer begins to rapidly expand its volume of written premium. [*Risk Financing* **V.A.4**]

surplus share—A form of pro-rata reinsurance in which the primary insurer cedes only the "surplus" liability above a specified retention. [*Risk Financing* **V.A.10**]

surrender—Withdrawing full cash value and surrendering a policy to the life insurance company.

survey—An insurance inspector's or surveyor's study of a risk used for underwriting purposes.

suspension of coverage endorsement—A commercial auto coverage endorsement that suspends certain coverages for specified vehicles when the vehicles will not be used for a period of 30 days or more. [*Commercial Auto Insurance* **XIII.E.2**]

syndicate—A group of companies or underwriters who join together to insure very high valued property or high hazard liability exposures. Insurance exchanges, such as Lloyd's of London, use syndicates to write insurance. See Lloyd's of London.

T

tail coverage—Another term for an extended reporting period under a claims-made liability policy. [*Commercial Liability Insurance* **II.C.7**]

target risk—In property reinsurance, a list of bridges, tunnels, fine arts collections, and property of similarly high value that is excluded from coverage under reinsurance treaties. Such risks require individual acceptance under facultative contracts.

tariff—In international insurance, refers to rates and coverages set and published by the rating bureau having jurisdiction. The rating bureau may be controlled either by an association of companies or by a foreign government.

tax factor—See Tax multiplier.

tax interruption coverage—Coverage for governmental entities that have taxing authority. Such policies cover the government's potential loss of income when the property of others subject to a property tax or sales tax, is destroyed. A specialized policy can be purchased in the excess and surplus lines market for this protection. Some public entities have also used the contingent business interruption form for this purpose.

tax multiplier—A component of a retrospective rating plan that represents the costs associated with taxes, assessments and other fees that the insurer must pay to the states on premiums written and collected. [*IRMI's Workers Comp* **XI.L.6** and *Risk Financing* **III.D.10**]

temporary partial disability—A workers compensation disability level in which the injured worker is temporarily precluded from performing a certain set of job skills but who can still work at a reduced level. Since the condition is temporary, compensation is based on the difference between the two earning levels. [*IRMI's Workers Comp* **III.C.7**]

temporary total disability—One of the four divisions of disability compensable under workers compensation. This level of disability reflects an injury that has rendered the employee completely unable to perform any job functions on a temporary basis. The employee is expected to make a full recovery and return to work. In the interim, compensation paid is usually a percentage of weekly wages until the worker returns to the job. [*IRMI's Workers Comp* **III.C.7**]

tender of defense—The act in which one party places its defense, and all costs associated with said defense, with another due to a contract or other agreement. This transfers the obligation of the defense and possible indemnification to the party the tender was made to. [*Commercial Liability Insurance* **V.G.3** and *Contractual Risk Transfer* **X.C.12**]

tender offer defense expense—Insurance that pays the expenses incurred by a publicly held company in combating a tender offer made by another company seeking to acquire it.

term life insurance—A policy that gives protection for only a definite period of time (e.g., 1, 3, or 5 years). If death occurs during the term for which the policy is written, proceeds are payable to the beneficiary. If the insured survives the term, the policy expires. There is no cash value build-up in a term policy. Guaranteed renewable term insurance can be renewed without proof of insurability. Under other types of term insurance, the insured must once again undergo an underwriting process (e.g., a medical examination).

terminal coverage—Coverage for damage to vehicles garaged or stored at a common location sometimes included in a property insurance policy or inland marine floater. This coverage is purchased by organizations that otherwise self-insure automobile physical damage exposures but desire to protect against a catastrophic loss affecting a number of vehicles garaged or stored together. [*Commercial Auto Insurance* III.H.3]

tertiary beneficiary—The third beneficiary in line to receive life insurance proceeds.

testing coverage—Coverage for the testing of newly installed machinery or equipment as well as overhauling engines. Testing coverage can usually be arranged in conjunction with builders risk insurance. [*Commercial Property Insurance* IX.J.8]

test modifier—An experience modifier calculated by or on behalf of the insured to estimate what the actual modifier will be when calculated by the National Council on Compensation Insurance or other rating bureau.

that particular part—A key phrase in the property damage exclusion of general liability and some umbrella coverage forms that eliminates coverage for damage to work performed by (or on behalf of) an insured contractor which arises from that work. The language precludes coverage for "that particular part of real property" on which the work is performed. The intent is to exclude the faulty work itself and yet cover resulting damage to work already in place. The phrase has been defined by the courts as "a single item of property which, though composed of many parts, is clearly a unit of property within itself, self-contained and a single item." [*Commercial Liability Insurance* V.D.32]

theft, disappearance, and destruction of money and securities coverage form C—Insurance Services Office, Inc., crime form (CR 00 04) that insures against loss by theft, disappearance, or destruction of the insured's money and securities inside the insured's premises (or insured's bank's premises) as well as outside the insured's premises while in the custody of a messenger. [*Commercial Property Insurance* XII.D.15]

thermal pollution—Discharge of heated water from industrial processes into a waterway or body of water in quantities that can harm plant or animal life in the water. One of the forms of pollution specifically addressed in the commercial general liability policy definition of "pollutant." [*Commercial Liability Insurance* V.D.23]

third-party administrator—A firm that handles various types of administrative responsibilities, on a fee-for-services basis, for organizations involved in cash flow programs. These responsibilities typically include: claims administration, loss control, risk management information systems, and risk management consulting. [*Risk Financing* VIII.G.1]

third party over action—A type of action in which an injured employee, after collecting workers compensation benefits from the employer, sues a third party for contributing to the employee's injury. Then, because of some type of contractual relationship between the third party and the employer, the liability is passed back to the employer by prior agreement. Additionally, there are instances in which the third party can circumvent the exclusive remedy doctrine of workers compensation and enjoin the employer in the action. Depending on the nature and allegations of the action, coverage may be afforded under the contractual liability section of the employer's commercial liability policy or the employers liability section of the employer's workers compensation policy. [*Contractual Risk Transfer* XI.T.1 and *IRMI's Workers Comp* VI.D.4]

30(b)6 deposition—To depose a corporate representative. Section 30(b)6 refers to that part of the Federal Rules of Procedure regarding deposing corporate executives.

threshold—The lowest dose of a chemical at which a specified measurable effect is observed and below which it is not observed.

threshold level—Time-weighted average pollutant concentration values, exposure beyond which is likely to affect human health adversely.

threshold limit value (TLV)—The concentration of an airborne substance that an average person can be repeatedly exposed to without adverse effects.

time element insurance—A property insurance term referring to coverage for loss resulting from the inability to put damaged property to its normal use. Insurance coverages in this group are so called because the amount of loss depends on how long it takes to repair or replace the damaged property. The best known types of time element insurance are business interruption and extra expense coverage. [*Commercial Property Insurance* II.E.1 and *Contractual Risk Transfer* XIV.P.7]

tontine—A pooling arrangement involving a group of people whereby dividends are paid to all individuals still living after a specified period of time has elapsed at the expense of those who have died. These arrangements are no longer legal.

tool and die floater—Inland marine coverage on metal molds and specialized tools needed to produce a customized metal part or housing. A tool and die policy may be necessary when such property is located at the premises of other manufacturers with whom the insured has contracted to supply certain custom components.

tort—A civil or private wrong giving rise to legal liability. [*Commercial Liability Insurance* V.L.15]

tortfeasor—A party accused of committing a tort; customarily, the defendant in a liability lawsuit.

total disability—As defined in a disability income policy, determines the liability of the insurer. Definitions vary from policy to policy, with some being very restrictive and some being very broad. The most broad disability income policies define this term as the inability to perform the functions of one's occupation. More restrictive policies define it to be the inability to perform the duties of any gainful occupation.

toxic tort—An action based on allegations that injuries or death were caused by contact with, use of, or ingestion of an insidious or poisonous substance, such as asbestos, PCBs, or insecticides.

trade disruption insurance—Political risk insurance that covers loss of gross earnings and extra expenses caused by a delay or nonarrival of supplies or stocks arising from foreign government actions or inaction. Such losses can arise from embargoes, expropriation, nationalization, interference with transportation, and similar actions.

trade libel—A standard peril covered under a media professional liability policy. Trade libel is also known as "product disparagement," and occurs when a product manufacturer makes untrue remarks about a competitor's product. [*Professional Liability Insurance* XVIII.C.2]

trading loss coverage—Coverage that may be added by an endorsement to a banker's blanket bond for employee dishonesty loss involving trading (usually of securities or currency).

trailer interchange insurance—A type of coverage available under either the truckers or motor carrier policy form, covers the insured's legal liability for damage to the trailers of others. Truckers frequently haul trailers that are owned by other truckers. This is often done through a "trade" of trailers that are in different locations to facilitate scheduling. A trailer interchange agreement makes the trucker who has possession of the trailer responsible for any damage to the trailer. [*Commercial Auto Insurance* X.E.1]

transfer of risk—A risk management technique whereby risk of loss is transferred to another party through a contract, e.g., a hold harmless clause, or to a professional risk bearer, i.e., an insurance company.

transit coverage—Inland marine coverage on the insured's property while in transit over land from one location to another. [*Commercial Property Insurance* IX.E.1]

transitional duties—A job assignment made to an employee returning to work while still recovering from a compensable injury. The employee can eventually return to the predisability position; however, this job fills the gap by providing work which takes into consideration the temporary physical limitations of the employee. [*IRMI's Workers Comp* XVI.E.8]

treaty—An agreement between an insurer and a reinsurer stating the types or classes of businesses that the reinsurer will accept from the insurer. [*Risk Financing* V.A.6]

treaty reinsurance—A form of reinsurance in which the ceding company makes an agreement to cede certain classes of business to a reinsurer. The reinsurer, in turn, agrees to accept all business qualifying under the agreement, known as the "treaty." Under a reinsurance treaty, the ceding company is assured that all of its risks falling within the terms of the treaty will be reinsured in accordance with treaty terms. [*Risk Financing* V.A.6]

trend factor—A factor used in the loss forecasting process that accounts for increases over time in the dollar amount of losses sustained by an organization. Trend factors are applied to convert historical loss data to current dollars. The Consumer Price Index and the U.S. Claims Cost Indexes are sometimes applied to past losses for this purpose. [*Risk Financing* III.B.3]

trespasser—One who, without authorization, goes on the private premises of another without an invitation or inducement, expressed or implied, but purely for his or her own purposes or convenience and where no mutuality of interest exists between him and the owner or occupant. Certain forms of trespass have been held covered under personal injury liability coverage. [*Commercial Liability Insurance* V.E.10]

trial court—The court that is assigned to preside over the trial, and in some instances, discovery, of a particular case.

trip transit insurance—Insurance written to cover a specific individual shipment, as distinguished from transit insurance written to cover any and all shipments that may occur during the policy term. [*Commercial Property Insurance* IX.E.10]

truckers downtime insurance—Business interruption coverage for truckers. Indemnifies for loss of earnings resulting from inability to operate because of damage to a tractor or trailer from an insured peril, e.g., collision or fire.

truckers policy—A commercial auto policy designed to address the needs of the "for-hire" motor carrier (i.e., trucking) industry. Coverages available include auto liability, trailer interchange, and auto physical damage; other coverages are available by endorsement. [*Commercial Auto Insurance* Section X]

trust agreement—An attachment to a life insurance policy stipulating that proceeds should be paid into a trust under certain conditions.

trust department errors and omissions coverage—Coverage for the liability of bank trust department personnel arising out of their acts as trustees. Examples of acts that may give rise to such liability include: improper investment of trust assets, failure of a stock transfer agent to effect the transfer in the required time limit, and permitting devaluation of trust assets.

trustee—A person appointed to manage the property of another.

twisting—The act of or attempt at inducing a policy owner to drop an existing life insurance policy and to take another policy that is substantially the same kind by using misrepresentations or incomplete comparisons of the advantages and disadvantages of the two policies. Most states have enacted legislation making twisting a crime.

U

uberrimae fidae—A Latin phrase meaning "in utmost good faith." Certain legal contracts, including insurance policies, are said to be executed in utmost good faith since they presume full disclosure of all pertinent facts on the part of both contracting parties.

ultimate net loss—A term used to specify insured damages in an umbrella liability policy. Most umbrella policies include a specific definition of the covered damages encompassed by the term. This will typically include amounts actually payable to claimants in settlement or judgment. If defense and other supplementary payments are included within the policy's limit of liability, they may also be included in the policy's ultimate net loss definition. [*Commercial Liability Insurance* **XI.B.6**]

umbrella liability policy—A policy designed to provide protection against catastrophic losses. It generally is written over various primary liability policies, such as the business auto policy, commercial general liability policy, watercraft and aircraft liability policies, and employers liability coverage. The umbrella policy serves three purposes: it provides excess limits when the limits of underlying liability policies are exhausted by the payment of claims; it drops down and picks up where the underlying policy leaves off when the aggregate limit of the underlying policy in question is exhausted by the payment of claims; and it provides protection against some claims not covered by the underlying policies, subject to the assumption, by the named insured, of a self-insured retention. [*Commercial Liability Insurance* **XI.B.1**]

unallocated benefit—A provision in health insurance policies that provides for reimbursement of miscellaneous hospital expenses without regard to a schedule but subject to a maximum.

unallocated loss expense—Salaries, overhead, and other costs related to the claim adjustment process that are not specifically allocated to the expense incurred for a particular claim. See Allocated loss adjustment expenses.

unauthorized insurer—An insurer not licensed to write business in a particular state.

unconditional settlement clause—A provision found in professional liability policies that requires the insured to approve all settlements proposed by an insurer. Under such provisions, an insured can reject an insurer's proposal and, unlike the standard "blackmail settlement clause," incurs no liability if the claim is ultimately settled or adjudicated for a larger amount. [*Professional Liability Insurance* **VII.B.18**]

underground property damage—Property damage to wires, conduits, pipes, mains, sewers, tanks, tunnels, any similar property, and any apparatus in connection beneath the surface of the ground or water caused by and occurring during the use of mechanical equipment for the purpose of

grading land, paving, excavating, drilling, burrowing, filling, backfilling, or pile driving.

underinsurance—A situation resulting from a failure to carry enough coverage on the value of a property, especially when there are coinsurance implications. [*Commercial Property Insurance* **II.D.17**]

underinsured motorist coverage—Provides coverage for bodily injury, and in some states property damage, incurred by an insured when an accident is caused by a motorist who is not sufficiently insured, e.g., when the limits of liability carried by the other motorist are lower than the uninsured motorist limits carried by the insured. [*Commercial Auto Insurance* **IV.D.1**]

underlyers—Policies occupying layers of coverage below the particular policy being referred to. For example, a general liability policy and an umbrella liability policy might be underlyers for an excess liability policy.

underlying coverage—With respect to any given policy of excess insurance, the coverage in place on the same risk that will respond to loss before the excess policy is called on to pay any portion of the claim. [*Commercial Liability Insurance* **XI.B.3**]

underwriter—Any individual in insurance who has the responsibility of making decisions regarding the acceptability of a particular submission and of determining the amount, price, and conditions under which the submission is acceptable.

underwriting agency—An agency given underwriting and policy writing authority by an insurer. This authority actually allows an agent to price and issue the physical policy to the insured. In return for this additional administrative work, the agency normally receives increased commissions from the insurer involved.

underwriting manager—The individual primarily responsible for achieving an underwriting profit at the local level. This person has operational as well as functional responsibilities. He or she is responsible for setting local underwriting policy based on various profit considerations.

underwriting member—Any person elected to Underwriting Membership of Lloyd's of London and subscribing to Lloyd's policies issued in accordance with the United Kingdom Insurance Companies' Acts and complying with the regulations for membership as laid down by the Committee of Lloyd's.

underwriting profit—The profit that an insurer derives from providing insurance or reinsurance coverage, exclusive of the income it derives from investments.

unearned premium—That portion of the policy premium that has not yet been "earned" by the company because the policy still has some time to run before expiration. A property or casualty insurer must carry all unearned premiums as a liability in its financial statement since, if the policy should be canceled, the insurer would have to pay back a certain part of the original premium.

unearned premium reserve—An insurer's liability for its unearned premium as of any given valuation date. This is typically the largest liability of an insurer.

unearned reinsurance premium—The portion of a reinsurer's premium that applies to the unexpired portion of the policies it has reinsured.

unilateral contract—A contract in which only one party makes an enforceable promise. Most insurance policies are unilateral contracts in that only the insurer makes a legally enforceable promise to pay covered claims. By contrast, the insured makes few, if any, enforceable promises to the insurer. Instead, the insured must only fulfill certain conditions—such as paying premiums and reporting accidents—in order to keep the policy in force.

uninsured motorist coverage—Provides coverage for bodily injury, and in some states property damage, caused by a motorist that is not insured. Uninsured motorists coverage allows an insured to collect from his or her own insurer as if it covered the negligent third party. [*Commercial Auto Insurance* IV.D.1]

unit statistical card—Also known as a "stat card," the instrument that provides the National Council on Compensation Insurance with necessary payroll and loss information to establish experience modifications. The payrolls reported on the unit cards are final audited payrolls by classification for each policy period. Also included are rates, premium, and experience modification used for

that policy period, and premium discount applied. [*Risk Financing* III.A.14]

universal life insurance—A very flexible life insurance product that pays much higher interest than conventional whole life and allows the insured to adjust the premium and death benefits.

unreported claims—Incurred but not reported claims.

unseaworthiness—The concept is based on general maritime law that warrants the vessel is reasonably fit for the intended use at sea. When the warranty is breached and the ship is shown to be unseaworthy, a no-fault liability is imposed on the shipowner or charterer to make restitution for the injury or death of the individual. [*IRMI's Workers Comp* VII.C.5]

upset coverage—Coverage for damage to a crane caused by its upset. Usually provided under an endorsement to an equipment floater. The endorsement usually specifies that if the weight carried by the crane at the time of upset exceeded the maximum rated load for the equipment, coverage will not apply.

use and occupancy insurance—Obsolete boiler and machinery insurance term for boiler and machinery business interruption coverage. [*Commercial Property Insurance* XI.H.1]

U.S. Longshore and Harbor Workers Compensation Act—See Longshore and Harbor Workers Compensation Act.

utility service interruption coverage—Coverage for loss due to lack of incoming electricity caused by damage from a covered cause (such as a fire or windstorm) to property away from the insured's premises—usually the utility generating station. Also referred to as "off-premises power coverage." Not provided in a standard property insurance policy but available by endorsement. Utility service interruption coverage endorsements vary widely as to what utility services are included, whether both direct damage and time element loss are covered, and whether transmission lines are covered. [*Commercial Property Insurance* II.D.14]

utilization review—A technique for controlling medical expenses by reviewing utilization patterns reflected in claims information. Types of, quantities of, and charges for medical services are evaluated to identify problem areas responsible for increasing costs. Specific diagnoses, procedures, service providers, and claimant groups responsible for increasing costs are identified.

V

vacancy permit endorsement—A property insurance endorsement that suspends some or all of the coverage restrictions that apply to buildings that have been vacant for more than a specified period of time (typically, 60 days). [*Commercial Property Insurance* VI.F.13]

vacancy provision—Property insurance policy provision found in most commercial property policies that severely restrict coverage in connection with buildings that have been vacant for a specified number of days (typically, 60 days). Some forms also restrict coverage in connection with buildings that have been unoccupied for a specified number of days. See Vacancy permit endorsement. [*Commercial Property Insurance* VII.C.22]

valuable papers and records coverage—Inland marine coverage that pays the cost to reconstruct damaged or destroyed valuable papers and records. "Valuable papers and records" usually is defined to include almost all forms of printed documents or records except money or securities; data processing programs, data, and media are usually excluded. [*Commercial Property Insurance* IX.G.1]

valuation—A provision in a property or inland marine policy that specifies the basis of indemnification when property is destroyed. An actual cash value valuation clause stipulates that the insurer will deduct depreciation from the cost to replace the property, whereas a replacement cost valuation clause stipulates that there will be no deduction for depreciation. [*Commercial Property Insurance* II.D.15 and *Contractual Risk Transfer* XIV.P.1]

valuation date—The cut-off date for adjustments made to paid claims and reserve estimates in a loss report. For example, a workers compensation loss report for the 1996 policy year that has a 1998 valuation date, includes all claim payments and changes in loss reserves made prior to the 1998 valuation date.

value reporting form—See Reporting form coverage.

valued business interruption coverage—Business interruption coverage that provides for the payment of a stipulated amount for each day of fully interrupted operations, rather than for payment of the amount of loss actually sustained. Also referred to as "per diem business interruption coverage." [*Commercial Property Insurance* II.E.2] Valued business interruption coverage is much more common in boiler and machinery insurance than in commercial property insurance. [*Commercial Property Insurance* XI.H.2]

valued coverage—Property coverage that provides for payment of a stipulated dollar amount (rather than the actual cash value or replacement cost of the property) in the event of total loss. Fine arts coverage is often written on a valued basis. Some states have valued policy laws which require that fire insurance on buildings be treated as valued coverage in the event of a total loss. [*Commercial Property Insurance* IX.I.7]

variable annuity—An annuity that provides lifetime income payments which vary in relation to the performance of the underlying investment portfolio managed by the insurer.

variable life insurance—A policy that provides a guaranteed minimum death benefit with the potential for increased benefits, without the necessity of paying additional premium dollars. Under such policies, the insured obtains a right to have the net investment return, in excess of the assumed rate of return, applied to increase his or her policy benefits.

vendor's coverage—Additional insured coverage, usually under a manufacturer's general liability policy, for specified vendors with respect to their distribution or sale of the manufacturer's products designated in the schedule on the endorsement. This endorsement gives products liability coverage to the vendors distributing or selling the named insured's product and eliminates the need for the vendor to purchase separate products liability coverage. [*Commercial Liability Insurance* VI.H.19 and *Contractual Risk Transfer* XI.C.24]

vendors dual interest coverage—Insurance purchased by financial institutions that covers physical damage to property (collateral) on which loans have been made. The premium is usually assessed against the borrower. Vendors dual interest coverage contrasts with vendors single interest coverage, in that it protects the interests of both the lendor and the borrower in the covered property.

vendors endorsement—A standard general liability endorsement (CG 20 15) that provides vendor's coverage.

vendors single interest coverage—Insurance purchased by financial institutions that protects against financial loss from physical damage to property (collateral) on which loans have been made. Such coverage applies in the event the borrower does not have physical damage coverage in place. Vendors single interest insurance covers only the outstanding balance on the loan. Even though the borrower frequently pays the premium, he receives no insurance protection of his equity under such policies.

venturi scrubbers—Air pollution control devices that use water to remove particulate matter from emissions.

venue—The location in which an action is brought for trial.

verbal threshold—A threshold based on a person's degree of injury that must be exceeded before a suit can be brought against the negligent party in a state with a no-fault insurance law. The verbal threshold is usually an injury that results in a whole or partial loss of a body member or function. [*Commercial Auto Insurance* IV.I.3]

vessel in navigation—A watercraft or any type of machinery which is intended for use in navigable waters as a means of transportation. This is one of the qualifications which must be established by an injured worker in order to make a claim under the Jones Act. See Jones Act. [*IRMI's Workers Comp* VII.C.3]

vesting—A process by which employees receive rights to values contributed on their behalf by their employer to a pension, profit sharing, or similar benefit plan.

vexatious litigant—An individual who overuses and abuses the legal system by filing frivolous lawsuits.

vicarious liability—The liability of a principal for the acts of its agents. Vicarious liability can result from the acts of independent agents, partners, independent contractors, and employees. [*Commercial Liability Insurance* VI.Q.1 and *Contractual Risk Transfer* III.E.1]

vis major—An act of God.

void—Without legal effect; unenforceable. A number of actions on the part of the insured can render coverage under an insurance policy void.

voidable—A policy that can be made void at the option of one or either of the parties to it.

voluntary compensation endorsement—Enables an employer to extend the benefits provided by the workers compensation act to employees who may not be entitled to benefits under the terms of the act, such as executive officers, partners, sole proprietors, farm workers, domestic employees, or employees traveling overseas. If such an employee is injured in the course of employment, he or she may elect to accept the scale of benefits provided by the designated workers compensation law or pursue common law remedies. [*IRMI's Workers Comp* VI.L.10]

voluntary compensation maritime coverage endorsement—Allows an employer with maritime workers compensation exposure to offer benefits of the state designated in the endorsement to an injured employee or survivors of a deceased employee. Used in conjunction with the maritime liability endorsement, which extends employers liability cover. The voluntary compensation maritime endorsement provides injured seamen an alternate remedy to legal action. [*IRMI's Workers Comp* VI.K.6]

voluntary market—A group of insurers who elect to write insurance in a competitive environment retaining the right to accept and reject business submitted. More specifically, the term also applies to the two types of mandatory insurance: automobile liability and workers compensation. In these instances, voluntary market refers to the insurers who provide coverage to desirable risks while rejecting the less attractive risks which must then be afforded coverage through assigned risk markets. [*IRMI's Workers Comp* **XII.J.3**]

voluntary reserve—An allocation of surplus not required by law.

voyage clause—A marine insurance policy provision specifying the period of time allowed for a voyage or series of trips that may be grouped together as one voyage.

W

WA—See With average.

WA 3%—See With average 3 percent.

wages, maintenance, and cure—See Maintenance, cure, and wages.

waiting period deductible—(1) A deductible provision sometimes used in business interruption and other time element policies, in lieu of a dollar amount deductible, that establishes that the insurer is not responsible for loss suffered during a specified period of time (such as 72 hours) immediately following a direct damage loss. [*Commercial Property Insurance* **XI.D.11**]

(2) A deductible mechanism in disability income policies and under workers compensation statutes that establishes a period of time which must pass following an accident or illness causing disability before salary continuation benefits are payable.

waiver—The surrender of a right or privilege.

waiver of inventory—A fire insurance policy provision that states inventory will not be required in the event of a small loss.

waiver of premium—The known relinquishment by an insurer of the right to collect premium from an insured.

waiver of subrogation—The relinquishment by an insurer of the right to collect from another party for damages paid on behalf of the insured. The waiver of subrogation condition in current liability policies is referred to as "transfer of rights of recovery." [*Commercial Liability Insurance* **V.J.17** and *Commercial Auto Insurance* **VIII.F.7**]

warehousemen's liability—Insurance coverage against liability that might be incurred in the business of warehousing property of others.

warehouse to warehouse clause—A marine cargo insurance policy provision that extends the protection from the warehouse at which the shipment originates to the one at which it terminates.

warranty—(1) A guarantee of the performance of a product. Product warranties are included within the definition of the named insured's product in general liability policies. [*Commercial Liability Insurance* **V.L.43**]

(2) A statement of fact given to an insurer by the insured concerning the insured risk which, if untrue, will void the policy.

war risk clause—An exclusionary clause eliminating coverage for losses arising out of war or warlike actions. [*Commercial Property Insurance* **V.Q.15**]

war risk insurance—Insurance against loss or damage to property due to the acts of war. It is freely written on marine exposures but is virtually unobtainable on property exposures. [*Commercial Property Insurance* **V.Q.15**]

Warsaw Convention—An international agreement setting limits of liability for freight, baggage, and bodily injury on international flights. Additionally, the agreement puts the responsibility on the air carrier to prove that it did not cause the loss to avoid reimbursement to the claimant.

waste load allocation—(1) The maximum load of pollutants each discharger of waste is allowed to release into a particular waterway. Discharge limits are usually required for each specific water quality criterion being, or expected to be, violated.

(2) The portion of a stream's total assimilative capacity assigned to an individual discharge.

waterborne equipment exclusion—A contractors equipment policy provision excluding coverage for equipment that is mounted on or being operated from a barge or other watercraft, when such watercraft is actually on the water. Equipment in transit by ferry, lighter, or car float is often covered by exception. This exclusion can often be removed or modified by attaching a waterborne equipment coverage endorsement to the policy.

water quality-based limitations—Effluent limitations applied to dischargers when mere technology-based limitations would cause violations of water quality standards. Usually applied to discharges into small streams.

water quality-based permit—A permit with an effluent limit more stringent than one based on technology performance. Such limits may be necessary to protect the designated use of receiving waters (i.e., recreation, irrigation, industry or water supply).

water quality standards—State adopted and Environmental Protection Agency-approved ambient standards for water bodies. The standards prescribe the use of the water body and establish the water quality criteria that must be met to protect designated uses.

weighted average loss forecasting—A method of forecasting losses that assigns greater weight, typically to more recent years, when developing a forecast of future losses. Recent years receive greater weight because they tend to more closely approximate current conditions (e.g., benefit levels, nature of company operations, medical expenses). [*Risk Financing* II.C.2]

welfare and pension plan bond coverage—Usually added by rider to a fidelity bond, this coverage protects funds and property in employee (labor-management) welfare and pension plans against loss by reason of acts of fraud or dishonesty on the part of administrators, officers, and employees of such plans. Bonding is required to safe-

guard these funds under the terms of the Federal Welfare and Pension Plans Disclosure Act. A guideline of 10 percent of the aggregate amount of funds handled, subject to a $1,000 minimum and a $500,000 maximum, is generally used to establish the required amount of coverage.

well control insurance—See Operators extra expense (OEE).

wellness program—A program initiated by an employer to promote a healthy lifestyle by employees.

whole life insurance—Permanent life insurance that provides for the payment of the face value upon death of the insured, regardless of when it may occur. This contrasts with term insurance, which pays benefits only if death takes place during the limited term of the policy. Under whole life policies, the insured pays a level premium rate all of his or her life. This approach results in an overpayment of premiums in the early years of the policy and an underpayment in the latter years—which averages out over the life of the policy. Whole life insurance also accumulates a cash value that may be borrowed or otherwise used by the insured.

wholesale health insurance—Also called "franchise insurance," essentially individual health insurance provided to groups of people in the same occupation or profession or to groups too small to qualify for true group insurance, e.g., less than 10 employees.

window plan—An early retirement plan in which an employer promises enriched pension benefits or credits workers for additional years of service if they retire early. Typically, early retirement windows are offered to employees for 60 or 90 days, and they give employers a humane approach to reducing their workforces without laying off employees.

with average (WA)—An ocean marine policy provision that covers partial loss of below deck cargo on the same basis as a total loss—that is, for loss by the same perils and regardless of what percentage of the total insured value is damaged or lost. Also see Free of particular average; Free of particular average (American conditions); Free of particular average (English conditions); Particular average; and With average 3 percent.

with average 3 percent (WA 3%)—An ocean marine policy provision that eliminates coverage for partial loss of below deck cargo amounting to less than 3 percent of insured value. Partial losses amounting to 3 percent or more of insured value are covered in full. Also see Free of particular average; Free of particular average (American conditions); Free of particular average (English conditions); Particular average; and With average.

without prejudice—When an offer or a dismissal is made "without prejudice," it is meant as a declaration that no rights of the party concerned are to be considered as waived or lost. A dismissal without prejudice allows a new suit to be brought on the same cause of action.

with prejudice—The opposite of without prejudice, it is meant as a final judgment of dismissal with the result as conclusive as if the action had been prosecuted to final adjudication adverse to plaintiff.

workers compensation—The system by which no-fault statutory benefits prescribed in state law are provided by an employer to an employee (or the employee's family) due to a job-related injury (including death) resulting from an accident or occupational disease. [*IRMI's Workers Comp* III.C.4]

workers compensation catastrophe cover—Excess of loss reinsurance purchased by primary workers compensation insurers to protect against an accumulation of losses resulting from a catastrophic event or series of events.

working layer—A dollar range in which an insured or, in the case of an insurer's book of business, a group of insureds, is expected to experience a fairly high level of loss frequency. This is the layer typically subject to deductibles, self-insured retentions, retrospective rating plans, and similar programs. Sufficient loss frequency in the working layer allows many organizations to provide some degree of statistical credibility to actuarial forecasts of the total expected losses during a specific period of time, e.g., one year.

workmanship exclusion—(1) A liability insurance exclusion that precludes coverage for damage to the insured's work resulting from that work. [*Commercial Liability Insurance* V.D.36]

(2) A builders risk exclusion that precludes coverage for loss caused by faulty workmanship.

worldwide insurance program—An international insurance program of a multinational company with a policy territory encompassing the entire world except for the country in which the insured is domiciled. See Global insurance program.

wrap-around risk financing program—A risk financing program in which two or more different risk financing approaches are combined into one overall program. Typically, a wrap-around is used for workers compensation insurance so that the most cost-effective program in each state can be used to an insured's advantage. For instance, in state A, an insured may have an exposure large enough to qualify as a self-insurer, whereas the requirements in State B may be such that another type of risk financing program is preferable. [*Risk Financing* IV.A.13]

wrap-up—See Consolidated insurance program.

writ—A party may "appeal" a nonfinal order issued by a trial court by use of a "writ."

write—In the insurance industry, it means to insure and/or to underwrite.

wrongful act—The event triggering coverage under many professional liability policies. Typically, a "wrongful act" is defined as an act, error, or omission that takes place within the course of performing professional services. [*Professional Liability Insurance* X.E.4]

wrongful termination—The act of terminating an employee in a manner which is against the law. In recent years, erosion of the employment-at-will doctrine has been the factor most responsible for the increase in claims alleging wrongful termination. Coverage for this exposure is provided under employment practices liability policies. [*Professional Liability Insurance* XX.I.4]

Y

York Antwerp Rules—A set of complex rules prescribed to by most nations that outlines the method of allocating general average losses between ship owners and cargo owners.

Z

Z-list—Occupational Safety and Health Act tables of toxic and hazardous air contaminants.

zone rating—A commercial auto rating system that divides the country into 50 zones with different rating tables applicable for each zone. Vehicles (excluding light trucks or trailers used with light trucks) that fall into the long-distance radius class are zone-rated. [*Commercial Auto Insurance* III.G.18]

zone system—A triennial insurance company solvency examination system developed by the National Association of Insurance Commissioners (NAIC). The system divides the United States into three geographical zones, and teams from states in each of the three zones examine the companies in their zones. All states then accept examinations from the other zones.

STATE REGULATORY AGENCIES

ALABAMA
Commissioner of Insurance
135 South Union Street
Montgomery, AL 36130-3401
205-269-3550, FAX 205-240-3194

ALASKA
Director of Insurance
Alaska Insurance Division
Department of Commerce & Economic
 Development
P.O. Box 11085
Juneau, AK 99811-0805
907-465-2515, FAX 907-465-3422

AMERICAN SAMOA
Insurance Commissioner
Office of the Governor
Pago Pago 96797
011-684-633-4116

ARIZONA
Director of Insurance
2910 North 44th Street, Suite 210
Phoenix, AZ 85018-7256
602-912-8400, FAX 602-912-8454

In Tucson:
Director of Insurance
Arizona Insurance Department
Room 152
400 West Congress
Tucson, AZ 85701
602-628-6370

ARKANSAS
Commissioner of Insurance
Arkansas Insurance Department
1123 South University, Suite 400
Little Rock, AR 72204
501-686-2900, FAX 501-686-2913

CALIFORNIA
Office of the Commissioner
California Insurance Department
45 Fremont Street, 23rd Floor
San Francisco, CA 94105
415-904-5410, FAX 415-904-5889

COLORADO
Commissioner of Insurance
Colorado Insurance Department
1560 Broadway, Suite 850
Denver, CO 80202
303-894-7499 ext. 311, FAX 303-894-7455

CONNECTICUT
Insurance Commissioner
Connecticut Insurance Department
153 Market St., 11th Floor
Hartford, CT 06106
203-297-3802, FAX 203-566-7410

DELAWARE
Insurance Commissioner
841 Silver Lake Boulevard
Dover, DE 19904
302-739-4251, FAX 302-739-5280

DISTRICT OF COLUMBIA
Superintendent of Insurance
P.O. Box 37200
Washington, DC 20013-7200
202-727-8001, FAX 202-727-7940

FLORIDA
Insurance Commissioner
State Capitol
Plaza Level 11
Tallahassee, FL 32399-0301
904-922-3100, FAX 904-488-6581

GEORGIA
Commissioner of Insurance
West Tower Rm. 720
No. 2 Martin Luther King Jr. Drive
Atlanta, GA 30334
404-651-7902, FAX 404-651-8719

GUAM
Insurance Commissioner
P.O. Box 2796
Agana, GU 96910
011-671-472-6940

HAWAII
Insurance Commissioner
Hawaii Insurance Division
Department of Commerce & Consumer Affairs
P.O. Box 3614
Honolulu, HI 96811
808-586-2790, FAX 808-586-2806

IDAHO
Commissioner of Insurance
Idaho Insurance Department
700 West State Street, 3rd Floor
Boise, ID 83720
208-334-4250, FAX 208-334-4398

ILLINOIS
Director of Insurance
320 West Washington Street
Springfield, IL 62727
217-782-4515, FAX 217-782-5020

In Chicago:
Director of Insurance
State of Illinois Building
100 W. Randolph Suite 15-100
Chicago, IL 60601
312-814-2420, FAX 312-814-5435

INDIANA
Commissioner of Insurance
311 West Washington Street, Suite 300
Indianapolis, IN 46204-2878
317-232-2385, FAX 317-232-5251
Consumer Hot line—
   INDIANA ONLY—1-800-622-4461

IOWA
Commissioner of Insurance
Lucas State Office Building, G23, 6th Floor
Des Moines, IA 50319
515-281-5523, FAX 515-281-3059

KANSAS
Commissioner of Insurance
420 South West 9th Street
Topeka, KS 66612
913-296-3071, FAX 913-296-2283

KENTUCKY
Insurance Commissioner
215 West Main Street
P.O. Box 517
Frankfort, KY 40602
502-564-6027, FAX 502-564-6090

LOUISIANA
Commissioner of Insurance
950 North Fifth Street
P.O. Box 94214
Baton Rouge, LA 70804-9214
504-342-5423, FAX 504-342-8622

MAINE
Superintendent of Insurance
Department of Professional &
   Financial Regulation
State House
Station No. 34
Augusta, ME 04333
207-582-8707, FAX 207-582-8716

MARYLAND
Insurance Commissioner
501 St. Paul Place
Baltimore, MD 21202
410-333-2521, FAX 410-333-6650

MASSACHUSETTS
Commissioner of Insurance
Massachusetts Division of Insurance
470 Atlantic Avenue
Boston, MA 02210-2223
617-521-7302,
FAX 617-521-7770 or 617-521-7771

MICHIGAN
Insurance Commissioner
611 West Ottawa, 2nd Floor
P.O. Box 30220
Lansing, MI 48909-7720
517-373-9273, FAX 517-335-4978

MINNESOTA
Commissioner of Commerce
133 East Seventh Street
St. Paul, MN 55101
612-296-6694, FAX 612-296-4328

MISSISSIPPI
Commissioner of Insurance
1804 Walter Sillers Building
P.O. Box 79
Jackson, MS 39205-0079
601-359-3569, FAX 601-359-2474

MISSOURI

Director of Insurance
301 West High Street, Room 630
P.O. Box 690
Jefferson City, MO 65101
314-751-4126, FAX 314-751-1165

MONTANA

Commissioner of Insurance
Mitchell Building
126 North Sanders
P.O. Box 4009
Helena, MT 59604
406-444-2040, FAX 406-444-3497

NEBRASKA

Director of Insurance
941 O Street, Suite 400
Lincoln, NE 68508
402-471-2201, FAX 402-471-4610

NEVADA

Commissioner of Insurance
1665 Hot Springs Road, Suite 152
Carson City, NV 89710
702-687-4270, FAX 702-687-3937

In Las Vegas:
Commissioner of Insurance
Insurance Division
Room 300
Bradley Building
2501 East Sahara Boulevard
Las Vegas, NV 89104
702-386-5313

NEW HAMPSHIRE

Insurance Commissioner
169 Manchester Street
P.O. Box 2005
Concord, NH 03301
603-271-2261, FAX 603-271-1406
Consumer hot line (for New Hampshire only)
1-800-852-3416

NEW JERSEY

Commissioner of Insurance
20 West State Street CN 325
Trenton, NJ 08625
609-292-6812, FAX 609-984-5273

NEW MEXICO

Superintendent of Insurance
PERA Building
P.O. Drawer 1269
Santa Fe, NM 87504-1269
505-827-4297, FAX 505-827-4734

NEW YORK

Superintendent of Insurance
160 West Broadway
New York, NY 10013
212-602-0429, FAX 212-602-0437

In Albany:
Superintendent of Insurance
Department of Insurance
State of New York
Empire State Plaza
Agency Building One
Albany, NY 12257
518-474-4550, FAX 518-474-4600

NORTH CAROLINA

Commissioner of Insurance
Dobbs Building
P.O. Box 26387
Raleigh, NC 27611
919-733-7349, FAX 919-733-6495

NORTH DAKOTA

Office of the Commissioner
North Dakota Insurance Department
600 E. Boulevard Avenue
Fifth Floor
State Capitol
Bismarck, ND 58505-0320
701-328-2440, FAX 701-328-4880

OHIO

Director of Insurance
2100 Stella Court
Columbus, OH 43266-0566
614-644-2651, FAX 614-644-3743

OKLAHOMA

Insurance Commissioner
1901 North Walnut Street
P.O. Box 53408
Oklahoma City, OK 73152-3408
405-521-2828, FAX 405-521-6652
Consumer hot line 1-800-522-0071

OREGON

Insurance Commissioner
440 Labor & Industries Building
Salem, OR 97310
503-378-4271, FAX 503-378-4351

PENNSYLVANIA

Commissioner of Insurance
Strawberry Square, 13th Floor, 1326
Harrisburg, PA 17120
717-783-0442, FAX 717-783-1509

In Pittsburgh:

Insurance Commissioner
Pennsylvania Insurance Department
Room 304
State Office Building
300 Liberty Avenue
Pittsburgh, PA 15222
412-565-5020

In Philadelphia:

Insurance Commissioner
Pennsylvania Insurance Department
Room 1701
State Office Building
1400 Spring Garden Street
Philadelphia, PA 19130
215-560-2630

In Erie:

Insurance Commissioner
Pennsylvania Insurance Department
P.O. Box 6142
Room 513
Baldwin Building
Erie, PA 16512
814-871-4466

PUERTO RICO

Commissioner of Insurance
Fernandez Juncos Station
P.O. Box 8330
Santurce, PR 00910
809-722-8686

RHODE ISLAND

Insurance Commissioner
233 Richmond Street, Suite 233
Providence, RI 02903
401-277-2223, FAX: 401-751-4887

SOUTH CAROLINA

Chief Insurance Commissioner
1612 Marion Street
P.O. Box 100105
Columbia, SC 29202-3105
803-737-6268, FAX 803-737-6205

SOUTH DAKOTA

Director of Insurance
South Dakota Insurance Division
500 East Capitol Avenue
Pierre, SD 57501-5070
605-773-3563, FAX 605-773-5369

TENNESSEE

Commissioner of Insurance
500 James Robertson Parkway, 5th Floor
Volunteer Plaza
Nashville, TN 37243-0565
615-741-2241, FAX 615-741-4000

TEXAS

Insurance Commissioner
P.O. Box 149104
MC 113-1C
Austin, TX 78714-9104
512-463-6464, FAX 512-475-2005

UTAH

Commissioner of Insurance
3110 State Office Building
Salt Lake City, UT 84114
801-538-3800, FAX: 801-538-3829

VERMONT

Office of the Commissioner
Department of Banking, Insurance and Securities
89 Main Street
Drawer 20
Montpelier, VT 05620-3101
802-828-3301, FAX 802-828-3306

VIRGIN ISLANDS

Commissioner of Insurance
Kongens Gade No. 18
Charlotte Amalie
St. Thomas, VI 00802
809-774-2991

VIRGINIA

Commissioner of Insurance
700 Jefferson Building
P.O. Box 1157
Richmond, VA 23209
804-371-9694, FAX 804-371-9873

WASHINGTON

Office of the Commissioner
Insurance Building
P.O. Box 40255
Olympia, WA 98504-0255
206-753-7301, FAX 206-586-3535
Consumer hot line for Washington only
1-800-562-6200

In Seattle:

Office of the Commissioner
Washington State Insurance Department
810 Third Avenue, Suite 650
Seattle, WA 98104
206-464-6262

WEST VIRGINIA

Insurance Commissioner
2019 Washington Street, East
P.O. Box 50540
Charleston, WV 25305-0540
304-558-3354, FAX 304-558-0412
consumer hot line—304-558-3386 or
1-800-642-9004 FAX 304-558-1610
(toll free—WV only)

WISCONSIN

Commissioner of Insurance
123 West Washington Avenue
P.O. Box 7873
Madison, WI 53707-7873
608-266-3585, FAX 608-266-9935

WYOMING

Insurance Commissioner
Herschler Building, 3rd Floor East
122 West 25th Street
Cheyenne, WY 82002
307-777-7401, FAX 307-777-5895

BOARDS, BUREAUS, AND STATE WC DEPARTMENTS

Workers compensation (WC) laws are enacted by the individual states. The organizations charged with administering the systems go by a variety of names, including state insurance departments, industrial commissions, and workers compensation bureaus.

The National Council on Compensation Insurance (NCCI), a bureau made up of member insurance and reinsurance companies that write WC insurance in one or more states, acts as the official statistical filing and rate-making organization for 36 states plus the District of Columbia. It formulates basic rules for writing WC insurance, which it publishes in its *Basic Manual for Workers Compensation and Employers Liability Insurance*. (A copy of the NCCI *Basic Manual* can be obtained by contacting the NCCI main Customer Service Center.) The NCCI maintains bureaus throughout the United States that administer the day-to-day activities in those districts. The addresses for the NCCI offices are shown.

Customer Service Center

NCCI is in the process of consolidating many of the functions of the district offices into one main Customer Service Center. Consumer questions should be directed to this office.

750 Park of Commerce Drive
Boca Raton, FL 33431-0998
407-622-4123
800-622-4206

Regional Offices

These offices deal with government affairs, such as item filings, rate filings, industry affairs, and legislation.

Northern Regional Office
998 Old Eagle School Rd., Ste. 1210
Wayne, PA 19807
215-964-8851

Southern Regional Office
750 Park of Commerce Drive
Boca Raton, FL 33487
407-997-4563

Western Regional Office
P.O. Box 5323
Denver, CO 80217-5323
303-695-8888

District Offices

These offices handle the day-to-day activities of NCCI members, such as experience rating (including calculation of experience modifiers), classification questions, assigned risk plan issues, etc.

Northeastern Division
1095 Day Hill Rd.
Windsor, CT 06095
203-298-9900; 800-622-4217

Atlantic Division
P.O. Box 3098
Boca Raton, FL 33431-0998
407-997-4633; 800-622-4206

Southern Division
10 Inverness Center Pkwy., Ste. 500
Birmingham, AL 35242-4819
205-991-7490; 800-622-4250

Midwestern Division
P.O. Box 19430
Springfield, IL 62794-9430
217-793-1100; 800-622-4207

Western Division
P.O. Box 5323
Denver, CO 80217-5323
303-695-8891; 800-622-4292

Northwestern Division
P.O. Box 8399
Portland, OR 97207-8399
503-228-4173; 800-622-4230

In the remaining states, an independent workers compensation bureau is responsible for promulgating and approving WC rates and forms. Delaware, Hawaii, New Jersey, New York, Pennsylvania, and Texas follow the rules established by the independent rating bureaus published in their respective manuals. California and Michigan require that insurers file their own manuals. However, California does publish the *California Uniform Statistical Plan,* which contains classifications and procedures for that state, and Michigan has a manual with rules for writing coverage in its residual market. Manuals published for use in independent states can be ob-

tained by contacting the administrative bureau listed below for that state.

Six monopolistic fund states (Nevada, North Dakota, Ohio, Washington, West Virginia, and Wyoming) have separate workers compensation rules and regulations. The addresses for monopolistic and competitive state fund states follow in the Monopolistic State Funds section.

The address and phone number of each state's rate-making and filing authority and department of insurance are provided below.

DIRECTORY OF STATE WC BUREAUS AND INSURANCE DEPARTMENTS

State	Administrative Bureau	State Insurance Department
AL	NCCI Inc.—Southern Division	Alabama Dept. of Ins., 135 South Union St., Montgomery, AL 36130–3401 (205–269–3556)
AK	NCCI Inc.—Northwestern Division	Alaska Ins. Div., Dept. of Commerce & Economic Development, P.O. Box 110805, Juneau, AK 99811–0805 (907–465–2515)
AZ	NCCI Inc.—Western Division	Arizona Ins. Dept., 2910 N. 44th St., Ste. 210, Phoenix, AZ 85018–7256 (602–912–8400)
AR	NCCI Inc.—Southern Division	Arkansas Ins. Dept., 1123 S. University, Ste. 400, Little Rock, AR 72204 (501–686–2900)
CA	WC Ins. Rating Bureau of Calif., Spear St. Twr., One Market, Ste. 500, San Francisco, CA 94105–1088 (415–777–0777)	California Dept. of Ins., 770 L St., Ste. 1120, Sacramento, CA 95814 (916–445–5280)
CO	NCCI Inc.—Western Division	Colorado Ins. Div., 1560 Broadway, Ste. 850, Denver, CO 80202 (303–894–7499)
CT	NCCI Inc.—Northeastern Division	Connecticut Ins. Dept., 153 Market St., 11th Fl., Hartford, CT 06106 (203–297–3802)
DE	Delaware Comp. Rating Bureau, The Widener Bldg., 6th Fl., One South Penn Sq., Philadelphia, PA 19107–3577 (215–568–2371)	Delaware Ins. Dept., 841 Silver Lake Blvd., Rodney Bldg., Dover, DE 19904 (302–739–4251)
DC	NCCI Inc.—Northeastern Division	D.C. Ins. Administration, 441 4th St., N.W., Washington, DC 20001 (202–727–8000)
FL	NCCI Inc.—Atlantic Division	Florida Ins. Dept., Plaza Level 11, The Capitol, Tallahassee, FL 32399–0301 (904–922–3100)

DIRECTORY OF STATE WC BUREAUS AND INSURANCE DEPARTMENTS (cont.)

State	Administrative Bureau	State Insurance Department
GA	NCCI Inc.—Southern Division	Office of Commissioner, 7th Fl., West Twr., Floyd Bldg., 2 Martin Luther King, Jr., Dr., Atlanta, GA 30334 (404-651-7902)
HI	Hawaii Ins. Rating Bureau, P.O. Box 4500, Honolulu, HI 96813 (808-531-2771)	Hawaii Ins. Div., P.O. Box 3614, Honolulu, HI 96811 (808-586-2790)
ID	NCCI Inc.—Western Division	Idaho Ins. Dept., 700 W. State St., 3rd Fl., Boise, ID 83720 (208-334-4250)
IL	NCCI Inc.—Midwestern Division	Illinois Ins. Dept., 320 W. Washington St., Springfield, IL 62767 (217-782-4515)
IN	Indiana Comp. & Rating Bureau, P.O. Box 50400, Indianapolis, IN 46250 (317-842-2800)	Insurance Dept., 311 W. Washington St., Ste. 300, Indianapolis, IN 46204 (317-232-2385; 800-622-4461)
IA	NCCI Inc.—Midwestern Division	Iowa Ins. Div., Lucas State Office Bldg., Des Moines, IA 50319 (515-281-5523)
KS	NCCI Inc.—Midwestern Division	Kansas Ins. Dept., 420 S.W. Ninth St., Topeka, KS 66612-1678 (913-296-3071)
KY	NCCI Inc.—Southern Division	Kentucky Ins. Dept., P.O. Box 517, 229 W. Main St., Frankfort, KY 40602 (502-564-6027)
LA	NCCI Inc.—Southern Division	Louisiana Ins. Dept., P.O. Box 94214, Baton Rouge, LA 70804-9214 (504-342-5423)
ME	NCCI Inc.—Northeastern Division	Maine Bureau of Ins., Station 34, State House, Augusta, ME 04333 (207-582-8707)
MD	NCCI Inc.—Northeastern Division	Maryland Ins. Div., 501 St. Paul Place, 7th Fl., Baltimore, MD 21202-2272 (410-333-2521)
MA	The WC Rating & Inspection Bureau of Mass., 101 Arch St., 5th Fl., Boston, MA 02110 (617-439-9030)	Massachusetts Div. of Ins., 470 Atlantic Ave., Boston, MA 02110-2223 (617-521-7302)
MI	The Compensation Advisory Org. of Mich., P.O. Box 3337, Livonia, MI 48151-3337 (313-462-9600)	Michigan Ins. Bureau, 611 W. Ottowa, P.O. Box 30220, Lansing, MI 48909-7720 (517-373-9273)
MN	WC Insurers Rating Assn. of Minn., 7760 France Ave. S., Ste. 640, Minneapolis, MN 55435 (612-897-1737)	Minnesota Ins. Div., Dept. of Commerce, 133 E. 7th St., St. Paul, MN 55101 (612-296-6694; 800-657-3602)
MS	NCCI Inc.—Southern Division	Mississippi Ins. Dept., 1804 Walter Sillers Bldg., P.O. Box 79, Jackson, MS 39205-0079 (601-359-3569)
MO	NCCI Inc.—Midwestern Division	Missouri Dept. of Ins., 301 W. High St., Rm. 630, Jefferson City, MO 65101 (314-751-4126)

DIRECTORY OF STATE WC BUREAUS AND INSURANCE DEPARTMENTS (cont.)

State	Administrative Bureau	State Insurance Department
MT	NCCI Inc.—Western Division	Montana Ins. Dept., P.O. Box 4009, Sam W. Mitchell Bldg., 126 N. Sanders, Helena, MT 59604 (406–444–2040)
NE	NCCI Inc.—Midwestern Division	Nebraska Ins. Dept., 941 O St., Ste. 400, Lincoln, NE 68508 (402–471–2201)
NV	See Monopolistic Fund Section	Dept. of Ins., Ste. 152, 1665 Hot Springs Rd., Carson City, NV 89710 (702–687–4270)
NH	NCCI Inc.—Northeastern Division	New Hampshire Ins. Dept., 169 Manchester St., Ste. 1, Concord, NH 03301–5151 (603–271–2261)
NJ	Compensation Rating & Inspection Bureau, 60 Park Place, Newark, NJ 07102 (201–622–6014)	New Jersey Ins. Dept., 20 W. State St., Trenton, NJ 08625 (609–292–6812)
NM	NCCI Inc.—Western Division	New Mexico Ins. Dept., P.O. Drawer 1269, Santa Fe, NM 87504–1269 (505–827–4297)
NY	NY Comp. Ins. Rating Bd., 200 East 42nd St., New York, NY 10017 (212–697–3535)	NY Ins. Dept., Empire State Plaza, Agency Building One, Albany, NY 12257 (518–474–4550)
NC	NC Rate Bureau, P.O. Box 12227, Raleigh, NC 27605 (919–828–5725)	North Carolina Ins. Dept., 430 N. Salisbury St., Raleigh, NC 27611 (919–733–7349)
ND	See Monopolistic Fund Section	North Dakota Ins. Dept., 600 East Blvd., Bismark, ND 58505 (701–328–2440)
OH	See Monopolistic Fund Section	Ohio Dept. of Ins., 2100 Stella Ct., Columbus, OH 43266–0566 (614–644–2651)
OK	NCCI Inc.—Southern Division	Oklahoma Ins. Dept., 1901 N. Walnut St., Oklahoma City, OK 73152–3408 (405–521–2828; 800–522–0071)
OR	NCCI Inc.—Northwestern Division	Insurance Div., 440 Labor & Industries Bldg., Salem, OR 97310 (503–378–4271)
PA	Pennsylvania Comp. Rating Bureau, The Widener Bldg., 6th Fl., One South Penn Sq., Philadelphia, PA 19107–3577 (215–568–2371)	Penn. Ins. Dept., Strawberry Sq., Room 1326, Harrisburg, PA 17120 (717–783–0442)
RI	NCCI Inc.—Northeastern Division	RI Ins. Div., 233 Richmond St., Ste. 233, Providence, RI 02903–4237 (401–277–2223)
SC	NCCI Inc.—Atlantic Division	SC Ins. Dept., 1612 Marion St., Columbia, SC 29202–3105 (803–737–6268)
SD	NCCI Inc.—Midwestern Division	SD Ins. Div., 500 E., Capitol Ave., Pierre, SD 57501–5070 (605–773–3563)

DIRECTORY OF STATE WC BUREAUS AND INSURANCE DEPARTMENTS (cont.)

State	Administrative Bureau	State Insurance Department
TN	NCCI Inc.—Southern Division	Commerce & Ins. Dept., 500 James Robertson Pkwy., Nashville, TN 37243-0565 (615-741-2241)
TX	Department of Ins., P.O. Box 149104, Austin, TX 78714-9104 (512-463-6464; 800-252-3439)	Department of Ins., P.O. Box 149104, Austin, TX 78714-9104 (512-463-6464; 800-252-3439)
UT	NCCI Inc.—Western Division	Utah Ins. Dept., State Office Bldg., Rm. 3110, Salt Lake City, UT 84144-6901 (801-538-3800)
VT	NCCI Inc.—Northeastern Division	Department of Banking, Ins. & Securities, 89 Main St., Drawer 20, Montpelier, VT 05620-3101 (802-828-3301)
VA	NCCI Inc.—Atlantic Division	Bureau of Ins., P.O. Box 1157, Richmond, VA 23209 (804-371-9694; 800-745-3926)
WA	See Monopolistic Fund Section	Office of Ins. Commissioner, 1212 Jefferson St., P.O. Box 40255, Olympia, WA 98504-0255 (206-753-7300)
WV	See Monopolistic Fund Section	WV Ins. Dept., 2019 Washington St., E., P.O. Box 50540, Charleston, WV 25305-0540 (304-558-3354)
WI	Wisconsin Comp. Rating Bureau, 2200 North Mayfair Rd., Box 26469, Wauwatosa, WI 53226 (414-476-6440)	Wisconsin Ins. Dept., 121 E. Wilson St., P.O. Box 7873, Madison, WI 53707-7873 (608-266-3585)
WY	See Monopolistic Fund Section	Wyoming Ins. Dept., Herschler Bldg., 122 W. 25th St., Cheyenne, WY 82002 (307-777-7401)

MONOPOLISTIC STATE FUNDS

There are six states that do not permit private insurers to write workers compensation insurance. Each of these states has its own monopolistic state fund which prescribes the rules and regulations, sets the rates, and administers all other activities for the writing of workers compensation insurance. Puerto Rico, the U.S. Virgin Islands, and St. Croix also have monopolistic funds. The list below shows the state and the industrial commission or department that administers the monopolistic state fund in that particular state.

State	Industrial Commission or Bureau
NV	Nevada State Industrial Insurance System, 515 East Musser Street, Carson City, NV 89714 (702–687–5220)
ND	North Dakota Workers' Comp. Bureau, 500 East Front Avenue, Bismarck, ND 58501 (701–224–3800)
OH	Ohio Bureau of Workers Compensation, 30 West Spring Street, Level 3, Columbus, OH 43215 (614–466–2950)
WA	Washington Dept. of Labor & Industries, Industrial Insurance Division, 905 Plum Street, Olympia, WA 98504 (206–956–5800)
WV	West Virginia Workers' Compensation Fund, P.O. Box 3151, Charleston, WV 25332 (304–558–0380)

State	Industrial Commission or Bureau
WY	Wyoming Safety & Workers Compensation, 122 West 25th Street, Herschler Bldg., Cheyenne, WY 82002-0700 (307–777–7441)
Puerto Rico	Fondo Del Seguro Del Estado, Oficina Regional De San Juan, Call Box 42006, Minillas Station, Santurce, PR 00940 (809–268–7400)
U.S. Virgin Islands, St. Thomas	Government Insurance Fund Department of Finance, P.O. Box 2515, St. Thomas, VI 00801 (809–775-5747)
St. Croix	Government Insurance Fund, K22 Hospital St., Christianstead, St. Croix, VI 00820 (809–773-0471)

COMPETITIVE STATE FUNDS

The monopolistic state funds should not be confused with the competitive state funds. In states with a competitive fund, private insurance companies also write workers compensation insurance. The state fund acts in almost the same capacity as an insurance company. They can, in some instances, write the coverage for less money but cannot provide coverage out of state. The states that have competitive funds and the organization which administers them follow.

State	Administrative Office
AZ	Arizona State Compensation Fund, P.O. Box 6967, Phoenix, AZ 85005 (602-631-2900)
CA	California State Compensation Insurance Fund, 1275 Market Street, San Francisco, CA 94103, (415-565-1234)
CO	Colorado Compensation Insurance Authority, 720 South Colorado Blvd., Suite 100 N, Denver, CO 80222-1909 (303-782-4000)
ID	Idaho State Insurance Fund, 317 Main Street, Boise, ID 83720 (208-334-2370)
KY	Employers Mutual Insurance Authority, Lexington Financial Center, 250 West Main, Suite 900, Lexington, KY 40507 (606-246-7800)
LA[1]	Louisiana Workers Compensation Corp., P.O. Box 98041, Baton Rouge, LA 70898 (504-924-7788)
ME[1]	Maine Employers Mutual Insurance Co., P.O. Box 11409, Portland, ME 04104 (207-791-3300)
MD	Maryland Injured Workers Insurance Fund, 8722 Loch Raven Blvd., Towson, MD 21286-2235, (401-494-2000)

State	Administrative Office
MN	State Fund Mutual Insurance Co., 900 Wilson Ridge, 7500 Flying Cloud Drive, Eden Prairie, MN 55344-3748 (612-944-3260)
MO	Missouri Employers Mutual Ins. Co., 200 East Walnut, Columbia, MO 65203 (314-442-2464)
MT	Montana State Compensation Insurance Fund, Division of Workers Compensation, 5 South Last Chance Gulch, Helena, MT 59601 (406-444-6490)
NM	New Mexico Mutual Casualty Co., 5840 Office Blvd., NE, Albuquerque, NM 87109 (505-345-7260)
NY	New York State Insurance Fund, 199 Church Street, New York, NY 10007 (212-312-9000)
OK	Oklahoma State Insurance Fund, Box 53505, Oklahoma City, OK 73152 (405-232-7663)
OR	SAIF Corporation, 400 High Street SE, Salem, OR 97312-1000 (503-373-8000)
PA	Pennsylvania State Workers' Insurance Fund, 100 Lackawanna Ave., Scranton, PA 18503 (717-963-4601)

---

[1]Legislature established the creation of privately funded companies to replace the assigned risk plan/pool and act similar to a competitive state fund.

State	Administrative Office	State	Administrative Office
RI	The Beacon Mutual Insurance Co., 1600 Division Road, Warwick, RI 02873-2366 (401-886-4400)	UT	Utah State Insurance Fund, P.O. Box 45420, Salt Lake City, UT 84145-0420 (801-288-8000)
TX	Texas Workers' Comp. Insurance Fund, 333 Clay, Suite 1550, Houston, TX 77002 (800-955-COMP)		

ASSIGNED RISK PLANS AND POOLS

The following table provides the type of assigned risk procedure (plan, pool, or state fund) used by each state, along with the board or bureau having jurisdiction. The addresses of the state WC bureaus can be found in the Boards, Bureaus, and State WC Departments section. NCCI is in the process of transferring the assigned risk application processing to a new Customer Service Center in Boca Raton, Florida. Contact them at the following address for the correct address for submission of assigned risk applications.

NCCI Inc.—Assigned Risk Department
P.O. Box 3078
Boca Raton, FL 33431-0998
800-622-4230; fax 407-989-6215

Where an organization independent of the state WC bureau or NCCI has jurisdiction over the state assigned risk plan, the address is provided below.

State	Type	Address
AL	Plan	NCCI Inc.—Southern Division
AK	Pool	NCCI Inc.—Assigned Risk Dept.
AZ	Plan	NCCI Inc.—Western Division
AR	Pool	NCCI Inc.—Southern Division
CA	State Fund	State Comp. Ins. Fund, P.O. Box 807, San Francisco, CA 94101 (415-565-1234)
CO	State Fund	Colorado State Comp. Ins. Authority, 720 S. Colorado Blvd., Ste. 100 N, Denver, CO 80222-1909 (303-782-4000)
CT	Plan	NCCI Inc.—Northeastern Division
DE	Plan	Delaware Comp. Rating Bureau
DC	Plan	NCCI Inc.—Northeastern Division
FL	Plan	NCCI Inc.—Assigned Risk Dept.
GA	Plan	NCCI Inc.—Southern Division
HI	Plan	Hawaii Insurance Rating Bureau
ID	Plan	NCCI Inc.—Western Division

State	Type	Address
IL	Pool	NCCI Inc.—Midwestern Division
IN	Plan	Indiana Comp. & Rating Bureau
IA	Plan	NCCI Inc.—Midwestern Division
KS	Plan	NCCI Inc.—Kansas Service Office, P.O. Box 1577, Topeka, KS 66601 (913-273-6660, fax 913-273-2060)
KY	Plan	NCCI Inc.—Southern Division
LA	[1]	Louisiana Workers Compensation Corporation, P.O. Box 98041, Baton Rouge, LA 70898 (504-924-7788)
ME	[1]	Maine Employers Mutual Insurance Company, P.O. Box 9500, Westbrook, ME 04098 (207-856-1300)
MD	State Fund	Injured Workers Insurance Fund, 8722 Loch Raven Blvd., Baltimore, MD 21286-2235 (410-494-2000)
MA	Pool	The WC Rating & Inspection Bureau of Massachusetts

---

[1]Privately funded company created by the legislature to replace assigned risk pool/plan (similar to a competitive fund).

State	Type	Address	State	Type	Address
MI	Plan	Comp. Advisory Organization of Michigan	PA	State Fund	State Workers Compensation Fund, 100 Lackawanna Avenue, Scranton, PA 18503 (717–963–4635)
MN	Pool	Workers Comp. Insurance Rating Assn. of Minnesota			
MS	Plan	NCCI Inc.—Southern Division		USL&HW Vol. Pool	Pennsylvania Comp. Rating Bureau
MO	Plan	NCCI Inc.—Midwestern Division	RI	1	The Beacon Mutual Insurance Co., 535 Centerville Road, Suite 301, Warwick, RI 02886, 401–886–4400
MT	State Fund	State Comp. Mutual Ins. Fund, P.O. Box 4759, Helena, MT 59601 (406-444-6490)			
NE	Plan	NCCI Inc.—Midwestern Division	SC	Plan	NCCI Inc.—Assigned Risk Dept.
NH	Plan	NCCI Inc.—Northeastern Division	SD	Plan	NCCI Inc.—Midwestern Division
NJ	Plan	Compensation Rating & Inspection Bureau	TN	Plan	NCCI Inc.—Southern Division
NM	Pool	NCCI Inc.—Western Division	TX	State Fund	Texas Workers Comp. Insurance Fund, 100 Congress Ave., #300, Austin, TX 78701-4042 (800–955–COMP, fax 512–322–3899)
NY	State Fund	New York State Ins. Fund, 199 Church Street, New York, NY 10007 (212-312-9000)	UT	State Fund	Utah State Insurance Fund, P.O. Box 4200, Salt Lake City, UT 84111 (801-538-8000)
NC	Plan	North Carolina Rating Bureau, P.O. Box 176010, Raleigh, NC 27619-6010 (919-783-9790)	VT	Plan	NCCI Inc.—Northeastern Division
OK	State Fund	Oklahoma State Ins. Fund, P.O. Box 53505, Oklahoma City, OK 73152 (405-232-7663)	VA	Plan	NCCI Inc.—Assigned Risk Dept.
			WI	Pool	Wisconsin Compensation Rating Bureau
OR	Pool	NCCI Inc.—Assigned Risk Dept.			

RISK MANAGEMENT/INSURANCE ORGANIZATIONS

ACORD
One Blue Hill Plaza
15th Floor
Pearl River, NY 10965-8529
Tel: 914-620-1700
Fax: 914-620-0808

Alliance of American Insurers
1501 Woodfield Road
Suite 400 West
Schaumburg, IL 60173-4980
Tel: 708-330-8500
Fax: 708-330-8602

A.M. Best Co.
Ambest Road
Oldwick, NJ 08858-9988
Tel: 908-439-2200
Fax: 908-439-3296

American Association of Insurance Services
1035 South York Road
Bensenville, IL 60106
Tel: 630-595-3225
Fax: 630-595-4647
E-mail: AAISinsure@aol.com

American Association of Managing General Agents
9140 Ward Parkway
Kansas City, MO 64114
Tel: 816-444-3500
Fax: 816-444-0330
E-mail: webinfo@mfassoc.com
Web site URL: http://www.mfassoc.com

The American College
270 South Bryn Mawr Avenue
Bryn Mawr, PA 19010
Tel: 610-526-1310
Fax: 610-526-1450
Web site URL: http://www.amercoll.edu

American Council of Life Insurance
1001 Pennsylvania Avenue, N.W.
Suite 500
Washington, DC 2004-2599
Tel: 202-624-2333
Fax: 202-624-2319

American Council on Science and Health
1995 Broadway
16th Floor
New York, NY 10023
Tel: 212-362-7044
Fax: 212-362-4919
E-mail: ACSHA/ACSH.org
Web site URL: http://www.ACSH.ORG

American Educational Institute
P.O. Box 356
170 Mt. Airy Road
Basking Ridge, NJ 07920
Tel: 908-766-0909
FAx: 908-766-9710
E-mail: TBA
Web site URL: TBA

American Institute for CPCU
720 Providence Road
P.O. Box 5016
Malvern, PA 19355-0770
Tel: 800-644-2101
Fax: 610-640-9576
E-mail: cserv@apauiia.org
Web site URL: http://www.insweb.com/
educator.aicpcu

American Institute of Architects
1735 New York Avenue, N.W.
Washington, DC 20006
Tel: 202-626-7300

American Institute of Marine Underwriters
14 Wall Street
New York, NY 10005
Tel: 212-233-0550
Fax: 212-227-5102

American Insurance Association
1130 Connecticut Avenue, N.W.
Suite 1000
Washington, DC 20036
Tel: 202-828-7100
Fax: 202-293-1219

American Nuclear Insurers
Town Center
29 South Main Street
Suite 3005 South
West Hartford, CT 06107-2430
Tel: 203-561-3433
Fax: 203-561-4655

American Prepaid Legal Services Institute
541 North Fairbanks Ct.
Chicago, IL 60611-3314
Tel: 312-988-5751
Fax: 312-988-5032

American Risk and Insurance Association
P.O. Box 9001
Mt. Vernon, NY 10552
Tel: 914-669-2020
Fax: 914-669-2025

American Society of Healthcare Risk Management
One North Franklin
Chicago, IL 60606
Tel: 312-422-3980
Fax: 312-422-4580

American Society of Safety Engineers
1800 E. Oakton Street
Des Plaines, IL 60018-2187
Tel: 847-699-2929
Fax: 847-296-3760
Fax-on-demand: 800-380-7101
E-mail: 73244.562@compuserve.com
Web site URL: http://www.ASSE.ORG

Arbitration Forums, Inc.
P.O. Box 271500
Tampa, FL 336388-1500
Tel: 813-931-4004
Fax: 813-931-4618

Automobile Insurance Plans Service Office
302 Central Avenue
Johnston, RI 02919-5095
Tel: 401-687-4501
Fax: 401-986-9716

Captive Insurance Companies Association, Inc.
655 3rd Avenue
New York, NY 10017
Tel: 212-687-4501
Fax: 212-986-9716

Casualty Actuarial Society
1101 North Glebe Road
Suite 600
Arlington, VA 22201
Tel: 703-276-3100
Fax: 703-276-3180
E-mail: office@CASACTSOC.coa
Web site URL: pending

College for Financial Planning
4695 South Monaco
Denver, CO 80237-3403
Tel: 303-220-4823
FAx: 303-220-0838
Web site URL: http://www.NEFE.ORG

College of Insurance
101 Murray Street
New York, NY 10007
Tel: 212-962-4111
Fax: 212-964-3381

Conference of Casualty Insurance Companies
Box 681098
3601 Vincennes Road
Indianapolis, IN 46268
Tel: 317-872-4061
Fax: 317-879-8408

Conference of Insurance Legislators
122 South Swan Street
Albany, NY 1221
Tel: 518-449-3210
Fax: 518-432-5651

Consumer Product Safety Commission
East West Towers
4330 East West Highway
Bethesda, MD 20814
Tel: 301-504-0530

The Council of Insurance Agents and Brokers
701 Pennsylvania Avenue, N.W. #750
Washington, DC 20004-2608
Tel: 202-783-4400
Fax: 202-783-4410
E-mail: ciab@ciab.com
Web site URL: http//www.ciab.com

Defense Research Institute
750 North Lakeshore Drive
Suite 500
Chicago, IL 60611
Tel: 312-944-0575
Fax: 312-944-2003
E-mail: dri@mcs:net
Web site URL: http://www.dri.org

Duff & Phelps Credit Rating Co.
55 East Monroe Street, #3600
Chicago, IL 60603
Tel: 312-263-2610
Fas: 312-263-4529

Employee Benefit Research Institute
2121 K Street N.W.
Suite 600
Washington, DC 20037-1896
Tel: 202-659-0670
Fax: 202-775-6312
E-mail: GebRi.org
Web site URL: http://www.ebri.org

Environmental Protection Agency
401 M Street, S.W.
Washington, DC 20406
202-382-2090

Federal Insurance Administration
500 C Street, S.W.
Washington, DC 20472
Tel: 202-646-2771
Fax: 202-646-3445

Food and Drug Administration
5600 Fishers Lane
Rockville, MD 20857
Tel: 301-443-1544

Foreign Credit Insurance Association
40 Rector Street
11th Floor
New York, NY 10006
Tel: 212-306-5000
Fax: 212-513-4704

Highway Loss Data Institute
1005 North Glebe Road
Suite 800
Arlington, VA 22201
Tel: 703-247-1600
Fax: 703-247-1595
Web site URL: http://www.carsafety.org

Independent Insurance Agents of America, Inc.
127 South Peyton Street
Alexandria, VA 22314
Tel: 703-683-4422
Fax: 703-683-7556

Inland Marine Underwriters Association
111 Broadway
15th Floor
New York, NY 10006
Tel: 212-233-7958
Fax: 212-732-3451

Institute for Civil Justice
1700 Main Street
P.O. Box 2138
Santa Monica, CA 90406-2138
Tel: 310-393-0411
Fax: 310-393-4818

Institute for Hazardous Materials Management
11900 Park Lawn Drive, Suite 450
Rockville, MD 20852
Tel: 301-984-8969

Insurance Accounting and Systems Association, Inc.
P.O. Box 51340
Durham, NC 27717
Tel: 919-489-0991
Fax: 919-489-1994

Insurance Committee for Arson Control
110 Williams Street
New York, NY 10038
Tel: 212-669-9245
Fax: 212-791-1807

Insurance Data Management Association
85 John Street
New York, NY 10038
Tel: 212-669-0496
Fax: 212-669-0535

Insurance Information Institute
110 Williams Street
New York, NY 10038
Tel: 212-669-9200
Fax: 212-732-1916

Insurance Institute for Highway Safety
1005 North Glebe Road
Suite 800
Arlington, VA 22201
Tel: 703-247-1500
Fax: 703-247-1678

Insurance Institute for Property Loss Reduction
73 Tremont Street
Suite 510
Boston, MA 02108-3910
Tel: 617-722-0200
Fax: 617-423-4620
Web site URL: http://www.iiplr.org

Insurance Institute of America, Inc.
720 Providence Road, P.O. Box 3016
Malvern, PA 19355-0716
Tel: 800-644-2101
Fax: 610-640-9576
E-mail: cserv@cpcuiia.org
Web site URL: http://www.insweb.com/educator/
aicpcu-iia

Insurance Library Association of Boston
156 State Street
Boston, MA 02109
Tel: 617-227-2087
Fax: 617-723-8524

Insurance Research Council
1200 Hager Road
Suite 310
Oak Brook, IL 60521
Tel: 708-572-1177
Fax: 708-572-9856

Insurance Services Office, Inc.
7 World Trade Center
New York, NY 10048-1199
Tel: 212-898-6000
Fax: 212-898-5525

International Advisory Council of the Chamber of Commerce of the U.S.
1615 H Street, N.W.
Washington, DC 20062
Tel: 202-659-6000
Fax: 202-463-5929

International Foundation of Employee Benefit Plans
18700 West Bluemound Road
P.O. Box 69
Brookfield, WI 53008-0069
Tel: 414-786-6700
Fax: 414-786-8670
Web site URL: http://www.IFEBP.org

International Insurance Council
1212 New York Avenue, N.W.
Suite 250
Washington, DC 20005
Tel: 202-682-2345
Fax: 202-682-4187

International Risk Management Institute, Inc.
12222 Merit Drive
Suite 1660
Dallas, TX 75251-2217
Tel: 972-960-7693
Fax: 972-960-6037

Moody's Investor Services
99 Church Street
New York, NY 10007
Tel: 212-553-0300
Fax: 212-553-4063

Mutual Atomic Energy Liability Underwriters
One East Wacker Drive
Chicago, IL 60601
Tel: 312-467-0003
Fax: 312-467-0774

Mutual Reinsurance Bureau
1780 South Bell School Road
Cherry Valley, IL 60116
Tel: 815-332-3155
Fax: 815-332-3265

National Association of Casualty and Surety Executives
316 Pennsylvania Avenue S.E.
Washington, DC 20036
Tel: 202-547-6616
Fax: 202-564-0597

National Association of Health Underwriters
1000 Connecticut Avenue, N.W.
Suite 810
Washington, DC 20036
Tel: 202-223-5533
Fax: 202-785-2274
Web site URL: http://www.nahu.org

National Association of Independent Insurance Adjusters
300 West Washington Street
Suite 805
Chicago, IL 60606
Tel: 312-853-0808
Fax: 312-853-3225

National Association of Independent Insurers
2600 River Road
Des Plaines, IL 60018
Tel: 708-297-7800
Fax: 708-297-5064

National Association of Insurance Brokers, Inc.
1300 I Street, N.W.
Suite 900 East
Washington, DC 20005
Tel: 202-628-6700
Fax: 202-628-6707

National Association of Insurance Commissioners
120 West 12th Street
Suite 1100
Kansas City, MO 64105
Tel: 816-842-3600
Fax: 816-471-7004

National Association of Insurance Women
P.O. Box 4410
Tulsa, OK 74159
Tel: 918-744-5195
Fax: 918-743-1968
E-mail: naiw@ad.com
Web site URL: http://www.naiw.org

National Association of Mutual Insurance Companies
3707 Woodview Trace
P.O. Box 68700
Indianapolis, IN 46268
Tel: 317-875-5250
Fax: 317-879-8408

National Association of Professional Surplus Lines Offices Ltd.
6405 N. Cosby
Suite 201
Kansas City, MO 64151
Tel: 816-741-3910
Fax: 816-741-5409

National Association of Surety Bond Broducers
5301 Wisconsin Avenue, N.W.
Suite 450
Washington, DC 20015-2015
Tel: 202-686-3700
Fax: 202-686-3656
E-mail: NASBP@aol.com

National Center for Policy Analysis
12655 North Central Expressway
Suite 720
Dallas, TX 75243
Tel: 972-386-6272
Fax: 972-386-0924

National Committee on Property Insurance
10 Winthrop Square
Boston, MA 02110
Fax: 617-722-0200

National Conference of Insurance Legislation
P.O. Box 217
Brookfield, WI 53005
Tel: 414-782-6669
Fax: 414-782-9607

National Council on Compensation Insurance
750 Park of Commerce Drive
Boca Raton, FL 33487
Tel: 407-997-1000
Fax: 407-997-4774

National Crime Prevention Institute
University of Louisville
Louisville, KY 40292
Tel: 502-588-6987

National Fire Protection Association
1 Batterymarch Park
Quincy, MA 02269-9101
Tel: 617-770-3000
Fax: 617-770-0700
E-mail: Librart@NFPA.org

National Insurance Association
P.O. Box 53230
Chicago, IL 60653-0230
Tel: 312-924-3308
Fax: 312-285-0064

National Insurance Crime Bureau
10330 South Roberts Road
Palos Hills, IL 60465
Tel: 708-430-2430
Fax: 708-430-2446

National Safety Council
1121 Spring Lake Drive
Itasca, IL 60143-3201
Tel: 708-285-1121
Fax: 708-285-1315

National Society of Insurance Premium Auditors
P.O. Box 323
Boys Town, NE 68010
Tel: 402-496-4700

Occupational Safety and Health Administration
Department of Labor
200 Constitution Avenue, N.W.
Washington, DC 20210
Tel: 202-219-8148

Oversees Private Investment Corporation
100 New York Avenue, N.W.
Washington, DC 20527
Tel: 202-336-8400
Fax: 202-336-8799

Pollution Liability Insurance Association
1333 Butterfield Road
Suite 408
Downers Grove, IL 60515
Tel: 630-969-5300
Fax: 630-969-4404

Professional Insurance Agents
400 North Washington Street
Alexandria, VA 22314
Tel: 703-736-9340
Fax: 703-836-1279

Professional Liability Underwriting Society
4248 Park Glen Road
Minneapolis, MN 55416
Tel: 612-512-2100

Property Insurance Loss Register
700 New Brunswick Avenue
P.O. Box M
Rahway, NJ 07065
Tel: 908-388-0157
Fax: 908-388-0537

Property Loss Research Bureau
1501 Woodfield Road
Suite 400 West
Schaumburg, IL 60173-4978
Tel: 847-330-8650

Public Risk Management Association
1815 N. Fort Myer Dr.
Suite 1020
Arlington, VA 22209
Tel: 703-528-7701
Fax: 703-528-7966

Reinsurance Association of America
1301 Pennsylvania Avenue, N.W.
Suite 900
Washington, DC 20004
Tel: 202-638-3690
Fax: 202-638-0936
E-mail: 6483481@mcimail.com
Web site URL: http://www.raanet.org

Risk and Insurance Management Society, Inc.
655 3rd Avenue
New York, NY 10017
Tel: 212-286-9292
Fax: 212-986-9716

Self-Insurance Institute of America
P.O. Box 15466
1700 East Dyer Road
Suite 165
Santa Ana, CA 92705
Tel: 714-261-2553
Fax: 714-261-2594
E-mail: JKinder120@AOL.COM

Society of Certified Insurance Counselors
3630 North Hills Drive
Austin, TX 78731
Tel: 512-345-7932
Fax: 512-343-2167

Society of Chartered Property and Casualty Underwriters
Kahler Hall 720
Providence Road (CB No. 9)
Malvern, PA 19355
Tel: 610-251-2728
Fax: 610-251-2761
Web site URL: cpcusociety.org

Society of Insurance Research
691 Crossfire Ridge
Marietta, GA 30064
Tel: 770-426-9270
Fax: 770-426-9298
E-mail: 104355.2510@compuserve.com
Web site URL: http://connectyou.com/ins/sir.htm

Society of Risk Management Consultants
c/o T.E. Brennan Co.
330 East Kilbourn Avenue
Suite 750
Milwaukee, WI 53202
Tel: 414-271-2232
Fax: 414-271-0104
E-mail: CONSUTL@tebrennan.com
Web site URL: http://www.tebrennan.com

Standard & Poor's Corp.
25 Broadway
New York, NY 10004
Tel: 212-208-8000
Fax: 212-509-8994

Surety Association of America
100 Wood Avenue, South
Iselin, NJ 08830
Tel: 908-494-7600
Fax: 908-494-7609

Underwriters Laboratories, Inc.
333 Pfingsten Road
Northbrook, IL 60062
Tel: 708-272-8800
Fax: 708-272-8129

Western Loss Association
c/o Hanover Insurance
333 Pierce Road
Itasca, IL 60143
Tel: 630-773-2882

Workers Compensation Reinsurance Bureau
Two Hudson Place
Hoboken, NJ 07030
Tel: 201-795-1700
FAx: 201-795-4441